Praise for

Engage!

"Social networks empower everyday people to become remarkable. How do you now earn their attention and also become remarkable in the process? *Engage!* is your answer."

—MC Hammer

"It's no longer an era of business as usual. Executives and entrepreneurs must embrace new media in order to not only compete for the future, but for mind share, market share, and ultimately relevance. This book helps you engage . . . without it you're competing for second place."

—Mark Cuban, owner, Dallas Mavericks, investor, entrepreneur,
Chairman of HDNet

"Affinity is personal and emotional. Without personifying the company and what it symbolizes, it's difficult for customers to connect with your brand. The concepts from this book can help your brand engage in a way that inspires communities to extend your message, promise, and reach."

—Tony Hsieh, CEO of Zappos.com

"The power of top-down, A-list influencer is winding down. Now brands must engage on a direct-to-many basis. Social media makes this possible, and Solis makes this happen. Read his book or be left in the dust."

—Guy Kawasaki, co-founder of Alltop

"Social media is changing everything about the way people relate socially, in commerce, and politics. *Engage!* gets you up to date regarding current trends and technology, and shows you how to build a serious social media strategy. It's the real deal."

—Craig Newmark, founder, Craigslist.com

"Brian Solis has shown once again his deep understanding of the power of new media. He shows how social media can give voice, credibility, and connections to both companies and their customers."

—Price Floyd, VP for Digital Media Strategy
BAE Systems

"What's the secret to a successful company? Seasoned business owners know that it's a combination of strong leadership and superior products. But that alone isn't enough anymore. The leader of the future needs to connect with the customer of the future when, where, and how the customer wants, and Brian Solis lays out some of the guidelines here, going far beyond the tools that are today's buzzwords."

—Scott Monty, Global Digital Communications, Ford Motor Company

"Brian Solis documents new media's evolution and its challenge to traditional marketing methods and corporate communications: Most profoundly, through social media the customer has become a more influential stakeholder. The book provides concrete guidelines on how companies must engage in the public conversation and how they must prepare for a new era of relationships with their clients, customers, and employees."

—Klaus Schwab, Executive Chairman, World Economic Forum

"New media is forcing the democratization of old media. It's how we engage that shapes our credibility and community . . . and ultimately our relationship with our newly empowered audiences."

—Joanna Drake Earl, COO Current TV

"The road from where you are to your business's future is neither paved nor marked. It's yours to discover and this book is your compass to leadership."

—Peter Guber

ENGAGE!

The Complete Guide for
BRANDS and **BUSINESSES** to
Build, Cultivate, and Measure Success
in the New Web

Revised and Updated

BRIAN SOLIS

WILEY

John Wiley & Sons, Inc.

Published by John Wiley & Sons, Inc., Hoboken, New Jersey.
Published simultaneously in Canada.

For general information on our other products and services or for technical support,
please contact our Customer Care Department within the United States at
(800) 762-2974, outside the United States at (317) 572-3993 or fax (317) 572-4002.

Wiley also publishes its books in a variety of electronic formats. Some content that
appears in print may not be available in electronic books. For more information
about Wiley products, visit our web site at www.wiley.com.

Library of Congress Cataloging-in-Publication Data:

Solis, Brian.
  Engage!: the complete guide for brands and businesses to build, cultivate, and
measure success in the new web / Brian Solis. — Rev. and updated
      p. cm.
    ISBN 978-1-118-00376-3 (pbk.); ISBN 978-1-118-07283-7 (ebk);
ISBN 978-1-118-07281-3 (ebk); ISBN 978-1-118-07279-0 (ebk)
    1. Internet marketing.   2. Social media—Economic aspects.   3. Customer
relations.   4. Online social networks.   I. Title.
    HF5415.1265.S65 2011
    658.8'72—dc22
                                                                    2010054031

Printed in the United States of America.

10 9 8 7 6 5 4

Contents

Foreword

New media is creating a new generation of influencers and it is resetting the hierarchy of authority, while completely freaking out those who once held power without objection. The truth is that most of the existing formulas, methodologies, and systems miss or completely ignore the role of new influencers to inspire action, cause change, spark trends, and recruit advocates. We are absent from the exact movement that can help us connect with those who guide their peers.

In light of the new media movement, how do brands approach this now? They spam the Web with useless rhetoric. (Who cares if you're on Facebook or Twitter?) They also distribute these horrible videos, uploading them to YouTube and then wondering why they never go viral. Look, you have seven seconds to entertain someone. If you don't grab them in seven seconds, then you can forget about someone sitting through the rest of the video—let alone having it go viral.

But if you know what people are looking for . . . if you know where people are interacting . . . if you know what moves people, you can engage the human algorithm to immerse viewers and trigger meaningful interaction and vibration across the social graph.

This is why we, we as in a collective of individuals who know what's best for us based on our passions, interests, and aspirations, are in charge of what compels us. To have any hope of attracting and earning our attention, you need to know who *we* are.

The roles are reversing and individuals and brands have the ability to reach and rouse powerful and dedicated communities without ever having to pay for advertising. I'm just part of the bigger movement of empowering the people who care enough to change the word. Social media is socializing causes and purpose, and inciting nothing short of a revolution in stature and influence, but more importantly, literacy and innovation.

As we engage, we learn. And learning is what this is all about. But we can't grow without admitting that we have something to learn and at the same time, we have to believe in ourselves and our ability to push things forward. In the end, everything starts with engagement.

This is our time. This is your time. Engage.

ASHTON KUTCHER
Co-founder of Katalyst

Preface

We are at the beginning of something new and incredible, and its paths and processes are for the most part undefined and far from standardized. Social media is a great equalizer and it's leveling the playing field for those who can adapt and lead. If this is you, it's time to speak up. It's time to show executives, peers, and stakeholders that you care. With a little homework, the case can be made quite easily and impressively. It just takes a little bit of extra time and passion to do so.

You are needed now more than ever to help the brand best position itself to compete in the *now Web* and for the future.

It takes a champion to rally support from within.

It takes a champion to connect customer needs with company solutions.

It takes a champion to become the customer the business needs to reach.

It takes a champion to guide decision makers within the organization on how to best implement social tools and services, how to use them, how to establish guidelines, and how to measure success and return on investment.

You're a purveyor of new media, but then again, so is everyone else, it seems. Suddenly, everyone is a social media expert, but very few are indeed champions and far fewer are change agents.

So what are you going to do to rise above the fray while also delivering true, uncontestable value to those you are helping?

Ask yourself . . .

Are you an evangelist or a consultant?

Are you an extension of your company brand or are you an employee?

Are you a leader or a follower, or are you meandering through your profession?

Are you confined to the role you're in now or do you represent something with longer-term value?

Everything that's transpiring around us is actually improving the existing foundation for our business, from service to marketing to product development to sales to executive management, and everything in between.

Social marketing revitalizes and empowers every facet of our workflow and its supporting ecosystem. Seeing the bigger picture and tying our knowledge to the valuable feedback from our communities will help us guide businesses toward visibility, profitability, relevance, and ultimately, customer loyalty.

In every single case, it doesn't take only an expert, it requires a champion to make an impact.

You are that champion.

Advancement doesn't come without investment, though. Social media may at first blush, look easy and free, but as any true champion can attest, it's so much more than we see superficially.

You may be saying to yourself, "I already have a full-time job that keeps me busy, more than busy, for eight to nine hours a day as it is. How am I going to squeeze in the time to learn everything required for this new role, and how will I balance my workload based on what I already have to do?"

Sorry. I don't have an easy answer or a shortcut for you.

What's taking place right now, right in front of you, is something so tremendous that to proclaim that a cheat sheet exists would actually cheat you from truly grasping this new opportunity for personal and professional growth.

This is something so much deeper than anything I could cover "for dummies." It's a matter of taking the easy route versus immersion. Success and maturation is tied to the latter.

The good news is that you have this book. Now let's work together to get you that MBA that will really help you excel in your career, wherever it may take you.

Think about it.

Investing extra time after hours and on weekends is the minimum ante to enroll in what I call the New Media University. With every day that passes, enrollment multiplies. The question you have to ask is whether you want to lead or follow. Please note that the risk of following is that the field will quickly become congested with competition and stagnation. In contrast, when you choose to take a leadership role, you will find that challengers are scattered and in short supply. The cost, however, is that you go back to school for the near future to help you learn and acquire the skills necessary to lead your brand into the future.

While many will ask questions, few will have answers. Which side of the dialogue do you choose?

Introduction: Welcome to the Revolution

By the time you read this book, you may have already heard or will soon hear whispers, rumblings, and rantings that social media is playing out.

Tune them out.

The truth is that social media may very well cease to exist as a category one day. However, while the term and category has and always will invite debate, social media's practices and benefits are indisputable and enduring. And they will always serve as an important and revered chapter in the evolution of new media.

This is not open to debate.

Influential conversations are sparked and steered by influential people right now and they exist and flourish outside of your organization. The practice of listening to and learning from these conversations in and around the social networks where they transpire is invaluable and indispensable.

New Media is simply a matter of digital Darwinism that affects any and all forms of marketing and service. In the world of democratized influence, businesses must endure a perpetual survival of the fittest.

Engage or die.

In June 2007, I wrote and published *The Social Media Manifesto*. What started as a blog post intended to help marketers grasp the emerging and rapidly shifting landscape of social media quickly ascended into the rallying cry for a new, in-touch epoch of direct-to-consumer engagement. *The Social Media Manifesto* introduced the methodologies, tools, and social networks that would eventually inspire a movement to evolve from top-down, broadcast programs to complementary forms of collaboration rooted in mutually beneficial exchanges. It served as the foundation to effectively redesign marketing communications and customer service organizations based on the art of observation, listening, engagement, learning, and adapting. It also introduced the mechanics and benefits for humanizing

Figure I.1

Source: Original drawing in honor of *Engage!* by Hugh MacLeod, author of *Ignore Everybody* and also blogger@gapingvoid.

and diversifying the company story based on the unique and varying needs of customers and peers who populate online communities and create channels of influence.

And here we are now: united in our efforts to discover meaning in the philosophies and processes we long operated without. We seek inspiration and we, too, endeavor to inspire. The people we attempted to reach over the years appear before our eyes as if they are long-lost friends and relatives. The faceless have revealed their identities through their actions and words. Socialized media and the people powering the convergence are accelerating an era of engagement driven by collective consciousness. It's inspiring a new type of business, one that is socially aware and participatory. After all, customer acquisition is only rivaled in value by customer retention.

The science of procuring attention is complemented by the delicate art of earning and cultivating relationships. Social media peeled back the layers of infrastructure, data, numbers, demographics, politics, procedures, and all of the corporate red tape that dug trenches between our brand and our customers.

This is our time to engage! In doing so, it is your declaration of independence, breaking the shackles that have bound us to hollow marketing practices of yesteryear. It serves as your framework to chart your own path and create your own destiny. It is your key to unlock the doors that prevent you from reaching your customers where they're interacting and seeking solutions today *and* tomorrow.

Together we are building the foundation for corporate and personal significance. We are the architects who are drafting the blueprint for a more efficient and yearned-for bridge between our story and the people who can benefit from it as well as the stories from which we can benefit.

Welcome to marketing providence. The crusade you join is growing in importance each and every day. You're surrounded by like-minded individuals who seek to improve the dynamics between people. The tools, methodologies, and stories shared within this book will reveal a wealth of *unmarketing* principles, strategies, and devices. It is this idea of unmarketing that inevitably extends all of the goals and objectives merited by traditional marketing, while also elevating the experience for everyone on both sides. This stimulates advocacy so that it can better expand your presence and impact in the mainstream and distributed communities that influence perceptions and decisions.

While the methodologies, theories, experiences, and social tools discussed in the original manifesto still stand, a deeper and more modern look is necessary to garner support and champion change from within—specifically an examination of what to do and how to measure success. It is through adaptation and engagement that we earn experience, connections, and prominence. There's no doubt that the proven tenets introduced in this book will ensure your success and career longevity. The doctrines that we examine and propose are in fact representative of best-of-breed ideals and methods unearthed and mashed-up from existing and extinct tactics to renew, edify, mature, and hone our proficiencies, conviction, knowledge, and experience.

Engage! will serve as a new manifesto, a reference point for all inward-outward-facing initiatives that incorporate two-way communication. And in the process, we'll see unmarketing emerge as one of the most effective forms of marketing, after all.

Until the proliferation of interactive media, traditional influence has followed a systematic top-down process of developing and pushing controlled messages to audiences, rooted in one-to-many faceless broadcast campaigns.

Personality wasn't absent in certain media, but it was missing from day-to-day communications.

For the most part, this pattern seemingly served its purposes, fueling the belief that brands were in control of their messages, from delivery to dissemination, among the demographics to which they were targeted.

It scaled and served very well over the years, until it didn't. . . .

Unbeknownst to many companies, a quiet riot has been amassing over the last two decades, one that we document clearly in this book. And slowly but surely, the whispers eventually intensified into roars.

The socialization of the Web and content publishing disrupted the balance and is now forcing a media renaissance that is transforming information distribution, human interaction, and everything that orbits this nascent ecosystem.

It is the dawn of a democratized information economy, which is fueling the emergence of champions, facilitators, and visionaries who are leading a more media literate society while transforming the way we engage with one another.

The interactive Web heralded the arrival of mainstream consumer influence and a global ecosystem that supports and extends their observations, complaints, opinions, referrals, and recommendations.

It served as a great equalizer, capsizing the existing balance and redistributing influence—and continues to do so.

Not only is it changing how we create, decipher, and share information, it is forever reshaping how brands and content publishers think about their markets and the people who define them.

Engage.

Chapter 1

The Social Media Manifesto

■ THE SOCIALIZATION OF MEDIA IS YEARS IN THE MAKING

In my 20-year marketing career, I've dedicated the last 14 years specifically to the practice of and experimentation in online interaction. My findings are based solely on the chemistry of failure, success, and, well, ambivalence, which equals either defeat or promise. The constant theme throughout has been the sustained balance between the pursuit of new influencers and the incorporation of proven traditional methods. This experience, and the experiences of others, ultimately serves as the foundation for creating a new communications bridge between companies and customers.

Socialized media has:

➤ Rewired the processes by which consumers share experiences, expertise, and opinions

➤ Broadened the channels available to consumers who seek information

➤ Changed how companies approach markets

➤ Altered how companies develop products

➤ Remodeled the processes by which companies connect with and show appreciation for their customers

➤ Transformed the method of influence, augmenting the ranks of traditional market experts and thought leaders with enthusiasts and innovators who self-create content-publishing platforms for their views

➤ Facilitated customers' direct engagement in the conversations that were previously taking place without their participation

A fundamental shift in our culture is under way and it is creating a new landscape of influencers, as well as changing how we define

1

Engage or Die

Source: Original artwork by Jesse Thomas (http://Jess3.com).

influence. By establishing an entirely new ecosystem that supports the socialization of information, this shift is facilitating new conversations that start locally, but ultimately have a global impact.

The days of "hear no evil, see no evil, speak no evil" have passed without lament.

Monologue has given way to dialogue.

The message is clear. Social media has introduced a new layer of influencers across all industries. It is the understanding of the role people play in the process of not only reading and disseminating information, but also how they create and share content in which others can participate. This, and only this, allows us to truly grasp the future of business, which is, for all intents and purposes, already unfolding today.

The socialization of information and the tools that enable it are the undercurrent of interactive media—and serve as the capital infrastructure that defines the social economy.

Content is the new democracy and we, the people, are ensuring that our voices are heard.

This is your chance to reinvigorate the tired and aging models of marketing and service, enliven a corporate brand, and increase revenue, all while paving the way for a brighter and more rewarding career.

How can companies implement an integrated social strategy quickly in this new social landscape? By focusing on desirable markets and influencers where they connect. This will have a far greater impact on brand resonance and the bottom line than trying to reach the masses through any one message, venue, or tool.

Our actions speak louder than our words.

New media is constantly evolving and has yet to reveal its true impact across the entire business publishing and marketing landscape. But, social media is only one chapter in a never-ending resource that continues to evolve as new media permeates every facet of every business. In fact, new media is only going to become more pervasive and, as such, prove to be a critical factor in the success or failure of any business.

The life of the information offered in this book is interminable. New tools and strategies will be revealed, and they will be tied to exciting case studies that document the challenges, tactics, lessons, and successes for each.

We're just getting started.

The evolution of new media is also inducing an incredible transformation within the organization, introducing opportunities for internal and external collaboration in customer service, product, sales, community relations, and public—its most dramatic evolution in decades. In the world of customer and product support, socialized media is putting the "customer" back in customer service. Likewise, in the world of communications, the democratization of media is putting the "public" back into public relations. It creates entirely new roles and teams within organizations to proactively listen, learn, engage, measure, and change in real time. And we'll soon see it have a profound effect in the financial sector.

This new genre of media is not a game played from the sidelines however. Nor is this book written merely to inform you of the benefits only to have you go back to your day-to-day routine. Those who participate will succeed—everyone clse will either have to catch up or miss the game altogether.

Businesses will evolve, customers will gain in prominence, and brands will humanize—with or without you.

■ THE FUTURE OF BUSINESS IS ALREADY HERE

The secret to successfully navigating the new landscape of marketing and service is understanding that social media is less about technology and more about anthropology, sociology, and ethnography. New media marketing and services are mash-ups of new and traditional media and processes that span across advertising, public relations (PR), customer service, marketing communications (marcom),

Figure 1.2

human resources (HR), sales, and community relations. We take the best practices from each and also introduce new social processes in and around them.

Communication, whether inbound or outbound, is now powered by conversations, and the best communicators always start as the best listeners. And the best listeners are those who empathize.

This is where and how the future of influence takes shape.

➤ It begins with respect and an understanding of how you connect with and benefit those whom you're hoping to help.

➤ Intent is defined by a genuine desire to evolve into a resource.

➤ Genuine participation is a form of new marketing, but is not reminiscent of traditional marketing formats and techniques—it's a new blueprint for *unmarketing*.

➤ Meaningful content can earn the creator trust, authority, and influence.

➤ Conversations can forge relationships, which are measured by social capital and trust.

Figure 1.2 shows the range of people you will be interacting with, from innovators to laggards.

■ WE ARE THE CHAMPIONS, WE ARE NOT MESSENGERS

While we lead the transformation of our company's marketing, sales, and service infrastructure, we must also ensure that our actions are discernible. Much in the same way that we attempt to create ambassadors by empowering our customers and advocates in the Social Web, we must become their ambassadors within—representing their concerns, ideas, questions, and experiences. Internal change is part of the game.

Since this is a powerful new form of *social* media, it begins with how we think and act. This is the point at which most companies fall down, when they rely on traditional marketing models instead of creating or adapting new methodologies.

Messages are not conversations. Targets and audiences are not people. The inability to know people for who they are and what they represent prevents us from truly seeing and hearing them—which then impedes our efforts to connect. As Doc Searls, coauthor of *The Cluetrain Manifesto,* wisely stated, "There is no market for messages."

The market for self-promotion is finite. Yet brands, even those that experiment with social media, confuse their role and place within these new digital societies. People do not create accounts on Facebook, YouTube, Twitter, or any other social network to hear from brands. The bottom line is that people are seeking answers and direction, not messages or sales pitches.

People just don't speak or hear things in the same way companies speak about their products and services. For us to be heard, we have to engage as though we were speaking person to person.

Social networks are hubs between the company and its customers. How we participate in each network defines our stature within them and also determines our ability to earn friends and followers while also promoting and instilling advocacy.

Everything we're integrating into the marketing mix is now aimed at sparking and cultivating conversations, as well as continuously expanding a network of lasting relationships.

■ CONVERSATIONS HAPPEN WITH OR WITHOUT YOU

In his great essay titled "We Are the People Formerly Known as the Audience," Jay Rosen introduced us to the people we're now trying to reach. In many ways, Rosen's essay served as a manifesto for the marketing, media, and advertising industries, serving as an eye-opener to the world of democratized influence and how to recognize and embrace the opportunity it represents.

To best reach people, we have to first figure out who they are and where they connect and how they share and find information. In the process, you'll quickly discover that there is no magic bullet for reaching everyone, all at once. The strategy is in how to segment active communities from audiences.

Social media is about speaking *with,* not *at* people. This means engaging in a way that works in a conversational medium, that is, serving the best interest of both parties, while not demeaning any actions or insulting the intelligence of anyone involved.

So what of those skeptics or apprehensive executives who claim that participating on social networks will only invoke negative responses and ignite potential crises?

As we're coming to realize, the social landscape is a vast sea filled with unforgiving predators—most of whom would love nothing more than to have marketers for every meal of the day. Nevertheless, succeeding here is the future.

The truth is that there will be negative commentary. However, that should not deter you from experimenting or piloting programs. Even without your participation, negative commentary already exists. In most cases, you just aren't listening in all of the right places. This is why I like to ask business leaders the following question: "If a conversation takes place online, and you weren't there to hear it, did it actually happen?"

Yes. Yes, it did and still does.

Assuredly, every negative discussion is an opportunity to learn and also to participate in a way that may shift the discussion in a positive direction. If there's nothing else that we accomplish by participating, we at least acquire the ability to contribute toward a positive public perception.

The conversations that don't kill you only make you stronger. And those negative threads that escalate in social networks will only accelerate without the involvement of inherent stakeholders.

■ SOCIAL MEDIA IS ONE COMPONENT OF A BROADER COMMUNICATIONS AND MARKETING STRATEGY

It's true that everything is changing. And in many cases, it's also true that everything old eventually becomes new again. The underlying principles of customer focus and service certainly aren't new. Instead, the attention on these elements may have waned, as businesses expand, contract, shift, and evolve based on market needs and trends, profit, and peer influence, as governed by the guidance of stakeholders and shareholders.

Social media force businesses to reflect and adapt to markets and the people who define them.

Social media are never-ending fountains of lessons and insight, and they flow both ways.

Social media present a means, not an end.

Social media spark a revelation that we, the people, have a voice, and through the democratization of content and ideas we can once again unite around common passions, inspire movements, and ignite change.

It's not a one-way broadcast channel. We are now part of the community and we don't own it. We must establish prominence and earn influence so as to amass attention, instill enthusiasm, empower ambassadors, and create a community of loyal collaborators.

The previous hierarchy of messaging has collapsed. Now, in order to appeal to customers, clients, or potential stakeholders, we must approach them from the top down, the bottom up, and side to side. We must outmaneuver the elusive. We must outthink the pessimists. We must sanction and amplify the experts and empower the emissaries.

■ BUILDING A BRIDGE BETWEEN YOU AND YOUR CUSTOMERS

Since our efforts are outward focused, visible, and indexable on the Web for all to see and find, everything we do now contributes to the brand we represent. Arming employees with knowledge, guidelines, and objectives, and accordingly empowering them to participate on behalf of the brand and greater mission, they can create an influential and community-focused organization that engages stakeholders. Doing so builds an active collective of participants, powered by influential voices, in addition to employees, who will shape perception, steer conversations, and provide help to those seeking advice. The community that once operated without us now becomes an extension of our outbound activities, beliefs, passions, and value propositions.

We are both architects and builders of strategic relationships and alliances, and we are creating the blueprints for and also constructing the bridge that connects customers and the people (you and me) who represent the companies we believe in.

To truly help businesses and the decision makers responsible for their direction, we need to learn through real work. We have to get our hands dirty. There's just no way around it. We can learn from the mistakes and successes of our peers, but actions speak louder than words. The last thing we need are more cooks in a crowded kitchen. At the same time, we need direction and lucrative movement. We need thinkers *and* doers. It is the only way to get smarter and, in turn, become more valuable to those you're consulting or helping.

Immersion equals incontestable experience, perspectives, and knowledge.

Let's get to work, build the bridge, and open up the gateways to traffic on both ends.

■ BEING HUMAN VERSUS HUMANIZING YOUR STORY

It takes so much more than an understanding of the tools and popular networks to inspire change and build long-term, meaningful relationships.

The ability to set up a profile on Facebook or Twitter, the wherewithal to update status in each network, the capacity to connect with people within each network, is in fact, child's play. This is a learned practice not unlike the sending, filing, and reading of e-mail, chatting through instant-messaging tools, placing IP-based calls on Skype, or sending a text message from your mobile phone.

There's a bigger, more significant opportunity to make a true impact within an organization. The tools are just extensions of you and your expertise and artistry. Everything starts with a deep commitment to the brand you're representing—its culture, personality, overall potential, and people. Without it, you're pushing the same old rhetoric in new places, which hardly helps you achieve your potential. And it certainly doesn't inspire anyone to concern themselves with the brand's presence in these emerging social networks that are so vital to our corporate economy. After all, why should I care about what you do in social media when you don't?

Don't speak to me in messages!

Stop trying to market at me!

Give me something to believe in. Give me something to let me know that you *know* whom you're talking to and why.

I am influential. I am a social consumer. I have built a valuable social graph. I'm the gatekeeper among gatekeepers who need direction, insight, and answers for me to accomplish the tasks in my life and meet my personal and professional goals. You could be just what I'm looking for, but in social media, where I dwell, I wouldn't know it based on how you are or aren't participating.

I'm a human being and so are you. Treat me as such . . . act as such.

Alas, being human is far easier than humanizing your story. Transparency is just not enough to convince me that I need to pay attention to you.

Get a little empathy going on and you'll begin to facilitate meaningful interaction. This is the necessary commitment to adopting and embodying a customer service mentality fueled by empathy and the desire to deliver resolution—one strategic engagement at a time.

Feel it.
Live it.
Breathe it.
Be it.

If you don't engage and become an internal champion, someone else will. That person may reside in your organization right now, or they may dwell in the cubicles of your competition's offices, or both. It's as simple as that. The key difference though, is that you can definitively demonstrate how your story can affect the day-to-day workflow of various important leaders and trendsetters, across multiple markets, because you, by default, have also become a new expert in the process of socializing your company. While intent counts, value talks and BS walks. It's the poetry of relationship building, versed in language and delivered by someone who knows how to speak to people because he is from the people.

■ SOCIAL SCIENCE IS NO LONGER AN ELECTIVE

As mentioned earlier, technology is not in or of itself the catalyst for change. Social tools facilitate the online conversations, but it's the people who are the instigators for change.

While Generation Y (the millennials) are entering the workforce with unprecedented knowledge of how to communicate with one another using social networks, micromedia communities, text messages, blogs, and all things social, their business discipline and work ethic are still rivaled by Baby Boomers and Generation X. And the technical aptitude of previous generations is locked in to a perennial cycle of catch-up and self-education. Each generation, however, is unique and representative of the reality that everyone, no matter which generation she represents, still needs to learn how to hear and see things differently. It's psychographics over demographics, and the only way to learn about and motivate people is to see and connect with those who band together through tastes, preferences, interests, and passions, regardless of age, location, and gender.

Psychographics: Any attribute relating to personality, values, attitudes, interests, or lifestyles; also referred to as IAO variables (for interests, activities, and opinions)[1]

Demographics: The physical characteristics of a population, such as age, sex, marital status, family size, education, geographic location, and occupation[2]

The knowledge of the tools is one thing. But it's what we hear, say, and learn that traverses seamlessly across generations and technologies—as it relates to those connected by relevant data and individuals who share their interests.

How people interact on Facebook is not the same as how they communicate on Twitter. Community interaction on YouTube is radically different from engagement on FourSquare. Each network cultivates its own culture—creating a unique society that fosters connections and socialization as determined by the people who connect, produce and share content, and who interact with one another.

Social sciences instruct us to study the social life of human groups. Conducting fieldwork in the form of listening, observing, asking questions, and documenting people in the natural environments of their online habitat reveals the insights necessary to successfully navigate our own immersion into each community. Social media require digital anthropologists, sociologists, and ethnographers.

Let's take a look at the definitions of sociology, anthropology, and ethnography to appreciate the similarities in the practice of social sciences as related to our work in social media.

> *Sociology: The study of society, human social interaction, and the rules and processes that bind and separate people not only as individuals, but as members of associations, groups, and institutions.*[3]

> *Anthropology: The scientific study of people, including the development of societies and cultures. It seeks to advance knowledge of who we are, how we came to be that way—and where we may go in the future.*[4]

> *Ethnography: A branch of anthropology that provides scientific descriptions of human societies based on people in their natural, or native, environments—where they live, work, shop, and play. Ethnography is based on objective fieldwork.*

Through sociology, anthropology, and ethnography, we're learning to peel back the layers of online markets to see the specific groups of people and document their behavior. As such, we can effectively visualize and personify the nuances that define each online community and the distinct subcultures within it. Through impartial examination, we gather the data necessary to effectively and intelligently cross over into societal immersion, in the networks that are relevant to our brand.

Specifically, we are looking to uncover:

➤ Material social networks.

➤ People linked through common interests that are germane to our business, industry, and marketplace.

➤ Keywords commonly used by community members.

➤ Patterns for discovering and sharing information.

➤ Influence of outside networks and also the effects of existing networks on external communities.

➤ Influential voices, tiered, and how they form distinct and over-lapping connections.

➤ The personality of networks and the specific communities.

➤ The nature of threads, memes, and associated sentiment.

➤ The language of inhabitants.

➤ The prevailing culture and our potential place within it.

➤ The tools people use to communicate in and around each network.

This critical element of preliminary fieldwork helps us adapt our outreach strategies and techniques, as well as construct the poignant information and stories we wish to share with potential stakeholders and advocates. And, through observation, we're able to find our real customers and those who influence them.

Later in the book, we'll uncover how to specifically identify the social networks and pertinent communities to your brand.

■ YOU ARE NOT ALONE

Everything starts with unlearning what you think you know and embracing everything you need to know in today's ever-advancing and transforming social climate.

We all need to determine what we need to know to compete for the future as professionals while helping the brands we represent compete for mindshare in an ever-thinning attention economy.

Whichever department we represent, the only way to evolve is to forge rewarding, long-term connections with the very people we wish to reach and compel. Success is tied to the ability to gain influence in our own right, within each community that affects our business and markets. Winning organizations will effectually shift outward activity from broadcast, us-versus-them campaigns to a one-on-one, and eventually to a one-to-many methodology that humanizes and personalizes our brand. What we're learning is that the ability to move and react is where most companies begin. Inevitably, however, the greatest advantages of social media reside in its ability for worthy individuals and companies to shape perception, steer activity, incite action, and adapt to the communities that establish the market.

Engage or die.

■ NOTES

1. Taken from Wikipedia.
2. Taken from Learnthat.com.
3. Wiktionary.org.
4. http://vlib.anthrotech.com/guides/anthropology.shtml.

Chapter 2

Making the Case for Social Media: The Five Ws+H+E

■ **THE RISE OF** *Unmarketing*

Fueled by a combination of popularity, curiosity, necessity, strategy, and trendiness, marketers are embracing a new recipe that injects a proactive, social approach to outbound communications and engagement—with or without all of the answers before they jump in. This approach, while courageous, requires faith, conviction, and champions who don't necessarily have access to metrics and case studies at the sole proprietor, small and mid-sized business (SMB), and enterprise levels. Many of the most, and also least, effective campaigns are implemented as a method of learning. As we all know, some social media campaigns excel while others publicly flop, which fosters cynicism and fear of embracing a transparent form of open and public dialogue. Some words of advice: Do not jump in to social media without fully understanding the five Ws and an H and E of social media.

1. Who: Define the brand personality and what it symbolizes.

     Social media is about people connecting with people, not avatars. Bring your business and your brand to life. Give it a persona, personality, voice, and presence. If your company was a person, how would it look, behave, speak, respond, or lead? Also, make the brand stand for something that's worthy and desirable. Give it a mission and a sense of purpose.

2. What: Listen to online conversations and learn from what's said.

     Assess how the brand is perceived today using search tools for the traditional and Social Web. Create a benchmark that captures what the world looks like today and pay attention to the general sentiment tied to your brand and competitors. Try Google, Collecta.com. Google Blog Search, and also Analytic.ly to get started. If you're working with a reasonable budget, also consider using services such as Spiral16 or Radian6.

3. **When: Pinpoint when your opportunities arise.**

Each tool mentioned here provides you with alert systems to let you know when your keywords appear online as they happen. Monitor the real-time Web to see the level of activity that takes place every day. Surface any conversations that represent opportunities for positive engagement as well as those that contribute to negative impressions.

4. **Where: Track down where your presence is required.**

Twitter, Facebook, YouTube, Flickr, and blogs are among the social networks most often discussed in popular media today. Using the same services discussed earlier, we get an exact idea of where your customers, prospects, and their peers are interacting online. Once we have this information, we can put together an action plan to become part of their conversations, learn how to build valuable relationships, and contribute to the loyalty and advocacy of the social customer.

5. **How: Become a part of the community.**

In your review, pay close attention to how people interact, and the culture and behavior that exists within the social networks that are important to you. Their words and actions reveal opportunities for value-added, not disruptive or offensive, engagement. Monitor the responses that follow each time we engage. They will offer feedback that teaches us how to improve and what steps we should take next.

6. **Why: Find the reasons that warrant your participation.**

Pay attention to recurring themes, topics, questions, insights, or the lack thereof. Doing so surfaces the reasons for initial engagement as well as the ideas that trigger creativity and value for engagement over time.

7. **To What Extent: Identify the individuals who can help you tell your story.**

Many individuals are earning authority within social networks, and what they say influences those around them. Their reach is expansive and is instrumental in effective word of mouth programs. We can identify who they are by using the same tools in Steps 1 through 6. Monitoring their activity and learning about who they are will also reveal their motivation.

While dollars evaporate from traditional budgets previously earmarked for advertising, public relations, events, and other return on investment (ROI) programs, individuals recognize social media as a cost-efficient venue for maintaining visibility, especially when compared to falling completely off the radar screens of potential customers, stakeholders, and influencers.

■ PEOPLE INFLUENCE BUYING DECISIONS, ONLINE AND OFFLINE

To most successfully capture mindshare and earn trust, we have to reverse the activities that have contributed to this negative perception held by consumers.

In 2010, Forrester Research Inc. released a survey that linked business buyers and their process of researching solutions to social media. The research group interviewed business buyers to learn about their social activity—in this case, more than 1,200 technology buyers in the United States, Canada, France, Germany, and the United Kingdom with 100 employees or more in seven major industries.

According to the responses, social media again proved to extend beyond consumers and business to consumers (B2C). In the real world of business-to-business research, analysis, and decisions, the Forrester data points to peer-to-peer influence and collaboration in social networks and blogs:

➤ 68 percent are *Spectators*—this group reads blogs, watches user-generated videos, and participates in other social media for business purposes.

➤ 31 percent are conversation lists—those who update their status on social networks.

➤ 33 percent are *Critics*—they contribute comments or react to content they see in social formats.

➤ 19 percent are *Collectors*—they use social technology to collect information and stay on top of trends.

➤ 59 percent are *Joiners,* who participate in social networks. Only 19 percent are *Inactives,* or nonparticipants.

This data demonstrates that social media is begetting trust as reinforced through genuine, sincere, and informative interaction between consumers, stakeholders, and brands.

■ THE DEMOCRATIZATION AND SOCIALIZATION OF BRANDED MEDIA

The democratization of content will only continue to further our global society. In the process it will transform traditional media and broadcast industries while also creating powerful platforms for everyday people with unique perspectives and ideas to cultivate global audiences. And every business, from mainstream brands to those run by you and me, will embrace social strategies to reach existing and potential customers to demonstrate value, solutions, and expertise.

This requires dedication, practice, and perhaps, most notably, an open mind and the patience to absorb a virtual fire hose of streaming information.

What you know today is quickly being leveled across an industry of people who are equally engaged and immersed—and thus becoming just as, if not more, knowledgeable than you. While new media is a great equalizer, it is also a source of motivation and inspiration to aspiring and ambitious students and professionals.

As a thought leader, you hold a power that most don't yet realize. You have influential people who follow and listen to you. This dynamic establishes authority and wields influence to further teach and change. You have the experience to create more effective teams that will work together to build an adaptive, customer-focused, and market-relevant organization. But you . . . we . . . are still learning. And we must practice what we learn so that we may gain proficiency. We need to make mistakes, experience triumphs, and observe when, why, and how we move the corporate needle, and galvanize communities through our work.

Businesses spanning every industry will empower employees to embrace the public through real-world and online interactions, requiring a renewed sense of adeptness, passion, and commitment. It's already underway and will one day simply become a function of most roles within an organization. The entire business will socialize.

Today's experimentation with socialized marketing will generate patterns, activity, results, and behavior that will serve as legitimate benchmarks for measuring metrics and ROI. It all starts with studying Web behavior and conversations to measure, monitor, and improve online experiences and activity. In a genre of social proficiency, we will leverage the insight gleaned from analyzing online events to develop more meaningful and compelling engagement initiatives, as well as transform our organization into one that can adapt to the real-world needs and wants of customers.

We need to be a genuine resource to the people who define the very communities that are important to us. As networks and new communities arise and thrive, we're experiencing a fundamental shift in content creation, distribution, and consumption—thus creating an active media-savvy society that is inspiring a more enlightened generation.

We have to relinquish any sense of entitlement we've earned or believe we've achieved over the years as the Social Web and the impending semantic Web (or, as Tim O'Reilly refers to it, "web squared") continues to advance.[1]

Lead by example.[2]

Embrace those who are learning along with you.[3]

Answer your own questions.[4]

We are all in this together, and truthfully, we could be so much more than we are today. Let's embody the change we wish to inspire and become the experts we seek to guide us.[5]

You are part of a new generation that[6] is humanizing the brands you represent. You are reshaping fundamental business dynamics and policies to establish, maintain, and cultivate loyalty and relationships with the people who define your markets. And, at the same time, the more you genuinely engage, create compelling and helpful content,[7] and share valuable information, you too will become a respected, trusted, and influential resource to your company and outside communities.[8]

■ NOTES

1. Internet Usage Statistics, www.internetworldstats.com/stats.htm.

2. "Russia Has World's Most Engaged Social Networking Audience," comScore (July 2, 2009), www.comscore.com/Press_Events/Press_Releases/2009/7/Russia_has_World_s_Most_Engaged_Social_Networking_Audience.

3. "Global Faces and Networked Places," Nielsen (March 2009), http://server-uk.imrworldwide.com/pdcimages/Global_Faces_and_Networked_Places-A_Nielsen_Report_on_Social_Networkings_New_Global_Footprint.pdf.

4. Jeremiah Owyang, "Social Media Playtime Is Over," Forrester Research (March 16, 2009), www.forrester.com/Research/Document/Excerpt/0,7211,47665,00.html.

5. "Is Social Network Advertising Ready for Primetime?" eMarketer (July 9, 2009), www.emarketer.com/Article.aspx?R=1007165.

6. Shar VanBoskirk, "Interactive Marketing Nears $55 Billion; Advertising Overall Declines," Forrester Research (July 7, 2009), http://blogs.forrester.com/marketing/2009/07/interactive-marketing-nears-55-billion-advertising-overall-declines.html.

7. Josh Bernoff, "People Don't Trust Company Blogs. What You Should Do About It," Forrester Blogs. http://blogs.forrester.com/jackie_rousseau_anderson/10-09-28-latest_global_social_media_trends_may_surprise_you.

8. Jose A. del Moral, "Facebook Becomes the Main Social Network in Most Countries, but in Asia and Latin America," Social Networks Alianzo's Blogs (February 22, 2009), http://blogs.alianzo.com/socialnetworks/2009/02/22/facebook-becomes-the-main-social-network-in-most-countries-but-in-asia-and-latin-america/.

Chapter 3

The New Media University

We are forever students of new media. While we learn through everything we read and practice, we should never strive to master something that evolves much faster than our ability to fully grasp its lessons, benefits, insights, and pitfalls. In the process, we learn a bit more about ourselves and our true potential.

For those versed in social media and the tools that connect us to those we wish to reach, enjoy this chance to hit *ctrl-alt-del* and restart with a fresh perspective. For those new to the socialization of media and influence, please take your time here. This is where everything begins.

Social media is a great equalizer and we share the desire and necessity to establish authority so we can better help those around us.

■ INTEGRATED MARKETING: THE TOOLS

The future of today's marketing integrates traditional media with social media elements intended to affect and renovate each and every department within the organization, from service to marketing to public relations (PR), information resources (IR), and human resources (HR) to sales and product development.

We're simply becoming aware of our markets, the people who define them, and our place within each community. It is a mandatory ritual of becoming socially adept.

While new media will always be new, the principles that govern behavior, interaction, and support remain constant. They're simply interpreted differently, based on intentions, objectives, and varying levels of customer empathy or ignorance. Social media is the latest in a series of chapters that determine the course of new media. The tools described in this book will change over time and that's why they're just the tools of the trade—right now. They help us connect with people. Over time, they'll help us connect more effectively. They'll help us identify the right people and spark communities based on an understanding of what we represent and what we're looking to accomplish. The Web is becoming a lot smarter and will eventually start to help us come together as peers to collaborate and innovate.

The landscape of current social tools and networks is vast. Let's open up the toolbox so that we may understand what's in it and why each tool exists, so that we can determine which tools make sense to place back in the toolbox that we will carry with us.

For a complete list of up-to-date tools and networks, please visit www.theconversationprism.com.

■ DEFINING SOCIAL MEDIA

Social media is many things to many people and represents much more than technology. It represents a societal renaissance that spawned a vibrant ecosystem supported by flourishing cultures and lifestyles.

Social media is:

➤ A platform for the socialization of media

➤ The online tools that facilitate conversations

➤ Connections between friends, peers, and influencers

➤ Collaboration

➤ The redistribution of influence

➤ A call for humanizing personas and audiences, and the stories that link them together

➤ Compassionate

➤ An opportunity and a privilege

When the original definition for social media was submitted to Wikipedia in 2006, it was, and still is, incomplete, inclusive, and worse, confusing. I've attempted to contribute to a more useful portrayal of social media over the years, only to find my words edited, revised, or deleted by scores of experts. I gave up and instead opted to write blogposts, publish ebooks, and write printed books to help clarify what social media is and isn't.

As I defined it several years ago with the help of Chris Shipley, Stowe Boyd, Chris Heuer, and Robert Scoble, among many others . . .

Social media is any tool or service that uses the Internet to facilitate conversations.

Of course, a longer version is always helpful.

Social media is the democratization of information, transforming people from content readers into publishers. It is the shift from a broadcast mechanism, one-to-many, to a many-to-many model, rooted in conversations between authors, people, and peers.

Social media is one chapter in the evolution of new media. Let's consider its affect on terminology.

■ WHEN WORDS LOSE THEIR MEANING

This is a subject that is garnering much of my attention and contemplation as the terminology that orbits the social media universe is in danger of spinning off course and into a black hole of obscurity.

We stand at a crossroads where the language of social media either matures and develops or depreciates and decays. As with anything, words become meaningless if overused and underpracticed. The words that appear in a glossary, specifically those used to capture and define the essence of social media and the tenets of successful engagement, education, and community building, are often misused, misinterpreted, undervalued, or thrown around as bragging rights.

Some of the words on the endangered species list include:

Transparency

Conversation, or dialogue

Listening

Relationships

Being yourself or being human

Engage

Viral

Authenticity

I suppose there's irony in listing *engage* on the list. The difference here is that we must engage rather than talk of its need. See, we must hold these words and their meanings sacred to create programs that exude integrity, instill advocacy, and earn trust. Conceived or devised in any other way, our efforts may lead to misperceptions that can cause angst and backlash within important communities, regardless of intent.

Authenticity and transparency are the minimum requirements in any exchange, online and in the real world. If authority, trust, and loyalty are what we strive for, then authenticity and transparency do not, in or of themselves, attain our goals. Authority, trust, loyalty, and their ability to inspire activity are earned gradually through every exchange where those involved are informed as a result of their participation. Engage!

Relevant information, consistency, and insight are the attributes of those who build credibility among their peers. Listening identifies relevant dialogue online. Transparency facilitates authentic conversations by being human and accessible. We start to turn words into action, which defines the formula for sparking relationships that create communities that spread our messages virally.

The essence and usefulness of each important and distinct word is slowly migrating into a hollow of obsolescence as we attach them to all things social media, without stopping to truly reflect on and observe their intent, definition, weight, and opportunity.

Before we go astray, it's now imperative to associate these words with sincerity, purpose, and action. It's not just a matter of authenticity versus authority, nor is it a race to listen and forge relationships by engaging through transparency. It's about transcending the ideas behind the words into something of significance, trustworthiness, education, and remembrance.

By way of illustration, what if we considered the differences between the following terms:

Believability versus transparency

Contribution or investment versus simple engagement

Participation versus conversation

Hearing versus listening

Collaboration versus relationships

Empathy versus being human

Hearing is much different from listening to what someone has to say, how they got to where they are, and where they need to go.

Listening, and truly hearing, profoundly affects how we improve or evolve our services or infrastructure.

Transparency is openness, but it's irrelevant without a cause to champion or the ability to convey empathy.

Authenticity is genuine, but people can be authentically misinformed and not even know it. Being yourself may not be enough to satisfy all parties and, no matter how amazing you are, if your personality and communication skills do not connect people to the personality of the company or brand you represent, missed connections become endemic. Intentions don't necessarily count. Purpose and mission must be defined so they can impart the intended perception and spark future activity.

Conversations are meaningless without substance, insight, collaboration, or a helpful exchange that offers mutual satisfaction.

It's not conversations that build relationships and spark word-of-mouth. Interaction, collaboration, and consistency help us build meaningful interactions that deliver value to contributors. It's how we earn trust and loyalty and establish significance that defines our stature and determines our diagnosis for just how contagious we are.

Purpose, empathy, and authority are, in fact, interrelated and entwined.

Perhaps what we learn is that authenticity + wisdom + engagement + reflection + adaptation = trust, loyalty, and authority.

Transparency and objectivity meets purpose and contribution.

Chapter

The New Media University 101

Blogs, Podcasts, and Livecasts

As we advance our knowledge of new media, its implications and its opportunities, we realize just how lucky we are to live in the time of the next Web.

At this stage, we review the platforms and tools that define the terrain of the Social Web so that we may build the roads, highways, bridges, and constructs of communications, community development, and goodwill.

But before we jump in, I'd like to introduce a concept to you—one that will make more sense as you scale your socialized communications efforts.

Building and organizing a social media program can be incredibly powerful. As people become increasingly connected and form relationships rooted in passions, interests, and circumstances, distinct communities emerge and evolve—endlessly. And, over time, these communities expand, contract, and shift as they foster dialogue.

These channels distribute information to people when and how they choose to receive, process, share, and interact.

You, me, all of us, we become media.

While once out of reach for most businesses over the years, we now possess the ability to transform any brand of any size into an independent media publishing, broadcasting, and service organization.

The implications are profound. We have the capacity to now reach people far beyond our local television and radio broadcasts and even beyond those of the most prestigious national media empires.

The difference is that this reach is not prescribed; it must be earned.

Unlike traditional broadcast mechanisms, information flows both ways, whether we choose to ignore it or embrace it.

We contribute to our perception through absence *and* participation.

We contribute to our presence *and* our reputation.

We define our contributions and benevolence through our actions *and* words.

We are the architects who are drafting the blueprint for a new bridge between our stories and the people who benefit from them.

■ BLOGS

No matter what we think we know about blogs, there's always something new to learn. Let's start with some interesting points of observation and reality so that we can frame blogs in a proper setting.

Forrester Research published a report shockingly titled "Time to Rethink Your Corporate Blogging Ideas."[1] To the surprise of many, it placed corporate blogs at the bottom of the credibility list. According to the study, only 16 percent of online consumers who read corporate blogs admitted to trusting them. As such, blogs ranked lower in trustworthiness than every other form of content in Forrester's list of corporate marketing and media tools, even below broadcast and print media, direct mail, and email.

However, don't let this deter you from starting or further developing your blog. The primary reason for the unpopularity of a corporate blog is directly attributable to the wariness that consumers have acquired through years of being barraged by propaganda, publicity, and hype. Many companies unfortunately have used the blog as yet another vehicle to push promotion over value. It's not a place to publish press releases, nor is it intended to serve as a stepchild of service or marketing.

Blogs are completely ineffective and only contribute to consumers' leeriness when used as a corporate platform for marketing, shilling, pitching, or broadcasting promotional messages.

The lack of seriousness and understanding toward blogs has unfortunately caused reverberating effects that are difficult to overcome. With that said, you are not burdened with the responsibility of transforming an entire industry, nor the perceptions associated with it. Your responsibility is to increase the collaboration between you and your peers, customers, and prospects. Your priority is increasing your value in the communities that affect your bottom line, and blogs are an important library for your digital legacy. The best corporate blogs are genuine and designed to help people, by becoming an industry resource through thought leadership, unquestionable passion, and solutions for the real-world pains of the marketplace.

The blog is your hub for demonstrating expertise, sharing vision, listening to and responding to customers, communicating progress, curating relevant market and trend information, and hosting dialogues to further the company's values and principles. It requires continuity, cadence, and a voice that readers can connect with.

What's the cause?

What's the intent?

How can we fill a void and, more importantly, how can we help solve problems?

What should readers take away from the blog?

Why should anyone link back to the blog?

Of all the blogs in the world, some of the most popular are, in fact, company blogs. Google, 37Signals, and Dell are among the most read and linked-to blogs in the blogosphere, and for good reason. They embody all of the points listed earlier. They live and breathe the human persona of the brand that they've created and have emerged as a frequented and must-stop destination for consumers seeking information, direction, discourse, and recognition.

It's important to point out that even to this day, executives and marketers question the efficiency and potential of blogs—even in the face of tangible evidence that proves its upside. Many believe that their time is better spent elsewhere and that finding contributors for insightful posts can become an unsustainable chore.

One solution resides in the outsourcing of post writing to outside experts who will gladly contribute unbiased, valuable, and interesting content for a price. Depending on the individual, posts can range from $25 to hundreds of dollars per article. But doing so links your blog to the network of each contributor, thus expanding its reach through value.

Marketers initially shied away from ghostwritten posts, whereas an uncredited, paid writer posts content under someone else's byline. Instead, communication and marketing professionals asked, or begged, for the participation of the influential voices of important individuals within the business, requesting them to blog as often as possible. While this is necessary in the art of blogging, it is not realistic to expect these focused business leaders to assume the role of blogger. It is rational, and effective, however, to encourage infrequent, yet scheduled, posts from them or to have their thoughts shared through an interview or Q&A. There's a reason why these people are leading the company, and their vision and experiences must receive attention in the most prominent platform for sharing that company voice and persona—the blog.

It's not only contract bloggers who represent a solution for filling the editorial calendar in between executive posts—other employees, stakeholders, and outside enthusiasts and customers are also willing to contribute. They just need direction, deadlines, and a framework. Many are more than capable of interviewing key executives, customers, partners, and influencers to feature their visions, experiences, and wisdom, without requiring them to write directly for the blog. We don't always need to hear from the spokesperson or the executive. Ford, for example, often introduces us to the people behind the story, allowing customers to make a human connection.

Everything must start with a plan, however.

Blogging for the sake of blogging, even with the best of intentions, is meaningless if the internal team cannot communicate an organized infrastructure. Essentially, someone must serve as an editor-in-chief for the blog or blog network. Someone must preside over the channel so it can better marshal the brand and ensure integrity. In the models in which multiple networks exist—for example, across product or business divisions—multiple editors must officiate the content for their dedicated channel, ultimately reporting to a chief editor. For those organizations in which tens, hundreds, or thousands of corporate-run or endorsed blogs exist, guidelines, best practices, standards, rewards, and consequences are not optional. They must exist and receive attention and governance. Otherwise, social chaos ensues, resulting in brand dilution and market confusion.

The challenges also lie outside the process of creating and publishing content. This is true for any form of social networking.

Nothing happens simply because you build a blog and publish a post. The delusions of grandeur or the misunderstanding of how people discover, respond to, and share information through blog sites leads to disappointment, and can cause the early termination of truly promising strategies.

Just because we host a grand opening doesn't necessarily assure us that we will host any guests. We have be in touch with our desired guests and invite them to the party.

There is an element of content promotion and marketing that is usually understated and neglected—mostly due to the lack of awareness or unfamiliarity with the processes. It crosses over, however, into ignorance when programs are disparaged or killed prematurely.

The truth is that everything related to content production, from blogs to podcasts to tweets, requires the active promotion of that content outside of your domain. Again, using the bridging metaphor, you must hand-deliver related information to those seeking it through unobtrusive, empathetic, and cooperative means.

With every link outward, every tweet back, every email, and every comment in other forums, we point people back to our work, not simply because we published something, but in view of the notion that we mindfully contributed value and insight to the greater conversation and were prepared to respond.

Yes, comments on other blogs are a form of both participation and unmarketing. Be sure to pay attention to relevant posts around the blogosphere and contribute relevant comments on both your blog and elsewhere. Some of the best conversations take place in the comments section, as people react to what you wrote, as well as the feedback from their peers.

The right comments boost visibility and contribute to a resume of experience, goodwill, and prowess.

Services such as BackType offer a window into comments across the entire blogosphere. It's a search engine for keywords and names, specifically in the comments sections of blogs. In contrast, blog search engines scour only the posts, but do not dive into the strings of conversations that transpire in the comments sections. BackType and new comment- and reputation-tracking systems that are integrated into blog platforms such as Disqus or IntenseDebate can say more about you than you imagine. These services align the comments that are strewn across the hundreds of thousands of (legitimate) blogs and give us clarity into each commenter.

As you blog, lead, or contribute to the blogging initiatives, make sure to link to all channels of influence each and every time they share something of significance—even if it's an older entry. This will send trackbacks to any outside blog post that may have inspired your post(s) and thus build tunnels between the blogs, allowing new readers to discover your content.

Extend your knowledge and acumen outside of your domain and into the online provinces that host and promote discussions that orbit your entity. Quite simply said, go where your customers are and not where they aren't. Give them something to read. Give them something to share. Give them reasons to respond.

Create a blogroll and link out to influential voices on the Web, whether they're reporters, bloggers, customers, analysts, or just excellent resources for inspiration and intelligence. Promote outside voices often.

■ BLOG EXAMPLE: SOUTHWEST AIRLINES AND DELL

Southwest Airline's blog (www.blogsouthwest.com), playfully named "Nuts about Southwest," keeps in line with the company's "Fun-LUVing" attitude. The site informs, with posts dedicated to the latest service changes or updates on its bid for Frontier Airlines. It entertains, such as by covering the wedding of two Southwest frequent flyers who prominently displayed Southwest peanuts packages at each table. And most importantly, the site aims to build a personal relationship between Southwest employees and customers. The blog extends beyond standard text posts to include multimedia. The page incorporates images; links to the Southwest Flickr group, an employee video blog; and also encourages user participation through ratings, polls, comments, and photo and video sharing.

In another example, Dell launched its blog, Direct2Dell, in July 2006, to engage customers, open up the lines of communication, and repair its reputation after dealing with a tarnished image and a firestorm of criticisms across the blogosphere. And the strategy is working. In Jeff Jarvis's *BusinessWeek* article in 2007,[2] it was reported that negative blog posts about Dell dropped from 49 percent to 22 percent.

Dell has participated openly and honestly—even posting photos of one of its exploded laptops on the blog. And the company launched IdeaStorm.com to solicit customer's suggestions, comments, and complaints. There's even been evidence that community feedback has driven product development at Dell (see http://is.gd/1YCUe).

■ PODCASTS

Podcasts are a powerful and portable way to reach people who prefer audio as a means of education, intellectual stimulation, or entertainment.

Podcasts are do-it-yourself (DIY)-easy and can provide a world of value to customers, peers, and influencers. Not only are podcasts portable, they're embeddable and shareable in websites and blog posts, are promotable just about anywhere to anyone looking for insight, and are distributed by Apple iTunes, which provides access to millions of potential users worldwide. The tools for recording, editing, and publishing podcasts are increasingly affordable and readily available from computer-based audio tools to handheld recording gadgets—making it practically a no-brainer to at least experiment with this medium.

Podcast content can focus on a variety of programming and can include shows dedicated to company milestones, industry trends and challenges, executive interviews, customer success stories, how-to instructions, and anything else in between.

■ PODCAST EXAMPLES: FIDELITY INVESTMENTS

Financial services provider Fidelity Investments offers its clients and the general public free podcasts at Fidelity Podcasts. Current and interested investors can listen to interviews with Fidelity mutual fund portfolio managers as they share investment strategies, expectations, and market analysis. No doubt this value-adding information keeps Fidelity in the spotlight for investors and helps establish their authority (see http://is.gd/1YBUF).

■ WIKIS

Wikis, a name that comes from the Hawaiian phrase *wiki wiki,* meaning *really fast,* are among the most efficient tools for tapping the wisdom of the crowds wherever ideas, information, directions and instructions, product or experiential feedback, brainstorming, process or event management, and myriad other applications are requested. In fact, one of the most successful and influential websites in existence is a wiki. You probably know it better as Wikipedia.

Wikis are designed to allow site visitors to add, edit, update, and amend information through any Web browser. They invite and promote collaboration among employees, as well as consumers and influencers.

Wikis are important to facilitate collaboration in a friendlier, more socially focused content creation and management system. It's not just about teams and document management or collaboration around a particular topic. Wikis can provide a vibrant forum for inviting content and suggestions from customers and partners to further ideas and dialogue in an ongoing, trackable, scalable, and measurable fashion.

Wiki software can run on any Web server, to host custom wiki pages as a stand-alone destination or as an extension to your website. Third-party wiki platforms are also widely available if you choose to host a wiki outside of your domain. URLs can still be customized and simply point to a different location.

Wikipedia entries regarding your company and market are highly influential to visitors who visit those pages. The Google page-rank function is incredibly strong in Wikipedia, and in most cases the leading result for any search in Google will direct you to the corresponding page in Wikipedia.

I've worked with several influential and famous people who did not appreciate the user-generated content associated with their Wikipedia entries and tried, numerously and unsuccessfully, to edit them directly or through the help of employees and outside experts. Their edits always reverted back to the previous version. Wikipedia operates on an earned trust and credibility system where accredited editors outrank everyday users. Find an expert to help you before you inadvertently lock up the page, which occurs when there are too many attempts to change it.

■ WIKI EXAMPLE: ORACLE

Oracle launched its official public Oracle wiki back in 2007. Designed for both employees and nonemployees (the main page bears the message "Oracle employees, this is not an internal site!"), the wiki is a place where members of the Oracle community can collaborate and share content on Oracle-related subjects—including installation guides, technical tips, and project documentation.

The Oracle wiki presents an interesting example for those companies grappling with the loss of control in the very public and transparent world of social media. While the wiki FAQs state that the site belongs to the community, Oracle (like Microsoft and others) has chosen to play the role of active moderator. The company has been criticized for removing negative statements about its products (which they claimed violated the terms of use). Of course, unlike the truly community-driven Wikipedia, corporate wiki owners always have a choice of when and how to moderate content on their site. In Oracle's case, they may have wanted to prevent damaging material from reaching their competitors—yet in the process of being careful and calculated, they run the risk of public backlash against perceived censorship and loss of goodwill in the community (see http://wiki.oracle.com).

■ NOTES

1. Josh Bernoff, "Time to Rethink Your Corporate Blogging Ideas," Forrester Research (December 2008), www.forrester.com/Marketing/Campaign2/1,6538,1946,00.html.

2. Jeff Jarvis, "Dell Learns to Listen," *BusinessWeek* (October 17, 2007), www.businessweek.com/bwdaily/dnflash/content/oct2007/db20071017_277576.htm.

ter

Media
y 201

ial Calendars,
sting

online provinces of blogs, pod-
examine the nuances, risks, ap-
ted with content communities,

COMMUNITIES

Online content communities exist to promote the human filtering of online information (or manipulation of it, depending on how you look at it). These unique communities are basically social networks that increase signal and reduce the noise from all of the information out there, fostering interaction around compelling content. These platforms tap the wisdom of the crowds to source, share, and show-case news, videos, pictures, music or other audio, and events. The most popular content is determined by the crowdsourcing of votes to determine popularity and visibility of entries as organized by the specific categories within the network.

These communities serve as a lens into what's hot, interesting, or promising, as dictated by the psychographics that connect demo-graphics. We'll open the curtains to reveal the groups of people pow-ering these networks later in the book.

33

Leading sites include Reddit, Digg, Mixx, and Fark, among others. Combined, these networks receive, on average, 55 million unique visitors per month. In comparison, CNN.com receives, on average, roughly 30 million unique visitors. Niche content communities exist for almost every vertical industry as well, and here may be more than one resource for you to learn and share with people who can help you and the company you represent.

The practice of curating content is pervasive in these networks, as well as in networks dedicated to social bookmarks (see the next section). Conversations take place in the form of comments and backchannel interaction where people usually ask each other for votes or spark private dialogues based on the comments for a particular entry.

These communities receive content from users who submit something that they find interesting on a news site, blog, website, or other social network (YouTube, Flickr, Vimeo, Photobucket, Picasa, Docstoc, and so on) directly into the community—usually by clicking *submit* or a similar command. To simplify the submission and promotion of content in user-curated communities, integrated (or user-installable) tools exist directly in the pages where the content is hosted. For example, if you're reading a news story or blog post, you may be guided to a "Digg This" or other button specific to a particular network of the publisher's choice, so you can either submit a story or vote it up for further visibility. Other aggregated services such as "Share This" enable publishers to offer one tool to connect users to the network of their choice.

The goal, of course, is to earn significant momentum within a finite time in order to hit the virtual front page, or at the very least, be among the most active within your given category.

The front page of Digg, for example, can yield upward of 20,000 to 50,000 unique visits in one week to that particular piece of content. And if it's a blog post on your corporate site or a video related to your brand or product, imagine how that traffic could directly convert into leads or prospects.

The activity that sends flurries of votes in any given direction is not always organic. In fact, in some cases, the process is calculated or paid. For example, in most social networks, many of the votes are driven by working with people in specific social graphs to vote for as a favor or as an investment, when something is needed in return. On the other hand, to make the front page of Digg, many of the "Power Diggers" will help you for a price ranging from $500 to $2,500 per event. Power users are connected and there's an incentive for them to leverage their networks to your advantage. Without them, it takes a very organized and orchestrated campaign to submit a story and then drive enough support for it to move naturally—pushed by the people you've aligned in advance to help.

Sometimes it's a combination of leveraging both power networks and the social graph to help push posts to the top.

The wisdom of the crowds begins with curation and is then propelled by word of mouth (WOM) or the physical act of endorsing or promoting content within the network and also across the social graph (in other social networks). Everything requires content promotion for any of it to grab the attention of those who are focused on everything else but what it is you're trying to share with them.

Earn their attention.

■ SOCIAL CALENDARS AND EVENTS

Nothing beats participation and relationship building like connecting in the real world!

Social calendaring networks transform email or website-based consumer invitation and RSVP management applications (such as evite.com) and provide a platform and supporting social network for those hosting or seeking events.

Want to see what your friends are attending?

Care to view upcoming events tied to your keywords in any city around the world?

Social calendars facilitate this ability and form paths to identify and connect with real world communities—or, as some refer to it, IRL (in real life).

Facebook events, Upcoming.org, Meetup, Twtvite (tweetups) and Eventful serve as sites that reach potential constituents by introducing or participating in relevant events, sorted by location and by topic or industry. In the case of companies and interest groups, these networks serve as tools to invite people to demos, polls, town halls, open houses, training, webcasts, trade shows, customer spotlights and Q&As, and live chats, among many other occasions and gatherings.

For example, you can list a particular event within a social calendar network. They can also invite inside and outside network friends to RSVP for the event. As people RSVP, their responses are visible across their social graph (those people connected to them within the social network and those who have set up their accounts to syndicate their updates across other social networks). If the event is listed in Facebook, each time someone RSVPs or comments, the activity appears on their newsfeed and in the newsfeed of all their friends. This brings greater awareness to the activity organically. For example, if you RSVP for a particular event in Facebook, I would see that activity in my timeline, "YOU have RSVPd for X event." The idea is that it would most likely motivate me to click through to view additional details about the event. This activity can also send updates to outside networks such as Twitter and Facebook, to reach an entirely different set of contacts. Did you know that millions of events are created each month within Facebook?

You'll notice that the events in each of the aforementioned services differ in organization, intention, and reach. For instance, Meetup.com is dedicated to recurring themed events. It's a vibrant, geographically expansive network that hosts regular meetups for everything from scrapbooking, photography workshops to branded dialogue around issues and opportunities facing particular industries.

I've hosted events for companies in our home cities using Meetup.com, Facebook, and Plancast, to experiment with event formulas, formats, and audiences that offer the most impact for attending guests while still building a community that extends from online to the real world. The idea was to create an event that appealed to customers, prospects, partners, and influencers to share and learn together. It also served as an installment series that provides ongoing insight and surfaces the most critical questions and concerns.

We invited customers and industry experts to speak about industry trends, challenges, and solutions, as well as answer questions related to the real-world experiences of those in the audience. Using Meetup.com, we're able to create a branded event that created a microcommunity within the larger community of users looking for related events. The goal was to find a format that proved effective, and that could be used locally on a monthly or quarterly basis, and create a template that could be reproduced by ambassadors around the country or world so they can provide resources for communities of users IRL.

We also experimented with events in which we used a combination of Upcoming.org, Facebook events, and Twitter for additional visibility to point back to one or both of the event hubs. Each network boasts its own group of contacts. Crossover may exist, but for the most part, distinct connections are anchored to each network. Contacts discovered and shared the events within their own networks and when combined with those targeted prospects who also discovered the affairs through search, the results were always outstanding—to the point of having to close sign-up lists or turn people away or both.

Another popular trend for meetups or tweetups centers on bloggers, local influencers, and visiting authorities who are in town for an event or conference.

As companies recognize the value, opportunity, and potential of blogger relations and engagement, extending a virtual hand to introduce bloggers to key executives is instrumental in establishing effective relationships that can garner attention and coverage in the future.

People are actively searching for relevant events. To reach them, we must earn a presence in the networks where they seek intelligence. It is imperative for every company to proactively and personally recognize bloggers and influencers as important to your business—not only for pitching stories, but also for establishing dialogue. Respect and admiration are not simply sentiments, they can be effective building blocks for strong relationships.

Building relationships within these communities, promoting events among those they benefit, and using the right tags and descriptions all play important roles in creating and attracting visibility.

Hosting events in the real world, even if they're organized on the Social Web, transcends online interactions and builds bona fide, real-world relationships—in fact, it ratifies them.

■ LIVECASTING

There was a time when only the most prosperous companies had access to the tools and services to shoot, edit, and broadcast audio or video. Over recent years, the Social Web has sparked remarkable innovation, substantially reducing the barriers to entry and the associated costs for creating and publishing online audio and video. Companies are, in essence, building full-fledged content networks online that can air live or episodic videos on demand.

As a result, a rising class of video networks exists that facilitates the streaming of live and prerecorded video channels that foster conversations around media.

Live video communities such as Ustream and Justin.tv, among others, enable livecasting and chat room interactivity. Services such as Qik and Mogulus also allow for livecasting, in addition to offering the ability to broadcast video and support chat room functionality from a mobile phone. Viewers can enjoy the videos from any PC or mobile device.

Live audio also represents a growing opportunity to reach important markets. Services such as BlogTalkRadio provide a sophisticated, but simple, platform for livecasting hosted audio discussions, similar to a radio talk show format. Imagine hosting a weekly interview series with executives, customers, or market experts to share insights with your community while introducing the personalities behind the business.

Livecasting networks also share many similarities with traditional social networks. Inherent in each network is a community of active affiliates. Users can "friend" other members to form micronetworks of contacts to interact in and around programming.

Many companies that I've worked with or observed have effectively leveraged these services to webcast training sessions, earnings reports, live chats with key personnel and special guests, HR and executive announcements, product reviews, marketing or industry events, lectures, and conference discussions, speeches, panels, and so on. Employees, partners, and customers can view and chat with one another during the sessions to ask and answer questions and solicit feedback. In every interaction, you're investing in and building a dedicated community of appreciative and loyal subscribers and patrons.

Chapter 6

The New Media University 301

Images and Multimedia

In this chapter, we study social networks dedicated to multimedia and focused discussions along with discussing the social media press release and the Social Media Newsroom.

■ IMAGES

One of the most understated categories of social networks is also one of the most established. Online photo sharing encourages views and interaction around images, transforming pictures into social objects.

People are, right now, looking for pictures related to products, companies, and brands, interesting people, places, events, and anything else you can imagine, by using keywords within these photo networks to find, react, utilize, remix, share, and republish.

Some of the more successful companies are already sharing art and customer-focused, exclusive content in communities such as Flickr and Facebook Photos. Just to give you perspective, Flickr alone receives on average, 30 million unique visitors per month. Facebook, now technically the largest social network for photos, receives more than 1 billion new photos every month.

On the most basic level, these new image channels can publicize and potentially circulate original artwork, previews and glimpses products, behind-the-scenes shots, events, screen shots, and beauty shots. Essentially all applicable media should be placed in social communities to benefit influencers, customers, stakeholders, and prospects. Create channels within these photo networks and organize the images by albums to attract interested parties, who will discover, appreciate, and hopefully interact and share.

The existence of these highly trafficked networks is changing our perception of how we create and distribute corporate artwork, events, and products. They also broaden the landscape and reach for artists (this is true for all forms of social media as well). It starts with letting go of control so as to effectually galvanize activity around your brand instead.

Before the socialization of the Web, copyrights prevented image usage. However, there are benefits to providing access to images and promoting free distribution. As pictures, as well as all forms of media, are social objects, the advantages that result from the extended interaction and visibility far outweigh controlled distribution. For that reason, many businesses and artists are adopting the use of Creative Commons licensing over traditional copyrights. Creative Commons is a nonprofit organization that increases sharing and improves collaboration. The tagline says it all, "Share, Remix, Reuse—Legally."

Creative Commons (CC) promotes the spirit of the Social Web by increasing the amount of creativity (cultural, educational, and scientific content) in "the commons"—the body of work that is available to the public—and securely encourages free and legal sharing, use, repurposing, and remixing. CC tools offer users a simple, standardized way to grant permission to their creative works, benefiting everyone from individual creators to large companies and institutions.

■ IMAGES EXAMPLE: JETBLUE AND THE AMERICAN RED CROSS ON FLICKR

JetBlue hosts a public group on Flickr that encourages customers, employees, and fans to post and share their own JetBlue-related shots. At the time this chapter was written, community members have posted 4,800 photos, videos, and drawings—ranging from shots of the plane on the tarmac to photos of the in-flight snacks and panoramas of skylines captured from the air. Sprinkled among the traveler's shots are photos clearly posted by JetBlue marketing teams and employees. Far from appearing like promotional fluff, these photos reveal the human side of the corporate brand, showing staff at corporate events or professional shots from various marketing events (see Figure 6.1).

Members of this Flickr group can comment on one another's photos. And without a doubt, employees and fans are connecting—sharing

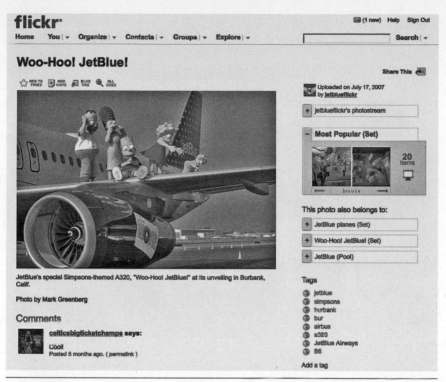

Figure 6.1   JetBlue's Simpson-Themed A320 Promotional Photo on Flickr

experiences and building relationships around travel memories and the brand (see www.flickr.com/groups/b6/).

After Hurricane Katrina, the American Red Cross launched a broad social media initiative to track people's sentiments about Red Cross–related issues and to strengthen the organization's relationship with the public. In addition to launching a blog, using WordPress to create disaster portals through which affected citizens can find resources, and sending Twitter updates with alerts on shelter locations, the organization is developing an active Flickr community in which people can share their photographs. At the time of writing, there are 393 Red Cross Flickr members and 1,627 images have been posted.

The Flickr site is designed to give Red Cross volunteers a place to visually share their unique stories and experiences and connect with others around the country who are passionate about the organization. Communities like this one on Flickr help the Red Cross strengthen its bonds with people who are already active in the organization, as well as increase exposure to its causes and services.

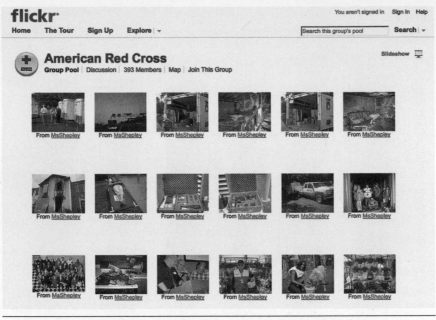

Figure 6.2   The American Red Cross on Flickr

Of course, remember that it's never just about one social media tool. While the Red Cross's Flickr community may be vibrant, they are leveraging multiple social media tools (blogs, Facebook, Twitter, and active brand monitoring across the Web), creating multiple touch points with volunteers and the general public. By cross-referencing updates, available resources, and communities across all these social media points, the Red Cross can increase visibility and drive traffic among its communities (see Figure 6.2 and www.flickr.com/groups/americanredcross).

Chapter 7

The New Media University 401

Dashboards, Social Networks, and Brands

I know: There's a lot to process here—not to mention that we are only beginning to discuss the evolution of media overall. Take solace in your state of understanding and in your surroundings. You are not alone. We are all in this together.

Learn with determination.

Breathe it in.

Discover.

Dream.

Imagine.

Lead.

Listen and engage in discussions with empathy and understanding.

Moving forward, we'll review social media dashboards, social networks, virtual goods, and branded, or purpose-driven, social networks.

■ SOCIAL MEDIA DASHBOARDS

The book will repeat this message throughout: We must produce and promote compelling material in the communities where our customers, peers, influencers, and prospects are active—using the consumption methods and means that they prefer.

Social media dashboards serve as a solution for arranging content from disparate networks into one cooperative digital menu.

Consumers may view one form of media, for example, a video on YouTube, but they may not necessarily be aware that the company offers additional insight through other forms of content beyond the YouTube video and profile. Sending viewers back to a company website is only going to hinder our goal of creating a bridge for interaction. For those curious visitors seeking a social directory in our domain, how do we steer them to our external social presences?

Chances are, a directory either doesn't exist or profiles are littered throughout the site and the Web.

A social dashboard is a dedicated microsite either within an existing corporate website or hosted at a dedicated URL that aggregates the disparate corporate social profiles and media—presenting them in one visually rich, easy-to-navigate destination that promotes outside connectivity and onsite interaction.

Dashboards can include video from YouTube, pictures from Flickr, blog posts, tweets, or other forms of updates from the *Statusphere,* social network activity, Facebook brand pages, a forum, events, and a directory to other social profiles. Each component of the dashboard can also provide individual RSS feeds or an all-inclusive feed (in online processor markup language, or OPML) for interested visitors who prefer to follow the updated content in their respective RSS readers.

In one such example, Chevy released VoltAge (see www .chevroletvoltage.com), a destination website to host and spark activity through a visually rich aggregated experience.

VoltAge offered unique content for visitors in the form of behind-the-scenes and custom videos and exclusive pictures of the Volt through channeled pictures (see Figure 7.1).

Chevy also integrated other forms of compartmentalized conversational content, such as a hosted forum for topical dialogues, blog posts, tweets from Twitter, news releases, polls with real-time results, upcoming events, and also Facebook Connect.

I worked with Anheuser-Busch to create a social dashboard to tell the story behind the company's Super Bowl commercials that year. The Dashboard went live before the big game and featured behind the scenes footage from the shoots, interviews with the director, discussions with the trainer of the famous Clydesdale horses, as well as pictures and other media. This content was less about promoting the company's new commercials and more about humanizing the intent and storyline behind the spots and the real people who brought it all together (see Figure 7.2).

Services such as Facebook Connect and Twitter Login provide a secure way to easily integrate into your hosted network, so that

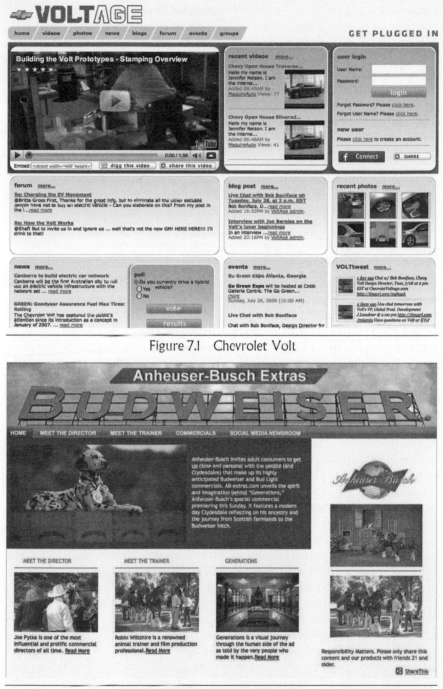

Figure 7.1   Chevrolet Volt

Figure 7.2   Anheuser-Busch Extras

visitors can access or contribute content without needing to create yet another profile or login account. Do not make users create new login credentials. By integrating (easily) the ability for people to login using their Facebook and Twitter IDs, the likelihood of participation is increased. It also aggregates the extracurricular activity back into Facebook, for example. The subsequent action of, for example, commenting on a video or blog post, will send that comment back to Facebook in their newsfeed and the feeds of their friends. If their friends see it, and if it's intriguing, it's likely that they may also click-through to see what engaged their attention.

It is a very simple and effective way of unmarketing content from your domain to the extended social graphs of those who appreciate the content you publish.

■ SOCIAL NETWORKS

Social networks such as Facebook and LinkedIn offer a variety of mechanisms to discover and connect with influencers and peers. Social networks also offer myriad other forms of collaboration and promotion. Opportunities range from comments and wall posts to groups and fan pages to events to customized applications, widgets, and games, and to virtual goods.

Community and brand managers can also create groups and or brand pages if they don't yet exist, so they can host dialogues with and solicit feedback from stakeholders. This group engagement also provides opportunities that pave the way for interaction, direction, or support.

In Facebook, for example, each group, event, application, or brand page can be promoted by organic means and also through email and in-network mail. It also provides a simple method for running a small visual ad tied to your chosen keywords, however, with which you can promote the page on a cost per 1,000 (CPM) or a cost per click (CPC) basis. CPM is used when trying to reach the broadest range of impressions possible. CPC is used when the goal of the program is to get people to click through (measured in a click-through rate, or CTR), and, in this case, join a group or page.

Many companies rush to create group or brand pages dedicated to their corporate and product brands without first considering the rationale for doing so or checking if one may already exist (usually started by a fan or an angry customer).

In some cases in which a popular group is already thriving, it may make more sense to align the brand with the group and take an active role in its direction. For example, on Facebook alone, there are thousands of groups and brand pages dedicated to Coke and Coca-Cola, with the most popular fan page hosting millions of fans. While Facebook rules state that fan pages can be created only by the company or authorized representatives, this page was started by Dusty Sorg and Michael Jedrzejewski in Los Angeles before the new rule took effect. When Coca-Cola was contemplating its Facebook fan page strategy, it realized that its greatest networking opportunity was to empower the duo to continue to run the page along with collaboration from the Coke team.

That's the trick of all of this. It's the art of garnering attention and then capturing and holding it now and henceforward. Everything requires promotion through the consistent and vigorous acts of connecting profiles and pages to those who will enjoy them. And once engaged, it's our job to keep them engaged.

Participation is key to growing the community and ensuring its integrity and associated activity.

■ BRANDED AND PURPOSE-DRIVEN SOCIAL NETWORKS

Indeed, the most popular social networks in the world offer the ability to create, host, and participate in subnetworks, or groups dedicated to your brand and products. They are not the only networks to establish a presence, however. In the spirit of reaching out to significant groups of people where they interact, there are several services that exist to facilitate the creation, promotion, and cultivation of stand-alone networks that are either hosted independently from your main Web presence or are also embeddable within your primary site.

These communities function similarly to other groups and networks, but differ in where they're hosted, how they appear, and their intended form and function. Simply said, brands can maintain multiple presences dedicated to fostering specific conversations spanning from sales and service to education to internal collaboration and dialogue related to specific products, lifestyles, and events—or simply a place that encourages consumers to share insights, ask questions, and contribute ideas on company and product direction.

Many brands seed to build loyalty-building networks in addition to existing social networks. And while I don't promote any brand spreading itself thin by dedicating resources to establishing presences in each and every network, it is typical to establish presences in multiple networks where customers are already active.

Communities such as Ning provide do-it-yourself (DIY) tools to build a very professional, customized social network dedicated to any theme or topic you choose. Ning is also a social network for social networks, in that it already boasts over one million niche groups and a significant user population that supports them. Ning gathers users together around common interests and therefore is an ideal location in which to establish a strategic presence and promote it inside and outside the rapidly growing network.

Other brands choose to socialize their main online presence, usually the corporate website, by adding social networking functionality on a particular page of the site. Some brands prefer the ability to aggregate worldwide Web traffic to a place where it can guide user click paths and ultimately capture leads or sales in one place. Leverage Software, Jive, Cisco, and Kickapps, among others, provide dedicated resources, services, and systems for creating and hosting inward- and outward-facing social networks. It's for this reason that Facebook has made its fan pages portable, allowing brands to embed a widget version of the brand page directly into websites. Doing so builds a bridge between the strong Facebook network and outside visitors to concentrate on promotion and community building.

Visitors to outside branded pages can securely log in with their Facebook credentials to interact with the widget to comment, like, and view the latest pictures, videos, posts, and so on. As fans participate, their activity is simultaneously shared within the Facebook community, further promoting the branded content within the personal news feed for Facebook friends and contacts to potentially view and click through.

Brands currently using the embedded Facebook fan page include BlackBerry, NPR, World Wildlife Fund, *Newsweek,* Roger Federer, and ABC News.

Remember, just because you build it, doesn't mean they will come. You have to start by recruiting. Go find your customers and bring them to you or engage them where they are right now.

■ BRANDED SOCIAL NETWORK EXAMPLES: PANASONIC LIVING IN HD

In conjunction with Crayon, a new media agency, Panasonic developed a dedicated social network surrounding its high-definition products and technology (www.livinginhd.com). Dubbed an HD playground, Living in HD (LiHD) encourages Panasonic HD customers, technology fans, and anyone else to share their insights, experience, creativity, and enthusiasm about the world of HD. To create buzz and incentives for joining, Panasonic offers valuable prizes, including a contest that gave away 30 HD products in 30 days to members.

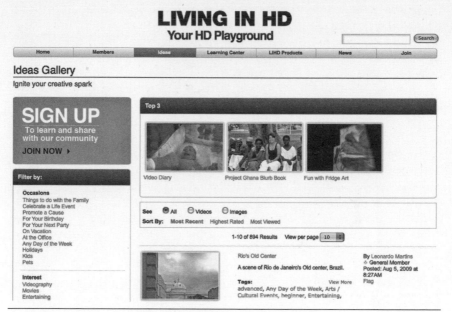

Figure 7.3　Panasonic Living in HD

Panasonic actively engages the LiHD community. For example, Greg Harper, the Panasonic Answer Man, offers community videos in response to questions from community members, on topics such as what to look for before making an HD purchase. LiHD also leverages the experience and wisdom of its community, as members frequently post and discuss tips and advice on various HD products. And recognizing that the fan base for HD products, particularly cameras and camcorders, is likely to be creative and expressive types, Panasonic offers community blogs within which members can express themselves through words, photos, and videos. They're creating a creative and collaborative atmosphere—all wrapped around the Panasonic HD brand (see Figure 7.3).

Chapter 8

The New Media University 501

Microblogs, Monetization, and Twitter

If there's one thing we're learning in the new world of socialized media, it's that our need for higher, modern education will always exist as technology advances and human behavior adjusts to accommodate the continuing rotation of pervasive applications. It's not only the study of the new tools and networks, and the intelligence that powers them, it's also the ongoing survey of the social sciences that reveal true cultures and behavior.

As our journey advances, we learn the value of aggregation and conversational threading in microblogs and microcommunities.

■ MICROBLOGS, MICROCOMMUNITIES

When this category was initially conceived, it was an industry sector that went by many names—microblogging, micromedia, micromessaging, and micronetworks, among others.

Of all of the micro services available today, Twitter is by and large the leader. FriendFeed, once embraced by the Web 2.0 elite, was later acquired by Facebook. Google introduced GoogleBuzz, but found it difficult to gain traction.

On average, there's a greater number of people updating their social status on microblogs than actually writing blog posts on a daily basis. More links are shared by micromessages than on any other form of digital media. And services such as Twitter represent a more approachable and usable gateway to social media than any of the networks serving as its predecessors.

Twitter has single-handedly forced businesses to pay attention to online conversations on a mass, and growing, scale. Communications, customer service, and even sales organizations are flocking to Twitter to participate in related conversations as well as attempting to foster communities around their brand and core values.

The magic of microcommunications is the human nature of the dialogue. Successful communities are built upon the fulfillment that consumers experience based on their conversations with real people who listen to and acknowledge their participation. It's driven by reciprocation and value-added updates, connections, and responses. The behavior associated with online engagement in these social networks is evolving. The techniques that captivate them today may no longer prove effective tomorrow. I challenge you to gaze at the horizon and determine what's coming next. Anyone reading this book or reading blogs or following influencers in social networks can design and implement copycat programs, but only you can customize a program that's specific to your business and the unique needs of your customers. Engage and activate a dedicated set of brand advocates.

Now, let's take a look at how to leverage these powerful microcommunities for macro impact, referencing the examples of today that can inspire tomorrow's programs.

■ TOP 10 MONETIZATION TRENDS FOR SOCIAL MEDIA AND MICROCOMMUNITIES

Let's take a quick look at some of the top ways that businesses are leveraging Twitter.

10. Advertising—promoted tweets, trends, accounts
9. Coupons and special offers
8. Lead generation
7. Competitive intelligence
6. Customer service
5. Commerce
4. Corporate social responsibility, making a difference
3. Ideation, collaboration for new products and services
2. Analytics; learning from customer conversations
1. Building a community of brand advocates

In the spirit of sharing monetization strategies, *Forbes* magazine assembled a visual list of Top 21 Twitter Tips[1] to help enterprise and small businesses learn how to engage on Twitter through the practices of those already successfully building online communities of customers and advocates. While many of the examples and quotes from company spokespeople remain the same, the article inspired me to modify the list, based on my experiences and observations. The end result is still a list of 21 Twitter Tips, but I believe this version may be more helpful and applicable to your world.

■ TIPS FOR TWITTER AND SOCIAL MEDIA FOR SOCIALLY SAVVY BUSINESSES

➤ Special Offers

We live in a society that is as distracted as it is informed. People are making decisions on what to read, view, purchase, visit, and sample based on the information that filters through their attention dashboards. At best, even the most qualified information sourced from the most trusted contacts will receive only a cursory overview. The trick is to concisely introduce the value up front. If the offer is compelling and affiliated with their interests, the consumer will make the connection to personal value and benefits and click through to redeem the special or coupon when ready or so inclined.

As Conway predicts, coupons and special offers will inject commerce into the social equation.

For example, @delloutlet uses Twitter and Facebook to send coupons to customers. In just one year, Dell recorded upward of $3 million in sales directly sourced from Twitter.

California Tortilla (@caltort), a chain of 39 casual Mexican restaurants based in Rockville, Maryland, sends coupon passwords through Twitter, which customers must say at checkout to redeem the offer.

➤ Ordering

While the distance between introduction and action is only separated by a link, many businesses are using Twitter to log orders. Coffee Groundz (@coffeegroundz) used the direct message channel on Twitter to receive and prepare orders. Using Twitter as a promotion and marketing channel, Coffee Groundz reports 20 to 30 percent increased sales and market share before management changed its focus.

As an aside, Pizza Hut offers iPhone and Facebook applications that allow hungry patrons to order pizza directly from Facebook and their mobile phone.

➤ Word of Mouth Marketing (There Is No Such Thing as Viral Marketing)

Moonfruit offered 11 Macbook Pros and 10 iPod Touches to celebrate its 10th anniversary. To qualify, contestants had to send a tweet using the hashtag #moonfruit. One month following the completion of the contest, Moonfruit site traffic was up 300 percent and sales also increased by 20 percent—and all because of a meager investment of $15,000. The company also realized SEO benefits, by landing on the first results page on Google for "free website builder."

Wendy Tan, Moonfruit's CEO, realizes that there's a fine line between effective and destructive #tweetowin campaigns: "Such campaigns must be courteous and fit with a company's brand, lest you draw the ire of the Twittersphere."

I discuss this challenge in more detail later in this book.

➤ Conversation Marketing

Zappos (@zappos) doesn't necessarily market on Twitter; instead, it unmarkets through conversations and engagement. At current count, 436 Zappos employees use Twitter, including CEO Tony Hsieh. For the record, Tony has more than 1 million followers.

Aaron Magness, director of business development at Zappos, acknowledges that proactively sharing the company culture and values creates a humanizing effect that invites people to be part of the community, and also acts as a sales driver. "It's easier for them to embrace openness," he said.

➤ Customer Service

Bill Gerth of Comcast (@comcastcares) and Richard Binhammer of Dell (@richardatdell) are paving the way for service-focused organizations on Twitter.

Eliason, whose title at Comcast is director of digital care, uses Twitter to help 200 to 300 subscribers a day. Frank and his 10-person help desk receive direct questions, but also proactively seek out complaints. His key to success lies in his desire to earn relations, not bark advice or chat people up. "If they want assistance, they'll let me know," he said.

➤ **Focus Groups**

Wisdom and creativity are widespread in social media. Tuning in to the frequency of conversations related to the brand or marketplace can serve as a real-time focus group for innovation and adaptation.

More than 3 million mentions of Starbucks populated Twitter in May 2009 and, as the company learned, the price for paying attention is less than for the cost of a caramel macchiato, but the value is priceless.

Brad Nelson, who leads @starbucks, recognizes the inherent wisdom and insight in Twitter: "There is a major element of Twitter that's about listening and learning. Twitter is a leading indicator," he said.

Morgan Johnston, manager of corporate communications at JetBlue, was inspired to change policy because of Twitter. He helped eliminate a $50 fee for carry-on bikes after hearing complaints through Twitter.

Johnston listens to the people who are active on the Social Web to help him improve company processes and customer service. "Think of Twitter as the canary in the coal mine. We watch for customers' discussions about amenities we have, and what they'd like to see made better."

➤ **Direct Sales**

Brian Simpson (@BSIMI) once helped the Roger Smith Hotel in New York monitor dialogue related to hotel stays and travel in order to offer specials in the hopes of attracting new guests. Using Twitter search, he can identify prospects and offer them a 10 percent discount on the lowest-rate rooms. Simpson estimates that Twitter and other forms of social media have netted between $15,000 to $20,000 in additional revenue.

Simpson also professed the necessity of cultivating community in social networks: "It validates us more when other people talk about us than when we talk about ourselves," he noted.

United Airlines and JetBlue use Twitter to provide customer service, in addition to using the micronetwork to offer followers first dibs on discounted fares and last-minute specials. Dubbed *cheeps* by JetBlue and *twares* by United, these tweets provide an already active and extemporaneous network with the ability to pounce on great deals by simply following these airlines and all the other companies that will soon follow suit.

➤ **Business Development**

Twitter, along with blogs, blog comments, and other social networks, is abundant with conversations that broadcast and echo dissatisfaction with brands and products. One company's crisis is another's opportunity.

Monitoring conversations (social reconnaissance) related to competitors provides the ability to save the day with better service or monetary incentives.

A word of caution on this front, however: Responding in the public timeline can be viewed by your competition. In my experience, following someone and offering to help through direct messaging has proven effective. Empowering your community to publicly respond is also powerful, as they can do so across networks and communities without regard for the ramifications of competitive awareness.

➤ Curation

I've written in the past that Twitter is not necessarily most advantageous when used as a conversation platform. Sometimes you can say more with less. Embracing it as a broadcast channel or a dumb pipe is also beneficial when used strategically.

For example, Google maintains more than 1.2 million followers, but only follows 160. It employs a strategy that I refer to as a *curation* feed. It compiles links to content and company posts elsewhere and aggregates them into one channel. I recommend that companies use this for information collected from customers and influencers, as well as to truly curate the best, most helpful content from around the Web while building goodwill in the process.

However, Twitter accounts can also create and portray a persona around an inanimate social object. For example Albion's Oven, a bakery in London, notifies followers when fresh croissants are ready.

➤ Information Networks

Unlike a curated network that keeps followers in sync with trends, services, and solutions, information networks can serve up helpful alerts and notices to help followers avert problems, change plans, and also pursue new opportunities.

The Michigan Department of Transportation uses Facebook and Twitter to alert friends and followers of traffic and road closures. Oakland County Parks uses Facebook and Twitter to spread the word about events and news and also conducts polls to improve local programs and services.

In 2009, I established @microjobs along with Christopher Peri (@perivision) to connect employers with job seekers on Twitter.

In business, customers could also benefit from updates and alerts that they might not have otherwise encountered on their own.

JetBlue tweets flight delays.

Comcast tweets updates on service interruptions.

United Linen, a linens and uniform company in Bartlesville, Oklahoma, alerts customers to delays in deliveries when weather becomes a factor.

➤ Dedicated and Branded Channels

Sometimes the pipes in social media become overloaded with general information, making it difficult to truly create and foster communities dedicated to particular topics, interests, or industries. Establishing exclusive channels or subchannels to share specific information increases signal versus noise.

On Twitter, Ford Motor uses distinct accounts for sharing information about specific models and products. For example, @forddrivegreen focuses on sustainability, whereas @fordmustang, well, you guessed it, shares content related to the Mustang.

Scott Monty, head of social media for Ford, recognizes that social media reveals the people who formerly made up the audience: "We give customers a choice as to how they want to consume information."

Whole Foods maintains independent channels, as well, to better serve customers. For example, the healthy foods retailer channels specific information and updates for wine and beer, cheese, and recipes.

➤ Mobile and Geo Location Marketing

This will prove to be among the most often-discussed examples of social media, and most specifically with Twitter. Local businesses are using social tools to identify customers in the area to attract new business and also extend the online interaction into a full-blown community in the real world. Because I was there when this story was just about to unfold, I will reference my good friend Mike Prasad and the great work he's done for Kogi, a mobile force of Korean BBQ taco trucks.

One night in Hollywood, California, Mike and I were talking about getting a late night snack. He told me about the company he was working with and how if we sent a tweet out requesting their presence, there was a good chance that they'd stop by the neighborhood to serve us dinner. Thirty minutes later, Kogi was indeed outside our hotel and a group of about 25 to 30 people immediately began proclaiming their appreciation for @kogiBBQ on Twitter. The rest is history in the making and will serve as the standard for local businesses building communities IRL.

Prasad echoes this sentiment and is helping to lead the way: "We try to foster a culture by interaction with the people around us. Now, Kogi isn't about getting a taco, it's about having an experience."

Expect to see this trend continue in mobile social networks dedicated to locale and accessible by mobile phones.

➤ Hosted Conversations that Generate Traffic and Referrers

Social media dashboards are the future of hosted and aggregated conversations. As we're observing, those sites that integrate Twitter chat functionality cannot only thread conversations in one place for easy following, but also send out tweets in the Twitter stream for all followers to see, and hopefully feel compelled or curious to join, as well.

During the 2009 NBA Eastern Conference Finals between the Cleveland Cavaliers and the Orlando Magic, Turner Broadcasting integrated Twitter into TNT.com with the help of Gigya Socialize. Visitors could log in to the site with their Twitter ID and respond directly in the hosted timeline. As such, their tweets not only appeared on TNT.com but also in Twitter, attracting more fans to the site.

➤ User-Generated Change

As we've seen and will continue to see, in social media tiny online social revolutions can manifest and ultimately ignite change.

Historically, the 2009 Iran election will serve as an inflection point for the rise of user-generated change. While the results of election itself weren't altered, the Iranian government was forced to respond.

Two services mentioned in the *Forbes* Top Twitter Tips article, Twitition and TinyPetition, are dedicated to organizing people on Twitter to officially call for change.

➤ Vendor Relationship Management

A form of relationship management introduced by *Cluetrain Manifesto* author Doc Searls, vendor relationships management (VRM) flips the workflow of CRM (customer relationship management) from companies to customers. Social media is a powerful vehicle for forcing or encouraging companies that have yet to embrace the Social Web to engage and participate through listening and evolution.

Whereas people are relegated to faceless customers when emailing or calling in to the service department, social media takes the power once held exclusively by the brand and injects balance.

United Kingdom–based Wiggly Wigglers, a marketer of farming and gardening supplies, was surprised to learn that British Telecom overcharged the company by $10,000. After five months of a stalemate and without any promise or hope of resolution, company owner Heather Gorringe took her story to the Twitterverse. Within 30 minutes, @BTCare responded with help and two days later, the bill was adjusted.

On a smaller scale, inciting responses on social networks is also a form of forcing companies to compete for your business in the public spotlight.

As the saying goes, a happy customer tells a few people, but an unhappy customer tells everyone. Social media serves as an amplifier to those seeking change, reform, and response.

I discuss VRM in a later chapter as part of the bigger discussion around sCRM (social customer relationship management).

➤ Ideation

As we've witnessed with My Starbucks Idea (http://mystarbucksidea .force.com) and Dell's IdeaStorm (www.ideastorm.com), crowdsourcing ideas cannot only be an excellent source for innovation, but also an effective means for establishing goodwill.

IBM uses Twitter to test concepts and solicit feedback and ideas through @ibmresearch.

➤ Employee Recruitment

Twitter is a magnet for people seeking information. It's one of the reasons that Christopher Peri and I created and released @microjobs. We realized that recruiters and hiring managers were turning to Twitter to seek referrals and applicants for open positions. Twitter and social media can spark a social effect that galvanizes community support and action. Not only can companies save a significant amount of money on listing and referral fees using traditional outlets and resources, the company essentially creates a presence through the practice of unmarketing itself through the process of seeking qualified candidates.

➤ Events

As we reviewed in the Social Calendaring section of Social Media 201, organizing and promoting events are natural applications for Twitter. Tweetups transcend online relationships and become real-world connections.

Using Coffee Groundz as an example again, the Houston-based business regularly organizes tweetups to draw hundreds of customers into the store for each event.

➤ Research and Intelligence

The Social Web is a real-time collective and assembly of valuable information that mostly goes unnoticed. A few existing services are dedicated to applying a magnifying lens into the dialogue that leads to insight, direction, creativity, and inventiveness.

For example, brands.peoplebrowsr.com and celebrity.people browsr.com provide real-time insight into the most actively discussed brands and celebrities on Twitter at any moment in time, while also revealing the sentiment that is most associated with each.

StockTwits provides an open, community-powered idea and information service for investments. Users can listen to traders and investors, or contribute to the conversation. The service leverages Twitter as a content production platform and transforms tweets into financial-related data structured by stock, user, and reputation.

➤ Fund Raising

This is a big opportunity and one that will yield amazing stories on how people are using Twitter and social media to raise money for charitable causes and capital for projects and companies. It's the art of spurring contributions through information and education, not solicitation.

When it comes to social media for social good, we don't have to look much further than anything Beth Kanter touches or spotlights. She's one of the most influential people in using social media for raising awareness and money for her causes. One of the projects that she remains dedicated to is helping orphans in Cambodia and, to date, it has raised more than $200,000. She has also used Twitter, widgets, and other social networks to help many other organizations and causes. In one live demonstration, which still leaves me in awe, she raised more than $2,500 to send a young Cambodian woman to college while she was on stage at Gnomedex in Seattle.

Jeff Pulver, founder of the 140 Characters Conference, and I decided to help prevent a single mother and her daughter from being evicted from their apartment by using an online payment service to collect money to go toward their rent. TipJoy is basically a PayPal for Twitter and was instrumental in tying together tweets, RTs, and contributions.

These examples will only grow in prominence as time passes.

➤ **Words of Wisdom**

As reiterated throughout these top tips, listening and responding is helpful and efficacious in luring new customers, empowering advocacy, and instilling loyalty.

Serving as a resource for your community or industry positions, proactively responding to online users who are posing questions, and assisting those who are seeking advice and guidance can garner trust, respect, and camaraderie for you and the causes you espouse.

There are measurable and also incalculable benefits to dedicating resources to lead individuals and organizations to resolution.

For example, @homedepot monitors dialogue related to the company, but also those individuals who are tackling home projects and seeking tips and instructions.

BestBuy's @Twelpforce has authorized its entire staff of trained employees to seek out discussions related to consumer electronics, home theaters, gaming, music, appliances, and technology, and to answer questions, whether or not they're directly tied to the BestBuy brand.

The examples are many, and the common thread is a willingness to share and a dedication to offering help.

■ NOTE

1. Dan Adler, "In Pictures: 21 Top Twitter Tips," Forbes.com (July 31, 2009), www.forbes.com/2009/07/31/top-twitter-tips-entrepreneurs -technology-twitter_slide_2.html.

Chapter 9

The New Media University 601

Mobile Marketing and Video Broadcasting

Higher education inspires us to strive for the insights that yield intelligence and personal significance. And here we are learning and sharing together—not about what we think we know, but mining for knowledge we don't yet possess. It's this ambition that broadens the gap between you, your goals, and everyone else. This is your time.

Let's now draw the curtains to reveal the windows into geo location and mobile networking, widgets and applications, and the immensely gripping and popular video broadcast networks.

■ GEO LOCATION AND MOBILE NETWORKING

One of the lesser-known, more interesting facts about Twitter is also one of its most legendary. Even though Twitter debuted in March 2006, it took one year and an onslaught of South by Southwest (SXSW) geeks convening in Austin, Texas, and the transient activity that would ultimately bring Twitter into the social media spotlight where it would stay for years later. For those who are unfamiliar with SXSW, it is an annual landmark event that combines music, film, and interactives to celebrate the artistry of the people who are engendering innovation and engaging communities in the real world.

During SXSW 2007, Twitter became the glue that connected everyone together during the pandemonium associated with the conference, which is attended by thousands of geeks from all over the world. Tweets flew back and forth, with attendees alerting friends and followers where they were and what they were witnessing, to share experiences and designate the next rendezvous. This rush of early adopters congregating in one city at the same time and using Twitter as a real-time human-powered positioning system helped to establish awareness for an application that initially struggled to find a market.

Even as Twitter was acquiring market share, it wasn't the first micromedia network designed to connect people through geography and location. At the time, Dodgeball was also competing for users as the essential network that bound together people and the locales they occupied online and in the real world. For several reasons, Twitter adoption outpaced Dodgeball, and subsequently Google eventually laid the service to rest.

With the launch of the iPhone and other smartphones, the rise of mobile networks flourished. Applications such as BrightKite and Loopt introduced a new element to micro and mobile networking. Not only are people encouraged to update their status, they're motivated to check in to specific locations, tying a place with an action.

Two years after Twitter stormed SXSW, a new service also emerged as the breakout application to consume attention (and bandwidth) during the popular show in Austin. Built by one of the original creators of Dodgeball, FourSquare united location-based networking with micronetworking, and introduced a gaming element to the experience.

Like Loopt, FourSquare uses the phone's ability to discern a location and, based on the privacy settings, can show nearby friends and the locations that they've visited on a map. FourSquare also rewards users and ranks them by city and by location. Updates are also transmittable to Twitter and Facebook for public consumption or as direct messages to stay connected to important contacts in both networks. While these mobile networks operate independently from Twitter, they are meant to extend the functionality of existing networks, not replace them.

With mobile networking, the world becomes a much smaller place. Mobile networking also uncovers new riches and interesting people within each neighborhood for discovery and exploration. It brings to life not only online and offline relationships, but also the local businesses and locales people are checking in to.

There's an interesting play here for businesses looking to promote a local presence and also attract new customers. Certainly, many of the applications mentioned in the Top 21 Tips for Twitter (see Chapter 8) will serve as inspiration. Coupons, offers, events, tips and advice, and to-do lists represent the initial opportunities to establish goodwill, create a presence, and forge loyal relationships. When tied to

Yelp, local-based networks can symbolize a potential windfall—when practiced genuinely, sincerely, and creatively.

For example, in FourSquare, an individual who repeatedly visits and checks in to a particular location eventually becomes the mayor of that establishment, until someone else overthrows her. In one example, San Francisco–based Marsh Cafe is promoting free drinks for the Foursquare Mayor. Thousands of businesses all over the world are following suit. And why not? Millions of people everywhere are already using the service. Every time someone checks in, he's essentially marketing and advertising a business or service—especially if he adds updates, tips, and to-dos around the location. It's peer-to-peer influence at its best and very engaging.

However, as in any social network, you must embrace and participate in the community if you wish to truly be part of it.

■ VIDEO BROADCAST NETWORKS

Video is the new frontier, again, and it's powered by the socialization of content. The ability to produce and publish online video is universal and the networks that host them can extend the reach of any person or brand globally, facilitating connections based on the content in a practically limitless array.

YouTube popularized the use of embedded code to encourage people to automatically add favorite videos to their websites, blogs, and profiles in social networks. It is this use of embedded code that further fueled the creation of other embeddable content, such as pictures, documents and presentations, animated media, and games.

In December 2010, Forrester Research released a powerful statistic: the average U.S. consumer now spends as much time online as watching television. Social networking and online video are among the top catalysts for the shift in attention.

Obviously the opportunity for finding online video audiences is tremendous. Getting and holding their attention, however, is different. Anyone can shoot and upload a video. We represent a brand, however, and that brand perception is defined through the content we produce and share. Quality, professionalism, creativity, and context speak volumes. Otherwise anyone, including your competitors, could win market share through the creation of amateur video.

There's a reason why I say that there's no such thing as viral videos and viral marketing. It's people that make something viral, not the video itself. Simply uploading a video to YouTube will not in and of itself earn attention, nor will it spark a flurry of views and shares.

Almost nothing goes viral without preparation and orchestration, with a little luck added for good measure.

Videos are mostly viewed as finite campaigns and not as dedicated channels to visualizing a company or brand story.

In one such example, which must unfortunately go unnamed, I was hired by a major consumer pet food company to help save its viral videos that debuted on YouTube a month earlier. The marketing team was frustrated that the videos hadn't received a significant volume of views and were prepared to kill the entire campaign. However, with a little strategy, guidance, and coordination, we resuscitated the videos through an informed, targeted, and substantial outbound program.

First, we removed the videos from YouTube and created a new, more intriguing, dedicated, and polished channel to house the content. We then cleverly titled and tagged the videos to promote social media optimization (SMO). This gave the videos a fresh start, with zero views and recent upload dates. Since time was of the essence, we didn't include the usual program element of assembling and managing a devoted digital street team to help us promote the videos across the Social Web. Note: these teams are either paid or rewarded with noteworthy or valuable stuff.

We then monitored conversations on Twitter, blogs, and other video networks related to dogs, bacon, and other key attributes of the video series and drafted clever, yet informational introductions to the video and encouraged people to view and share. For Twitter, we used Search.Twitter.com and PeopleBrowsr (now ReSearch.ly), and for blogs we used blogsearch.google.com and Technorati (we searched blogs by topic, not keywords). The video earned 20,000 views within the first 24 hours, and that number only continued to skyrocket as time progressed. Not that views account for success, but in this case, views were used as the metric from the inception point.

In other cases we tied an action to the end result to help us truly measure the effectiveness of the video. When we were introducing a particular online social bookmarking tool, we realized that its greatest market opportunity resided with the vertical markets of users seeking to document, share, and plan activities and projects around information discovered online. We shot a four-minute demonstration video as a screencast (a video that captures what's on the computer screen) along with narration from the user perspective. The goal of the video was to inform people that a new solution existed that could help them. Our metrics were determined by how many people watched the video and clicked through to download the application. With these two parameters in mind, we drafted a script and storyboard that would entertain, capture attention, and motivate people to click through to install the software based on their needs. Again, titled and tagged strategically in YouTube as well as promoted among the people we discovered who were already looking for a solution like this on Twitter, blogs, and other social networks, we earned 70,000 views in one week with almost 60 percent of those translating into direct downloads. The campaign continued effectively and would ultimately spark a new series of videos that demonstrated its advantages to specific markets.

With reference to digital street teams, they can be a highly effective group when directed and managed. They must be held to metrics, which should be defined before the formation and official deployment of the team. Viral marketing agencies exist and they can help you produce and promote videos. They're not inexpensive, but they can orchestrate popular, far-reaching campaigns. Ultimately, it's the intent and goals of the video that determine the content and promotion strategies.

Many businesses film their spokespersons or project leads demonstrating or discussing a product or service and in most cases, it never truly connects or resonates with viewers. That's marketing of old as they're usually presented in a top-down messaging format, showcasing the features and benefits that the presenter thinks makes for interesting viewing. Other videos feature interviews with executives or key personnel, but much like the demo videos, most are not terribly interesting, revealing, or gripping. Online videos aren't necessarily gimmicks nor are they intended to provide the same old broadcast messages using new mediums. We learned otherwise.

This is storytelling.

This is entertainment.

This is education.

This is your chance to genuinely connect with people in ways and in places where their attention is focused and impressionable, using a human voice or creative narrative. It's where they already search for interesting videos tied to the keywords that are important to them. What's there to represent you now?

Videos can range from short demos, screencasts, or event footage, to entertaining "day in the life of" snippets, collages, customer or hero interviews, original episodes related to your value proposition, or behind-the-scenes footage, to helpful guides and did-you-know segments that appeal to viewers as well as help them learn, solve, or perform something they couldn't do before watching the video.

In 2010, when Ford was set to introduce the all-new Explorer, it decided to break the rules. Instead of launching the car at an auto show like every car manufacturer has done over the years, Ford took to Facebook, creating a custom tab to host the debut. As part of its Reveal campaign, it reached out to bloggers and influencers to alert them of a unique campaign that would reveal the new Explorer on Facebook using social video as the key ingredient to tell the story. On the hour, Ford released a new video, each with a different perspective on the story behind the story. Rather than use typical spokespersons, the company relied on the people who brought the new Explorer to life. It was their story and with it, pride and gratification beamed through. According to Scott Monty, Ford's head of social media, the Reveal campaign earned as many impressions as a Super Bowl commercial for far less. And, it made an emotional connection with viewers.

Now before you jump in to the director's chair, think about the video strategy and the associated branding of your online video presence. I highly recommend creating one master channel and also dedicated channels to specific programming and company divisions. These channels also need satellite channels such as Facebook. This keeps everything focused, organized, and highly brandable without cluttering or diluting the brand through the saturation of various videos housed in one massive location.

Also, it's essential that each video is titled, described, and tagged with SMO using the keywords that are important to your market as well as the keywords that your customers and prospects are using to find relevant information.

Figure 9.1   Home Depot on YouTube

■ VIDEO EXAMPLE: HOME DEPOT

Home Depot serves as an excellent example of a brand publishing relevant and educational video content that won't be dismissed as overly promotional or gimmicky. The company launched a Home Depot branded channel on YouTube (www.homedepot.com/youtube) that features know-how videos on relevant material—anything from programming a thermostat for optimal energy efficiency to installing a bath fan (see Figure 9.1). While a step-by-step video on retiling the shower doesn't have mass appeal, it's going to be highly relevant to a key demographic—those interested in do-it-yourself home renovation projects (and those most likely looking to buy bathroom tiles and other needed supplies).

What's particularly successful about Home Depot's approach is that the videos lack outright product pitches by blatant spokespeople. Instead, we see Home Depot employees offering practical advice and walking through each step in a very natural, friendly way. It's almost as if someone walked in to their local Home Depot and asked a store associate a question. Of course, Home Depot is promoting their merchandise, but more importantly, they're establishing themselves as a trusted and friendly resource for whatever home improvement task is on the front burner.

Chapter 10

The New Media University 701

Social Media Optimization, SEO, and Content Distribution

In the 701 series of the New Media University program, we undergo initiations that introduce us to the technology undercurrent as well as the philosophies and social sciences that govern and enrich human behavior on the Social Web.

■ SOCIAL OBJECTS

The topic of social objects will force us to think about social media as the connection of abstract objects that trigger related dialogues and activities.

In social media, these objects are personified by the pictures in Flickr, the videos on YouTube, the events in Upcoming, the profiles in Facebook, links shared in Digg, the places in FourSquare, the documents in Scribd, a destination or service in Yelp, a Tweet, a thought shared in the comment of a blog post, and so on.

Essentially, social objects in social networks take the form of content or media and can induce responses in each network.

Subscribing to the school of thought that aligns effective social media strategies with anthropology and sociology, social objects therefore represent the epicenter for distributed micronetworks that are formed within larger, established social networks, yet connected by interests. Social objects become the hubs for specialized discourse at the point of introduction.

Introducing social theory into the mix of social media allows us to understand the behaviors that regulate and affect the culture and influence of objects within respective groups of individuals that share interests.

According to social theory,[1] the comprehension of natural phenomena is predicated on the understanding of social phenomena. The interpretation of natural phenomena is a social activity. To better understand the nature and prospect of resulting activity associated with social objects, we must embrace social theory as it relates to objects of similar traits and targets online. Altogether, this is not unlike the fieldwork and observational studies performed by anthropologists and sociologists.

Typically, we view the connections established within social networks as symbolizing relationships between people. We therefore look at the number of friends and followers as a metric for authority. However, as we discuss in Chapter 20, which visualizes "human networks," we learn that in social media, the pattern for forging connection is migrating toward themes and interests. It's the idea that social graphs also break out into interest graphs, which also mimic how we communicate and form groups in real life.

In 2009, Bernardo A. Huberman, Daniel M. Romero, and Fang Wu of the Social Computing Laboratory at HP Labs issued a report that examined relationships on Twitter. Their findings, published in "Social Networks That Matter: Twitter under the Microscope,"[2] revealed that the driver of usage is actually a sparse and hidden network of connections that defines the declared set of friends and followers.

In the abstract, HP Labs disclosed, "The scarcity of attention and the daily rhythms of life and work make people default to interacting with those few that matter and that reciprocate their attention."

As the HP Labs report states, people do interact with those few who matter and reciprocate recognition. But they did not account for the viral potential of social objects. They did, however, qualify it and helped associate credibility for the consumption and sharing of the content within their social graph as well as the respective graphs of their contacts.

The backchannel, which is practically immeasurable for the time being outside of our dominion, is also incredibly influential in the volume and extent of interaction, as well as the lifespan of any social object.

The backchannel represents the communication, connections, cooperation, favors, deals, and alliances that take shape outside public view—usually through in-network messaging, traditional email, and events that take place offline. The back channel is instrumental in the success of programs designed around social objects. If you remember the Ford Reveal campaign that we reviewed earlier, the Ford team was active in the back channel ensuring that all of the right people shared links back to the Facebook tab. Conversations and traffic were not just left to chance. Ford didn't just connect with anybody. The team spent years building relationships with connected individuals in ideal markets.

The contacts that we leveraged in these cases were distinct in their association with the nature of each social object. Said another way, people didn't connect to or share content in the long term just because we placed it in front of them and asked them nicely to view and promote the content. An emotional or intellectual bond must eventually exist—even in the cases of established, healthy, and vibrant relationships.

Forging relationships before the introduction of social objects, reinforced by interaction and recognition, serve as the foundation for the introduction, adoption, and distribution of relevant social objects.

Having described the benefits of the backchannel, I should mention that its effectiveness is not without limits. While there may be a natural enthusiasm as new objects are presented, without scrutiny, restraint, respect, and, most important, reciprocation, we foster exhaustion. We wear thin our relationships.

It's about awareness trumping promotion, social alliances, not socialism, and collaboration over hierarchy.

Building these communities to support social objects represents only one way to engage and earn engagement. Also, online support of social objects is readily available for hire. Service providers, consultants, and marketing agencies dedicated to creating visibility for social objects are a dime a dozen these days. Their art, techniques, and playing fields have transformed with every technology (r)evolution, including social media.

■ GETTING NOTICED: SOCIAL MEDIA OPTIMIZATION A NEW CHAPTER OF SEO

As discussed earlier, at the center of any social media program is the social object. Content indeed serves as the foray into the conversations that ultimately define the place and perception of any brand.

Uploading content into a social network simply guarantees that it will have a place to reside online. Visibility and the socialization of the content however, are not assured. Contrary to perception, objects don't inherently generate gravitational pull. The laws of attraction are not unlike those in the wild kingdom. Specifically, we have to integrate digital seduction in the objects we wish to earn attention and notoriety.

Much in the same way that SEO helps Web pages gain greater visibility in searches, SMO increases the likelihood of objects within social networks. Everything is tied to relevant keywords, inbound links, and clever promotion.

For example, YouTube is among the largest destinations for search, not for websites, but for video related to keywords. The point is that if you want your content discovered, it requires social media optimization to increase its discoverability.

■ WHAT IS SOCIAL MEDIA OPTIMIZATION?

Social media optimization (SMO), at the moment, is less scientific than search engine optimization, but not less important. At a minimum, SMO refers to the deliberate acts of aligning keywords with social objects to improve the association of your content with search queries in specific social networks as well as traditional search engines.

To clarify, there are several forms of search today; understanding them helps us.

Traditional search: Searches performed in the search engines that have existed since the dawn of the Web, such as Google, Yahoo!, Bing, and the like.

Real-time search: The emerging category of search, spawned by the adoption of Twitter search, where content is discoverable as it's uploaded online, whether it's on a website, blog, or any social network, including Twitter. Real-time search engines include Collecta, Topsy, and others.

Social network search: A manual form of search within each social network, in which keywords or keyword strings are manually input into the search boxes of each network.

Social Search: This is a hybrid search category that combines traditional search with the social graph. Google, Bing, and also Facebook are introducing social search features that tie search results to the related activity of friends.

SMO specifically is defined by the elements used for organization in each social network. For example, when a social object is uploaded to its respective social network, you're provided with the opportunity to further categorize the content through the titles, descriptions, and tags. To get a bit geeky here, this is technically referred to as metadata. Quite specifically, metadata is the data that defines other data. It is this metadata that proved instrumental in Web 2.0 to help classify and organize user-generated content uploaded to social networks and blogs everywhere. Unknowingly, we became the Web's librarians and helped to index the volumes of social objects to help others discover them quickly and easily.

Yes, tags, descriptions, and keywords collectively contribute to the discoverability of social content.

■ TITLES

Titles refer to the official designation or name of the content. Specifically, when you upload a video, image, or any other social object, the headline serves as the main moniker. The art of headline writing is not unlike that of magazines or newspapers. It must grip the viewer immediately and compel them to act and hopefully share. In social media, the headline must also contain the keywords that explicitly match the search patterns of the people you hope to reach, even at the cost of creativity. Keywords must prevail!

■ DESCRIPTIONS

Descriptions further refine the context of the social object to entice visitors to view and hopefully circulate it among their social graph. Usually the description falls either beneath the title or below the media preview. The description field is your chance to frame an object so as to boost its discoverability and further entice the viewer to spend a portion of his precious time clicking through. Descriptions also help set the stage for how someone connects with the intended messages and desired sentiment and takeaways. Make sure that the description includes at least three or four keywords related to your business or brand and target viewers.

■ TAGS

Tags are basically keywords that further organize the object within the social network. Tags are based on folksonomy,[3] a system of classification derived from the practice of collaboratively creating tags to categorize content within specific networks. Tags also add a contextual wrapper to each object, helping provide a frame of reference.

The same process of matching content based on metadata can work in your favor in almost every social network where titles, tags, and descriptions are woven into the content fabric.

Moving forward, let's presume that tags and keywords are identical when referring to SMO, and that keywords are the social beacons that match keywords used in search queries.

Keyword ranking is referred to as the dark art of SEO, and it is powerful. We borrow the basics from the black book of SEO to help us increase visibility for media within social networks. And it is these keywords that serve as one side of the social media optimization equation.

It is essential to not only attach the words and descriptors that we think best describe the content; we must also audit the queries used today when searching for related information. This will help increase the exposure of our content, as it better matches it to how people are already searching.

One way to do so is to use an online keyword tool to help analyze the trends, obtain ideas, and most importantly, to visualize popular terms that others may use in addition to or in place of your keywords or phrases. One such tool (and it's free) is Google Adwords. We enter the words we believe to be important and Google Adwords will also show us what consumers are already using as the most popular keywords. The service is located at https://adwords .google.com/select/KeywordToolExternal, or simply google "Google keyword tool."

In some networks, tags also serve as grouping mechanisms in addition to keyword anchors that facilitate the categorization of social objects within a social timeline, helping people find them at later times. In particular, the use of #hashtags in Twitter serve as keywords or tag markers, which surface all of the discussions related to either a social object or topic through a standard Twitter search.

■ CONTENT DISTRIBUTION

On the other side of the social media optimization equation is content distribution, which metaphorically establishes presences in strategic networks and points back to the original content to increase visibility and findability.

If we upload a picture worthy of viewing for any number of reasons, we would then organize community-supported activity to help attract targeted visitors—after we effectively titled, described, and tagged the image, of course. The next step could employ a strategy through which we promote the content within those networks dedicated to the sharing and promotion of social objects, such as a Digg, StumbleUpon, and blogs, of course.

Inserting the object into the network isn't enough, however. An organized, thorough, and significant effort is also imperative to earn votes and bookmarks (diggs in Digg, stumbles in StumbleUpon). Blogger relations is often complementary whereby reaching out with embeddable social objects helps to entice bloggers to include compelling content in their post. Combined with the incorporation of SMO within each network, this orchestrated campaign of promoting the object can generate tens of thousands of unique views.

Through a content syndication plus SMO strategy, the social object can also earn prominence in Twitter, Facebook, and other social networks to entice views and also bookmarks, additional sharing, likes, favorites, and comments. All of this activity also improves the chances of your social object appearing in traditional search engines as well.

■ LINKS

In SEO, the quantity of inbound links increase the Google page rank for any given website. In blog ranking, inbound links contribute to the authority of the blog. In social media, inbound links increase the weight and visibility of social objects. These links serve as orbiting satellites that beam signals (or traffic) back to the source and can be measured in views, ratings, retweets, likes, and favorites. This boosts stature and credibility for perception when someone stumbles upon the object. Depending on the host network, the gauges are viewable by visitors and hosts alike.

For example, in Flickr and YouTube, the quantity of views is readily present. In Digg, that benchmark is visible in the number of diggs. In Twitter, we can view the number of retweets. In Facebook, we calculate the sum of likes and comments.

Of course, many of these social networks have earned prominence as measured by the ranking and authority that traditional search algorithms use to measure relevance. This weight determines the placement and ranking of specific social objects in search engine results pages (SERPs).

The folksonomy that served as the underpinning of Web 2.0 will be augmented as the Social Web progresses. The next generation of the Web, referred to as Web Squared (by Tim O'Reilly, the visionary who coined the phrase *Web 2.0*), and also called the Semantic Web, will inject intelligence or semantics into the foundation of the Web to connect data, metadata, and personal preferences based on individual activity, as well as the related activities of those in the individual's immediate social graph.

■ LIKING: MICRO ACTS OF APPRECIATION YIELD MACRO IMPACTS

Like is basically similar, in principle, to the *favorites* feature found in many popular communities, such as Twitter, which essentially served as an in-network bookmarking system. This small but important feature nonetheless has the ability to reinforce relationships between friends and followers.

Made popular by services such as FriendFeed, now owned by Facebook, the idea of liking an update is much stronger than merely bookmarking or favoriting (*favoriting* is now a verb, too) updates from friends and contacts for later reference or sharing. Liking is the epitome of the relationship-based culture encouraging reciprocal interactions on the Social Web. It's a powerful form of recognition, which serves as a nod from someone else. Essentially, likes are forms of social currency that combine an endorsement with the network effect.

The deed of liking an update resonates within and outside the social graph, as those who follow your activity will receive your signal in a news feed. In many cases, it serves as a trigger for them to view what it is that has caught your attention. If they in turn like the object, this further amplifies the source post by placing the object within the social streams of their friends and followers as well as their network of friends of friends (FoFs).

Likes are incredibly powerful because they share the love. It is the digital curation of relevant content that binds us contextually. Liking sets the stage to not only introduce new content to new people, but also to facilitate the forging of new friendships in the process.

As the Social Web and new services continue to migrate into and permeate everything we do online, we're faced with an increasingly thinning state of continuous partial attention (CPA)[4] . It's affecting how and what we consume, when, and more importantly, how we react, participate, and share. That something is forever vying for our attention and relentlessly pushing us to do more with less, driven by the omnipresent fear of missing out on what's next. This is important, as it encourages us to introduce more relevant and valuable objects that people will indeed like. We are competing for the moment and competing for attention.

■ NOTES

1. "Social Theory," Wikipedia, http://en.wikipedia.org/wiki/Social_theory.

2. Bernardo A. Huberman, Daniel M. Romero, and Fang Wu, "Social Networks That Matter: Twitter under the Microscope," Social Computing Laboratory at HP Labs (January 2009), www.hpl.hp.com/research/scl/papers/twitter/.

3. "Folksonomy," Wikipedia, http://en.wikipedia.org/wiki/Folksonomy.

4. Linda Stone, "Continuous Partial Attention—Not the Same as Multi-Tasking," *BusinessWeek* (July 24, 2008), www.businessweek.com/business_at_work/time_management/archives/2008/07/continuous_part.html.

Chapter

The New Media University 801

Syndication, Illustration, and Aggregation

Collectively, we contribute to the wisdom or irrelevance of the crowds that rule the Social Web. The brilliance of social media is that at any point in time, we can gauge the sentiments and impressions, perceive the states of affairs and hot spots, glean insights, and trendcast opportunities to diagnose, discover, and predict the fate of our brand. This real-time digital sampling is infinite in its benefits and its promise.

Let it guide you.

Be thoughtful.

Make me care.

Inspire me to follow you.

Help me learn.

Earn my respect and trust.

■ ESTABLISHING A SYNDICATION NETWORK

The benefits of a syndication network serve as the mechanics of SMO. Also, a well-established and thoughtfully constructed syndication network can not only improve SEO and SMO, but also reach a greater audience. Similar to the social dashboard we discuss in Chapter 7, a syndication network operates on the premise that people don't necessarily find and follow objects and the individuals who interest them in the same ways. It's our job to serve as a bridge between the interesting content we create and those who are seeking it—in the networks where they're actively searching for it.

While directly participating in the social networks of significance (a topic we discuss further in our review of "The Conversation Prism" in Chapter 18), the mere act of producing a pulse in outside networks is beneficial in establishing a community around a pure informational source.

Remember, in this section, we're not discussing the actions necessary to cultivate a community through direct participation. Here, the social object becomes the participant and the greater visibility it receives through distribution increases the potential for discovery, appreciation, and redistribution.

Thus the dawn of syndication and aggregation is upon us.

Syndication symbolizes our ability to upload one object and have it simultaneously appear across multiple networks.

■ SYNDICATING SOCIAL OBJECTS: AN ILLUSTRATION

Aggregation refers to the content consumption patterns of those seeking content in one place, and therefore we can create branded activity streams that funnel our distributed content into one timeline (see Figure 11.1).

Figure 11.1 Syndicating Social Objects

■ CHANNELING ILLUSTRATION: AN ACTIVITY STREAM

Building a framework that unites the distributed objects published in disparate networks is a primary goal of our social aggregation strategy (see Figure 11.2). In parallel, ensuring that individual social objects are beamed to other networks to balance our content marketing program is a chief objective of a social syndication strategy.

Aggregation + Syndication = Extended presence for scattered social objects and improved organic SMO and SEO

Everything starts with building a framework that extends from one source to other predefined profiles that accept outside feeds. We then build varying levels of activity feeds in designated networks to activate the content firehose for those consumers who prefer following full data streams.

When we talk about publishing one post across multiple networks simultaneously, we are syndicating that content. If we pull our diverse content from the multiple networks where they're hosted into one

Figure 11.2   Aggregating Social Objects

place, we're aggregating it. The confusion emerges when we realize that certain networks are both aggregating and possibly syndicating content simultaneously.

I know this seems a bit overcomplicated, so let's step back for a second to look at syndication and aggregation from a byte-sized perspective to further examine these concepts.

■ AGGREGATION: ASSEMBLING THE PIECES

Aggregation networks—also referred to as brand streams, activity feeds, or activity streams—collect the various feeds you specify and channel everything into a single branded presence (see Figure 11.3). These specialized services are hosted within dedicated social networks and allow followers to subscribe to your complete content stream for viewing, commenting, and sharing. Examples of aggregation networks include dedicated blogs, the Facebook news feed, Twitter, and more specifically, Plaxo Pulse, Tumblr, SocialThing, and Lifestream.fm.

In essence, we create a profile and presence in one or more of these networks. We then define which services we wish to funnel into these profiles, such as blog posts, Twitter updates, Flickr pictures, YouTube videos, documents from Scribd, and so forth. These services offer built-in features for automating and simplifying the process for

Figure 11.3   Channeling Social Objects into One Aggregated Stream

adding a wide variety of feeds and presenting them in an easy-to-follow, aesthetically pleasing data river.

■ EXAMPLE OF ACTIVITY STREAM

Activity feeds also offer in-network response mechanisms, similar to blog posts, Twitter, and Facebook, for followers to respond to your updates through comments, repost in their feed, bookmark, or send to Facebook, Twitter, Digg, StumbleUpon, and so on (see Figure 11.4).

Naturally, syndicating your content in these activity streams further enhances organic SEO and Web visibility around important keywords.

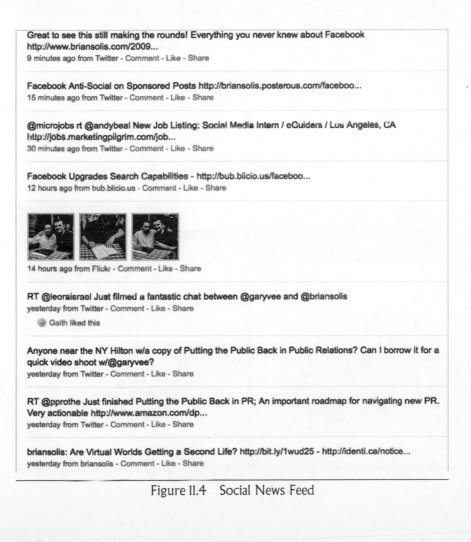

Figure 11.4   Social News Feed

■ IN-NETWORK AGGREGATION

Initially, social networks were islands: The content that was uploaded within each network was exclusive to it. Over time, network architects realized that the more people shared, the more conversations would ensue. Thus, social networks opened up the ability to import outside feeds into their profiles to increase in-network interaction—similar to activity streams—capturing and holding the attention of users in one network. It's just good for business.

Facebook, for example, offers the ability to pull feeds from almost any network into your news feed through its settings option. It provides a seamless process for choosing which streams you wish to pull and, in turn, publish in your Facebook news feed to thus be potentially discovered by those friends who choose to receive your updates in their timeline. As you publish new content from each respective network, the objects are automatically syndicated to Facebook. It's now very common to host simultaneous conversations wherever the content appears. For example, a blog post can entertain dialogue at the host site, but now that it also appears in your news feed (which is visible by friends and followers) reactions are likely to occur within Facebook concurrently (see Figure 11.5). Reactions require your attention and often your response. So many brands feed their content into their brand page on Facebook, only to never respond to fans.

Figure 11.5   Facebook Social News Feed

Even though content is apparently up to date, it's nothing more than a ghost town. Hello . . . is there anyone here?

Twitter is also a channel for creating and circulating original content (tweets), as well as an activity feed for sharing aggregated social objects from other social networks directly into your Twitter stream. Those who follow you on Twitter can receive your tweets plus the other social objects from outside networks. If your target consumer base is active in Twitter, this will prove as a highly valuable system for channeling additional content in and around your Tweets. Therefore, Twitter, like Facebook, is both an aggregation tool and a fundamental component of a broader syndication channel.

If you so choose, your Tweets, as well as updates from other dedicated content networks, can also broadcast to other networks, including Facebook, as part of your syndication strategy, which we discuss next (see Figure 11.6).

■ SYNDICATION: WEBCASTING SOCIAL OBJECTS

To illustrate the potential for the syndication network, let's examine the prospective audiences for a standard blog post. With syndication tools, we can sync the availability of a blog post from the

Figure 11.6   Twitter Social News Feed

host site and have it automatically repost in additional networks such Facebook, Twitter, Ning, and Tumblr, among many other networks of choice—thus amplifying its visibility considerably. Likewise, we can publish a video on YouTube, an image on Flickr, or post a Tweet, and have this particular object propagate immediately to all of our predefined channels.

■ AUTOPOSTS AND SYNDICATION

Those people who choose to follow your brand in any or all of these communities can receive the full portrait of the brand persona through your content. That's the point of all of this, I suppose. We are what we produce and visible where we publish.

Tumblr is an ideal microblog for publishing short-form original material. It also facilitates the aggregation of syndicated content into one channel. Contrarily, Posterous represents a new genre of intelligent microblog that also helps producers easily create short-form original posts. But instead of channeling syndicated content, it encourages publishers to autopost content sourced from Posterous Web-wide to blogs, Twitter, Flickr, Facebook, Tumblr, and so forth. It also offers a unique syndication option in which you can easily dictate which posts are sent to which outside networks. It's essentially up to you whether you send updates to all or a combination of networks as dictated by the nature of the content and the communities you host within each.

Other services such as Ping.fm offer a discrete solution for publishing one update across popular services.

It is vital that you establish a functional and targeted social architecture that complements the activity of other individuals and groups within the company, as well as the social presences they create and promote.

■ DON'T CROSS THE STREAMS

As we weave together our syndication and aggregation networks, we must remain acutely aware of each channel and where it sends or receives content to ensure that we don't cross the streams.

Let's walk through an example of a tangled feed. If you automate the publishing of a blogpost to Twitter and have your Tumblr account set to receive either the blog post or the Twitter feed, and Twitter is automatically fed to Facebook, you've seamlessly broadcasted one post to three networks without any potential issues of crossing the streams. However, this one sentence shows that the intersection of content can potentially occur.

Let's say we publish a blog post and it's sent to Twitter and Tumblr, and ultimately Facebook. We have to ensure that Tumblr isn't set up to receive duplicate feeds from the blog or Twitter. Likewise, we also need to ensure that the Facebook settings are instructed to receive only one of those signals. Otherwise, it's quite feasible to have the blog post fed to Twitter and Tumblr, while Tumblr might also publish both the post and the tweet about the post, and then, in Facebook, we could view the post, the tweet about the post, the Tumblr post about the post, and the Tumblr post with the aggregated tweet from the post.

"The Conversation Prism" (Chapter 18) will serve as your central source for revelation and direction in the intersections of posts.

■ DESTINATION UNKNOWN: DEFINING THE JOURNEY THROUGH YOUR EXPERIENCE

Through the creation and distribution of online videos, blog posts, tweets, images, status updates, or a combination thereof, social objects rife with thoughtful content and intentions become an effective form of unmarketing. If we're creating content in disparate networks, we are indeed reaching people where they seek content, in the formats they prefer. But for those who choose to visit our site after viewing the media we publish in their respective network, we must ask ourselves—where are we sending these prospects and what is the impression they form or action they take once they get there?

By way of illustration, if a customer, influencer, or peer viewed a video on YouTube or picture series on Flickr, stumbled across a story on Digg, became a member of our Facebook brand page, or retweeted us, what is the next action that we're defining? How do we connect that person to other relevant information, content, and outcomes? Does our website, as it stands, suffice for those who choose to click through to the home page or designated product pages?

Did you just hear those brakes screeching?

It's an all-too-common occurrence that, rather than socialize the experience from introduction to action, we send prospects to a static dead end at our website.

Participating and engaging is only part of the process. Defining the experience and guiding people to a destination that invites further interaction and steers, enhances, and reinforces positive sentiment strengthens the branded chain of events. (See Figure 11.7.) It is also an opportunity to capture user information and promote commerce.

Figure 11.7 Defining the Experience

As we syndicate our story and value proposition, we must funnel attention to its designated channel of relevance—a dedicated hub that serves as a visual menu for people seeking to connect, learn, communicate, and collaborate. Today, when we participate and engage in the Social Web, we directly and indirectly drive consumers to review our profile page to learn more about us. From there, it's usually unclear where they go unless we establish a click path. But most of the time, we send them to our home page or we send them into the ether, and none of it is guided or intended. Referring people to a traditional landing, or home page, in the Social Web is not only immeasurable, it's ineffective.

At the beginning of any social media initiative, we must establish an endgame—what is it that we are hoping to accomplish and how are we going to measure it?

The first step in answering this question is to realize that social media is not relegated solely to the creation, production, and distribution of social objects.

There's no shortage of businesses, and, more specifically, the individuals who represent them, seeking insights, answers, and directions to make decisions. The Web has both simplified and complicated the process of decision making. We mistakenly take comfort in the assumption that our customers already view us as a source of guidance and wisdom. However, it's not enough to create content. As you know, anyone with an opinion, a keyboard, camera, or microphone, fueled by the desire to share, can do so at will nowadays. The question is, how do you, as an authentic marketer, business leader, and service professional convince prospects that you're believable, qualified, and ready to lead?

Our job is to build the bridges that connect what we represent to those seeking direction. Once we understand how to build these bridges, we ultimately become experienced social architects.

As we're learning, however, the bridges we build between people and social objects and the experiences they encounter along the way are fragmentary if not steered and managed. These bridges need to lead to destinations that not only provide information, but also lead the followers to resolution. Therefore, social engagement is routed through the roads, highways, off-ramps, and ports of call that are constructed by thoughtful social engineers. It is this social engineering that enables the interconnection of experiences and perception.

Partnering with the Web team is paramount, and not optional. To best guide people to action, we have to engineer and build a cohesive experience that connects social networks and social objects to our overall brand, its defining tenets, and desirable outcomes.

But, what about the corporate website?

What about the company's commerce site and associated search and reviews engine?

How about the hosting of conversations directly on the company site in addition to conducting dispersed social interactions across the Web?

What about building links between our brand and the objects and networks where it's syndicated?

The experience must be complete and dynamic from the point of introduction to the point of action, tied together by the intentions we wish to instill. Regardless of social or broadcast or static presences, we must always purport, represent, embody, and personify oneness. (See Figure 11.8.)

We are one.

But the paradox of oneness in social media is that we relinquish control of the brand and the message—either unknowingly or willfully or both. Contrary to popular belief, a brand is not completely crowdsourced, nor should it be.

In a report published on ClickZ in July 2009,[1] Bill McCloskey, in partnership with StrongMail, observed the email marketing campaigns of top brands and how they integrated social presences into the corporate fold. The data he analyzed revealed that top brands were reviving email campaigns with the inclusion of links to social profiles, specifically Facebook and Twitter.

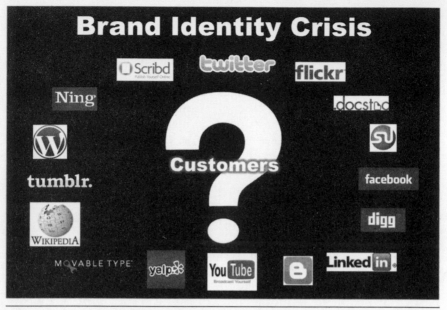

Figure 11.8   Brand Identity Crisis

In the ClickZ article, McCloskey reported that top brands such as Nike, Intel, The Gap, Pepsi, Sony, HP, Home Depot, Lane Bryant, Circuit City, Saks Fifth Avenue, Polo Ralph Lauren, Lands' End, and J.C. Penney included social media within email marketing messages. But, where were they sending people? And what was the mission and purpose behind the social strategy?

We need a hub that's consistent with the experiences consumers expect inside and outside our mission control.

H&R Block's Digits site (http://digits.hrblock.com) is an H&R-branded community that offers tax and personal financial resources through Q&As, forums, videos, podcasts, blogs, and more. The site provides a wealth of information from H&R experts to help people navigate the murky waters of mortgage refinancing, economic stimulus benefits, and tax preparation and deductions. Digits also provides a host of widgets, such as Economic Stimulus FAQs and Tax Answers, to further spread the company's resources across blogs and social sites. American Express Open Forum for Small Businesses, www.openforum.com, is also designed around the social experience. The destination site is literally an idea hub that features advice, information and also the expertise of prominent small business and social media bloggers such as Guy Kawasaki of AllTop, Adam Ostrow of Mashable, Henry Blodget of Business Insider, and John Jantsch

Figure 11.9   American Express Open Forum

of Duct Tape Marketing. The hub also offers tips for one's life and work balance, essentially providing a complete experience for business owners to focus attention rather than scour the Web in search of direction (see Figure 11.9). There's more to the story, however. American Express has extended the Open Forum experience to Facebook and Twitter to engage with business owners outside the site. And with the inclusion of many notable bloggers who maintain quite prominent presences in the Social Web in their own right, they use their social channels to distribute their contributions, thus further extending the American Express Open story.

Oneness therefore doesn't assume just one presence, just one mission, purpose, or resolve across the entire Web. The previous examples represent destinations that extend and focus the company's corporate message at the market or product level, while still building equity for the brand overall. If we evaluate the typical sales process that customers experience, we can intertwine a messaging platform that's consistent across social networks and objects:

1. Need/want/desire is recognized
2. Search for information
3. Evaluate options
4. The action of purchase
5. After-purchase evaluation

Adding to the list of attributes that are fundamental drivers for creating effective online presences and corresponding communities, we should also include those seeking:

1. Recognition
2. Affinity/association
3. Purpose
4. Insight
5. Entertainment
6. Rewards
7. Empowerment
8. Resolution
9. Access
10. Exclusive content

Addressing each of these points with content, design, structure, and click paths will inspire new, enriched, and socially effective experience-driven programs not unlike what we might expect to see in a standard experiential marketing initiative. For those not familiar with experiential marketing, it is the art of creating an experience in which the result is an emotional connection to a person, brand, product, or idea.[2] In social media, people engage others directly and indirectly through conversations and conversational objects. It is an emotional landscape.

At the very least, the marketing, communications, services, and sales teams representing the brand in social and traditional media must collaborate on the redesign of all online entities, especially the corporate focal point—that is, the main website.

You must ensure that the landing, or home, pages feature social objects, opportunities for interaction, spotlighting of customers and visitors, and also a directory of external social presences and aggregated content from each, within one location. Also, be respectful of the thinning attention span of those who have intentionally clicked through to your site. Grab and hold their attention and walk them through their paths of choice, making it simple and rewarding to take action, but define that action before you attempt to channel it.

Define the experience you wish them to take away.

More specifically, when you are actively participating in the Social Web and when you are establishing the profiles, pages, and communities in each respective social network, make sure that you point them to predetermined destinations within the corporate site or to a hub in which action can be captured.

This is how we focus attention, trigger activity, and set forth the metrics to capture a return on our investment.

■ NOTES

1. Bill McCloskey, "Twitter Surpasses Facebook as Top Link in E-mail," ClickZ, sponsored by StrongMail (July 30, 2009), www.clickz.com/ 3634551.

2. "Experiential Marketing," Wikipedia, http://en.wikipedia.org/wiki/ Experiential_marketing.

Chapter 12

The New Media University 901

Brand Personality, Discovery, and Promise

We travel through many places in our expedition toward social media adeptness, and most of it is unfamiliar territory—from social science to active listening and linguistics to experiential marketing and engagement rooted in empathy to social architecture and engineering and everything else that emerges in between. But this is why these times are so exciting and promising.

We're about to review a topic that is instrumental in defining the face, voice, and personality of a brand in socialized media and the ideas and lessons that materialize will most likely affect your next steps.

■ ESTABLISHING AN ONLINE PRESENCE AND DEFINING THE BRAND PERSONA

In the era of the Social Web, we are all brand advocates and managers—whether we know it or not.

I spend a significant portion of my time sharing the importance of listening and engaging noteworthy conversations and studying the enveloping cultures that define relevant online communities. When it comes to participation and engagement, however, identity and branded personalities are often an afterthought.

When it comes to engagement, we unknowingly risk brand dilution. Without defining and reinforcing the brand personality as intended is no different in social media from any other form of

97

media. This is only complicated by the addition of human personalities into the equation, as they may or may not embody or personify the brand essence and as a result, they dilute the brand in every update and interaction.

Many brands still approach this with a "ready, fire" approach and just jump in without aiming. Once there, it's easy to get caught up in the treadmill of listening, learning, responding, and listening again, without ever stopping to ask:

What is it that we want to accomplish?

Who are we trying to reach and why?

How do we wish to be viewed?

How are we contributing to the depiction of the brand?

What do we stand for?

What are our core values?

How does my personal brand affect the company brand and vice versa?

■ ONLINE PROFILES SPEAK VOLUMES ABOUT YOU AND YOUR BRAND

Yes, for many, everything starts with the username and the profile you create within the specific social networks of influence.

These data fields, while simple in their design and intent, can potentially speak volumes for the brand when the company representatives aren't there to speak on its behalf. At a minimum, profiles and bios serve as brand beacons to position and reinforce the company, brand, value proposition, and mission.

Visually, profiles provide canvases for painting the picture that symbolizes our brand. Less is more in social networks and therefore we should seek influence and direction from the school of minimalism, a movement in various forms of art and design, where the work is stripped down to its most fundamental attributes and features.[1]

Usernames are also an important factor in establishing online identities and the presentiment established upon encountering the online persona—before official engagement. This is pivotal, as our usernames can benefit from a consistent presence across the Web—for the company and products, as well as the people representing them. To clarify, there are several username strategies to evaluate and plan: the company, the products, and the personal brands that personify them in respective social networks.

■ MULTIPLE PERSONALITY DISORDER

The inevitability of a brand identity crisis is caused by the saturation of online presences untethered from a centralized strategy. Essentially, chaos and anarchy are inevitable as various company divisions, representatives, and worse, unauthorized representatives swarm the Social Web and involuntarily contribute to multiple personality disorder.

But before we design backgrounds, define usernames, create profile pages, and populate information fields, we first have to take a step back to assess the state of the brand, its eventual direction, and its goals. We begin with an identity assessment and planning strategy to create a center of gravity and parallel orbits around a brand axis. We must define what we represent and also distribute this credo to orbiting brand satellites in the social media universe.

Our profile should reflect our corporate soul and personality. It is our job to introduce the elements, essence, and purpose that attract the individuals seeking alliance and rapport with others possessing similar attributes.

Many companies view the tactical process of establishing online profiles as a simple check-item on the to-do list, when in fact, this is the proverbial book cover on which we're judged.

Without going through a renewed branding exercise at the beginning of the social process, we inadvertently invest in multiple, differing personalities further diluted by the personalities of the people who interact on behalf of the company. Even something as seemingly harmless as not maintaining a consistent username or profile across social networks contributes to brand disarray.

Before jumping in, establish objectives, procedures, and a plan for social branding from the top down. This becomes the style guide that other aspects of the business then base their plans.

■ MULTIPLE PERSONALITY ORDER

One of the more important conversations that will earn prominence now and over time is whether or not a professional should participate in the Social Web as oneself or as a branded representative. Matters become a bit more convoluted when the discussion as to which profile the individual uses comes into play—personal, professional, or both?

There isn't a right or wrong answer to this. But however you engage, it must be practiced in a genuine, helpful, and endearing fashion. It's not unheard of to build two online personas: one personal and the other professional. And it is this strategy that I strongly urge you and your business and teams to consider.

Dell and Zappos, for example, created branded user accounts for each individual. For example, at Dell, we see names such as Richard@Dell and Lionel@Dell. At Zappos, we see a pattern based on FIRSTNAME_Zappos. Also, Zappos boasts more than 250 Zappos-branded employee accounts. They are careful, as anyone on the Social Web should be, with what and how they share. Their activity must collectively build relationships while also boosting the brand and, in most cases, these accounts are used exclusively for work or professional interaction, while a separate, personal account is maintained to publish personal content.

At the point of introduction of any brand in the Social Web is the brand *you*. Ideally, your character and behavior are in alignment with that of the brand you represent. In many ways, this is a role you play and that role is defined differently from the personality you exude in real life.

The question to ask yourself is: Who do you want to be, as defined by different groups of people with whom you wish to connect over time? For example, you obviously connect differently with friends and family and peers and customers. You share content accordingly. At the same time, you will produce content and interact differently among professional contacts when you're on duty for work. In your day job, you may share special offers, interesting observations about market trends, updates about new products and services, or details regarding an upcoming event.

While being human is consistent throughout the cycle, you are indubitably a different person to different people in different circumstances. You further fortify these dedicated personas irregularly, making it difficult to establish meaningful connections among your multiple online personalities. In some cases, these ties overlap, but most of the time, they are divergent in nature, intentions, and outcome. To put it bluntly, I really may not care about one or the other, based on the essence of our connection.

All of this is about bringing it together, the right way, even if they're maintained separately. In other words, it's far more beneficial to you and the brand(s) you represent to maintain multiple accounts, at the very least, one for each professional and business persona online.

Case in point: Richard Brewer-Hay, online media maven for eBay, maintains dual personalities on Twitter. For friends, family, and peers, he maintains @ESBAle, an account dedicated to Elizabeth Street Brewery, a name that affectionately refers to the residence of his family, which also houses a "pub by the people for the people." This is where you get to know the person behind the persona. Simultaneously, Brewer-Hay also manages the @ebayinkblog account to share updates, news, observations, and conversations related to eBay, a company that in and of itself hosts many accounts dedicated to varying divisions, each communicating exclusive content, dialogue, and notifications.

As individuals embrace social media, in due course, they will find themselves at the crossroads of choosing an equitable personal versus professional branding strategy that's scalable, enduring, and portable. Ultimately, this discussion precipitates the necessary requirement to establish the online brand personality, attitude, spirit, and behavioral traits that will synthesize all concerned brands now and henceforward.

■ DISCOVERY AND ACTUALIZATION

This is the beginning of the modernization of a traditional brand style guide. We are, in the least, bringing the brand to life. To get us started, I borrowed from the school of personal development to help us uncover the attributes that are beneficial to the professional, personal, and corporate brands we represent. I included an initial version of a brand reflection cycle (Figure 12.1) to assist in the navigation of brand discovery, definition, and direction. Copy it, recreate it, change it. Whatever you do, make sure to use it or some variation of the cycle to help you assess and dictate the voice and bearing of the brand (and the personal brands supporting it).

This process is not unlike the identity circles used in methods for reflecting on inner qualities. They help us assess strengths, recognize weaknesses, and identify growth qualities as a means of promoting self-awareness and efficacy and also building collaboration in team dynamics. It's how we recognize where we are, where we need to be, and how to get there.

Everything begins with an assessment of the brand's journey through the past, to where it is today, and, in the fullness of time, where it will reside in the future. A brand continually evolves, and it's defined not only by the characteristics we place around this chart, they're also fortified through the words and actions that emanate during engagement, thus contributing to the overall impression post-rendezvous. In any exchange, we must account for twists in the message based on the individual encounter and the reality of what we say and how it's perceived through the filters and biases that establish individual character and identity.

Brand Reflection Cycle

Establishing Online Identity + Persona Through Introspection

1. Core Values
2. Pillars
3. Promise
4. Aspirations
5. Brand Characteristics
6. Opportunities
7. Culture
8. Personality

Figure 12.1   Brand Reflection Cycle: Establishing Online Identity and Persona through Introspection

Storytelling: Remember, in every experience, there are always three sides to storytelling—what's said, what's heard, and the pure state of the story in and of itself, in between.

■ SHAPING THE BRAND PERSONA

To begin the process of brand identification and personality definition, we must establish a body and a supporting process of governance.

This board will also be instrumental in the development of social media guidelines, training, processes, and growth. Depending on the infrastructure of your organization, it may or may not be necessary to invite representatives from executive management, sales, product development, customer service, marketing, legal, human resources, and public relations.

Those departments should interact on behalf of the brand and participate at some level in the definition of the brand as it relates to specific circumstances. This is to safeguard against the common fallacies that assume that one audience exists purely for the consumption of our corporate messages and therefore responds to each directive.

The brand reflection cycle will uncover a series of important revelations that illuminate the brand, its personalities, and its characteristics, in addition to those of the individuals representing it online. I also find this process valuable in that it allows us to revisit the mission. Would someone tweet our mission statement as it exists today? I think not. Humanizing the company is one thing. Making the company and its mission more collaborative and relevant sets the stage for affinity and aspiration.

Run through each of the following reflection cycles and fill in the blanks, as a team, and finalize the top traits to serve as a blueprint for building the brand persona. For fun, run through it as the brand exists today, on your own, to create a sense of urgency or simply to contrast and compare.

■ THE CENTER OF GRAVITY: CORE VALUES

The audiences, surrounding environment, and the circumstances in which we exist define our disposition and character. Ergo, the process of corporate soul-searching may generate varying brand attributes. We need at the very beginning to establish a common center of gravity to support the orbiting characteristics to interplay seamlessly in different situations and under a variety of conditions.

This hub is defined by our core values, and they must be consistent in defining our brand persona in the Social Web. Revisiting our core values is central to substantiating our stature, intentions, and purpose as reinforced by our actions and words. They serve as the framework for our culture and the communities we build. The goal at this stage is to identify and define our core values, as well as relate each of them to intentional behaviors. Try to strive beyond *genericism,* that is, those bland qualities that could define any and every company. Instead, dig deep and determine what your brand stands for, and why customers and prospects should care.

Remember, why should I care, when you don't?

■ BRAND PILLARS

Pillars are the support objects that serve as the foundation to support the brand. These qualities help us stipulate the essential properties that govern perception and connection—in a variety of conditions and affairs. In many respects, it is these pillars that influence every aspect of the social identity cycle.

It is during this stage where we establish the principal central themes and hallmarks.

What is unique to our brand that people need to know as it exists today? What are the hooks for affinity?

■ BRAND CHARACTERISTICS

Defining the brand characteristics will help us establish the traits we wish to associate with the brand. It, of course, includes the qualities and characteristics that define the brand today. Consequently, these properties should adapt to the nuances and expectations of the individuals we aspire to join and inspire.

What is it that we aim to portray?

What are the words customers and peers use to describe us?

What primary characteristics describe our competition?

What are the terms that designate our desired depiction?

In societal domains, they may differ from our presumptions and assumptions.

What are the words we want our customers to use to describe who we are, not today, but tomorrow?

■ PROMISE

The promise of any brand is not necessarily linked to its aspirations— however, it is this pledge that paves the way to its meaning and direction.

The brand promise should answer a simple, yet momentous question: What is our mission?

This is not a marketing exercise.

While searching for the answer, we will discover our ambitions and commitments and rally a team of leaders around a more meaningful corporate guarantee.

This response will serve as the backbone of the brand ethos as well the communications doctrine that affects all outbound marketing, service, and sales materials—essentially, this process defines the mission statement.

■ BRAND ASPIRATIONS

No brand is inanimate. The characteristics defined in the process of social personification require purpose and vision for it to maintain relevance. The attributes we define today must continually evolve along with the evolution of online media. Reaction is not our stimulus. The objective of defining brand aspirations helps us establish a goal that symbolizes those attributes we hope to embody. Branding is an unending story, narrated through experience and maturation. Like a fine wine, it gets better over time.

We are continually redefining what our brand symbolizes in each network and in each instance, while aspiring to typify promise, community, exemplification, and guidance. We need to give people a reason to connect with us and willfully share their affinity.

■ OPPORTUNITIES

Part of the process of merging brand attributes and personality characteristics is the unplanned reward of exposing hidden opportunities for direction and enlightenment.

As we fill out the brand reflection cycle, we identify the attributes that are missing based on the conversations we monitor in each respective network. These conversational trends affect us, as they should, and require us to adapt, based on the possibilities that recurrently appear. Note that I'm not purporting the behavior of simply moving and reacting and thus becoming a brand that exudes an opportunistic presence. I envision an organization that can accept the need for growth and maintain the ambition to transform itself into a more customer- and market-focused partner wherever it is warranted and expected. These attributes are communicated through the brand presence and personality in every social transaction and interaction.

■ CULTURE

The term *culture* can refer to many different facets of anthropology, knowledge and learning, sociology, organizational and human psychology, and ethics—with each carrying its own definition. When establishing a brand persona for the Social Web, we can focus on the interpretation of culture as the beliefs, social forms, and material traits of a particular group. Culture also represents the shared attitudes, values, goals, and practices that characterize an organization (see Merriam-Webster's definition).[2]

Using the brand reflection cycle chart (Figure 12.1), your brand team must search the corporate soul to associate the words and personality attributes that help define, strengthen, and protect the brand, and earn the respect, confidence, and loyalty of those who join the brand's culture. Culture is at the epicenter of affinity. There must be a cultural fit between you and your customers. This is projected through profiles, social objects, and engagement.

■ PERSONALITY

If we haven't determined so by this point, it is absolutely crucial to contemplate and designate the elements that we wish to illustrate. It is a combination of these traits that forms our unmistakable brand personality.

While filling out the brand reflection cycle, we explore, identify, embrace, and manifest the personality and temperament of our brand and how we wish to portray it within each social object and community.

Through this process, we reveal the threads that weave the brand to key characteristics, to best match them to the personalities within our organization, and vice versa. This marriage of brand personality to individual dispositions pivots on how we merge into one persona that personifies the brand as we've designed it and nurtured it.

■ NOTES

1. "Minimalism," Wikipedia, http://en.wikipedia.org/wiki/Minimalism.
2. "Culture," Merriam-Webster, www.merriam-webster.com/dictionary/culture.

Ch*apter* 13

The New Media
University 1001

Attention and Word of Mouth Marketing

In the spirit of the New Media University metaphor, we've now graduated and are pursuing advanced learning, the same way we would seek to earn an MBA in continuing education.

■ FROM INTROVERSION TO EXTROVERSION

As you may or may not know, I'm a big believer in, and also forever a student of, the social aspects of new media. I've dedicated a significant amount of time to studying the sociology behind the technology, as well as the implications of technology in society and how we interact with one another. Indeed, I believe the implications are much bigger than we think. In many cases, the promise of online sociology are still greatly underestimated.

The staggering adoption numbers of social media bring to light a quantum shift in our behavior. We are, without a doubt, empowering a new genre of digital extroverts, encouraged by what I playfully refer to as the *Verizon Network*—the armada of virtual friends and peers who journey with us as we traverse online and offline. Perhaps this is more accurately defined as a personal support system or quite possibly a socialized ego system that champions free thought and speech, while instilling confidence and self-esteem with every comment, retweet, reaction, and connection we earn.

This observation is much more profound than we may initially expect. And its implications for the future of media and marketing are not yet fully understood. As we examine the social landscape and our place within it, acknowledging this cultural (r)evolution will only promote individual-focused media. Context, not content, becomes king.

■ THE NOW WEB

We are witnessing a shift in power. Once tightly controlled by publishers, broadcasters, and corporations, the power to publish and connect messages and stories to people was considered a luxury only a matter of a few years ago—a privilege many of us never would have experienced without the introduction of social platforms. Technology is a change agent, and the capabilities and accompanying benefits that social media offers are liberating our channels of influence. Information is now democratized and we the people are making our voices heard.

The simultaneous advantage and disadvantage of new media is exemplified in its reach, inertia, and volume.

Twitter, Facebook, Tumblr, and other microcommunities that define the real-time Web (or the *now Web*) are captivating and distracting our focus. But, while many argue that they're decreasing productivity, they're also engaging a more active and enlightened community of media-literate socialites.

Twitter is the culprit and is proudly holding the smoking gun. When the ability to search the billions of tweets that were flying across our screens materialized, we were bestowed with a gift of instant insight and revelation.

This is the dawn of the real-time Web, and it's further feeding our insatiable appetite for information as it's published.

When it comes to searches, the most notable comparison between traditional and real-time discovery is represented in the difference between human memory and consciousness. The experience of searching for relevant information is personified in the context of what you're doing and not necessarily what you're typing into the search box. The Internet is more biology than technology.

The patterns for real-time search offer an augmented reality, mapping who we are on the Internet. The constructs of what, where, how, and to whom we communicate and share information are converging through related activity and a syndicated architecture designed to connect the dots and amplify our voice. What we're learning through Twitter and real-time search is that people want access to the immediacy of conversations tied to keywords, regardless of the authority, page rank, and SEO.

It's the difference between finding the right content on the Web and finding the right content, right now, across the Web and social media.

As Gerry Campbell, CEO of Collecta, a real-time platform puts it, "I want to know what people are saying about my topic, right now. The minute you put rankings and filters on search, it stops representing real time. Every minute, stories are told on the Web. Yet in traditional search, most are usually ranked out of the results and therefore, people don't get a chance to see them."

In 2008, I introduced the Conversation Prism, (www .theconversationprism.com), with Jesse Thomas to map the social landscape as a way of gaining *real* insights into the conversations transpiring across social networks, where and when they occurred. The dream was, of course, to have a search window into the Social Web and the social graph, in real time. Specialized tools such as Collecta, Topsy, Radian6, and PeopleBrowsr's Research.y are peeling back the layers of society, focusing our attention to change how we listen. These tools are also plugging us directly into the conversations that shape perception. We'll discuss these search tools in a later chapter on listening and monitoring.

While searching the entire spectrum of the Conversation Prism in real time is not yet fully realized, it is imminent and it is powerful.

Real-time search of the now Web reveals a river, while traditional search architectures discover oceans.

■ THE RISE OF THE STATUSPHERE

In 2009, Twitter stole the spotlight with millions of passionate users not only promoting Twitter, but also ushering in a new generation of real-time, searchable conversations. Twitter is one of many social networks that provide a platform to do so, usually prompted by a question for you to answer in your intentionally limited short post or update.

I call this new form of posting the *statusphere*,[1] a play on other descriptors of social media such as the blogosphere, Twitterverse, and socialmediasphere. The statusphere is what defines and shapes the *egosystem*.

To define it more precisely, the statusphere is any network in which your post is intended to answer questions related to activity or thoughts. The idea is simple: Provide a quick update in a short form and click "update." This short-form response is much easier to produce than a blog post, podcast, webcast, or video, which may require long and involved production cycles. It made media more conversational.

At the moment, Twitter, Facebook, and other microcommunities define the statusphere and are driving action and determining the direction and course of individual attention.

The statusphere is particularly important for brands, since publishers and consumers are losing the luxury of infinite awareness and qualifying their information sources—meaning that they are narrowing their focus to only those voices and peers who share their interests, passions, and insights. We are at the center of our social graphs, and our connections determine how information finds us. As a result, we are now forging contextual networks within networks, to improve our signal to noise ratio.

We can now readily identify and connect directly to existing contacts and also forge new friendships to create a series of interconnected contextual networks within broader networks. Essentially, we can find the right people who may be interested in our story without having to shotgun our value proposition to the masses. This sets the stage for the social effect, a connection of targeted social graphs, or interest graphs, that propagates pertinent information to the right people.

It's in the way that you use it.

Yes, the statusphere is brimming with unimportant chatter, but it is also overflowing with highly curated and valuable information, important questions and answers, influential opinions and observations, breaking news, trending activities, feedback, and personal insight, all of which would otherwise go unnoticed in the volume of online chatter.

Producing and posting updates that people find insightful, entertaining, and enriching is how you build a meaningful foundation for which people follow, admire, and trust you.

■ NEWS NO LONGER BREAKS, IT TWEETS

While we may argue over the degree of intelligence behind the wisdom of the crowds, the ability to swiftly spark word of mouth to propel information across the Web is incontestable.

Twitter, Facebook, and other social networks are defeating even the most nimble news agencies and bureaus, and it's changing the way we find and share news.

Without having to do anything other than open the window to your social graph of choice, you have immediate access to information, as it happens, curated by your friends and contacts, even before the traditional media has time to report it. Think about it. Over the last four years, we have had access to the following information in real time, as told by people, who report live from the center of activity:

➤ News of earthquakes and other natural disasters

➤ The passing of celebrities

➤ An airplane making an emergency landing in the Hudson River

➤ The election in Iran

➤ Terrorist bombings

➤ Sports scores and updates

➤ Earnings reports and stocks

➤ Gossip

➤ Updates from live events

Now and in the future, information will find *you*. And it will be spread through the vision and words of our peers and other citizen reporters who are compelled to leverage their networks of influence to unite people around information that captures the heart, mind, and soul.

The real-time Web also serves as a telltale source for trends and represents a leading indicator for any topic related to your interests or business.

The era of *now* is fueling new media. The pursuit of now is conditioning us to expect information as it happens, whether it's accurate or developing.

The question is: How will this latest chapter of community-powered news and information production, distribution, and consumption affect your ability to connect with your customers?

As now media continues to mature, its impact is clear. The opportunity for social media lies in our ability to build a two-way information bridge between the point of our content introduction, alternative sources for information, and the people looking for insight and direction. To build a community, we have to be an active participant in it.

Today's news and trends no longer break through traditional news sources, voices, or wires; they're captured through the camera lenses, mobile phones, and laptops of people who serve as both witnesses and reporters.

■ THE ATTENTION RUBICON

We're experiencing an increasingly thinning state of focus resulting from volumes of information flying at us within our networks of interest. It's affecting how and what we consume, when, and, more importantly, how we react, learn, and share. It's the quest for an unquenchable thirst for something we cannot yet define. And that something is forever vying for our attention, pushing us to do more with less, driven by the omnipresent fear of potentially missing what's next.

For those attempting to capture attention, this section reveals the state of awareness, to help produce a more substantive signal that effectively rises above the noise.

Attention is a precious commodity. And if you subscribe to the theory of *attention economics,* we're indeed living in an era of information overload that is pushing us to the edge of attention bankruptcy.

Attention economics suggests that human attention is a scarce commodity and attempts to resolve the management of information and its associated challenges through the application of economic theory.[2]

Linda Stone, a widely recognized visionary and thought leader, observes that attention is "the most powerful tool of the human spirit. We can enhance or augment our attention with practices like meditation and exercise, diffuse it with technologies like email and Blackberries, or alter it with pharmaceuticals. In the end, though, we are fully responsible for how we choose to use this extraordinary tool."[3]

The Social Web and new services that continue the permeation into everything we do online are proving that attention is, as expected, not scalable. However, the rate of information that flows to and past us only continues to escalate.

As documented in an August 2009 article in the *Wall Street Journal* written by John Freeman,

> *In the past two decades, we have witnessed one of the greatest breakdowns of the barrier between our work and personal lives since the notion of leisure time emerged in Victorian Britain as a result of the Industrial Age. It has put us under great physical and mental strain, altering our brain chemistry and daily needs. It has isolated us from the people with whom we live, siphoning us away from real-world places where we gather. It has encouraged flotillas of unnecessary jabbering, making it difficult to tell signal from noise. It has made it more difficult to read slowly and enjoy it, hastening the already declining rates of literacy. It has made it harder to listen and mean it, to be idle and not fidget. This is not a sustainable way to live. This lifestyle of being constantly on causes emotional and physical burnout, workplace meltdowns, and unhappiness.[4]*

He then asks the reader, "How many of our most joyful memories have been created in front of a screen?"

Freeman's assertions are accurate and I don't disagree with him. As I've long maintained, social media is fueling our Industrial Revolution.

As brands and content publishers, we must understand the psychology and sociology governing the socialization of online information. Those contributing to the egosystem are not yet ready to step off the treadmill per se. We're actively investing in our intelligence and social capital as much as we're defining the new boundaries for discovering and sharing material information.

Instead of inhibiting the pace and breadth of information flow, we must channel relevant details and data.

It's part technology, part science, and part conditioning of the mind.

This is what I refer to as the *Attention Rubicon*.

A rubicon is defined as a limit that, when passed or exceeded, permits of no return and typically results in irrevocable commitment.[5] We have hit an information crossroads and many of us are unknowingly contributing to the Attention Rubicon as we increasingly consume, and interact with, social objects and people.

The Attention Rubicon is the acceptance that our appetite for information has passed the point of no return. Therefore, we must concentrate our energies on innovation, technologically and psychologically, to process and parse data more effectively. Embracing this Attention Rubicon and investing in our ability to learn, share, and contribute is how we will thrive in today's attention economy.

Linda Stone offers a solution to this dilemma. She refers to it as *Continuous Partial Attention* and defines it this way:

> *Continuous partial attention describes how many of us use our attention today. It is different from multitasking. The two are differentiated by the impulse that motivates them. When we multitask, we are motivated by a desire to be more productive and more efficient. We're often doing things that are automatic, that require very little cognitive processing. We give the same priority to much of what we do when we multitask—we file and copy papers, talk on the phone, eat lunch—we get as many things done at one time as we possibly can in order to make more time for ourselves and in order to be more efficient and more productive.*
>
> *To pay continuous partial attention is to pay partial attention—continuously. It is motivated by a desire to be a live node on the network. Another way of saying this is that we want to connect and be connected. We want to effectively scan for*

opportunity and optimize for the best opportunities, activities, and contacts, in any given moment. To be busy, to be connected, is to be alive, to be recognized, and to matter. We pay continuous partial attention in an effort not to miss anything. It is an always-on, anywhere, anytime, anyplace behavior that involves an artificial sense of constant crisis. We are always on high alert when we pay continuous partial attention. This artificial sense of constant crisis is more typical of continuous partial attention than it is of multitasking.

Whatever we call it, we are in truth learning to publish, process, and react to information in *Twitter time.*

■ CHANNELING OUR FOCUS: THE ATTENTION DASHBOARD

Attention is engaged at the point of introduction. Retweets (RT) and favorites in Twitter, likes and comments in Facebook, posting shortened links that connect friends and followers back to the source, have changed our behavior.

We are in control of what we read and learn, and responsible for what we share.

As technology transforms, our sources for discovering and consuming information also continue to evolve. With the pace of information published through the activity streams we follow, our attention spans are overloaded and scattered.

Our intentions are limited by available time, daily responsibilities, usual distractions, and the realistic ability to process only part of the sheer volume of data that flows through our social streams.

Conversations and social objects are distributed beyond our reach and they are tugging at our attention and focus.

In 2009, the introduction of tools and services that funneled information from multiple social networks into one aggregated stream gave rise to a new type of reader.

These tools essentially channeled updates from one or multiple social networks such as Twitter and Facebook into one easy-to-read activity stream. This allowed individuals to stay up to date on information and trends, click through to shared content, respond directly in the timeline, and also read and send private messages to their contacts. Tools such as TweetDeck, Seesmic, Co-Tweet, and HootSuite, among others, thus served as the attention dashboards for the social consumer.

I introduced the concept of *attention dashboards* in 2008 in reference to Twitter and Facebook specifically, as they served as the window to the social world. I suggested that these windows were open for the majority of the day and provided the ability for us to stay connected and keep our ears to the ground, while allowing our attention to focus on other responsibilities. As such, these social feeds serve as our centralized attention dashboards and determine what we read, what we say, and who responds, simply by the information that continually flows through it. We're engaged at the point and place of introduction and bound by context and time.

Businesses must tap in to these attention dashboards for them to earn awareness and, more importantly, build relationships. As we're learning, noticeable content sparks curiosity and dictates our next move and subsequently the next moves and reactions of friends and friends of friends. The most successful initiatives require a personalized engagement strategy to consistently vie for consideration. The laws of attraction and relationship management will support your efforts when you create compelling content and transparently connect it to the people whom you believe will benefit—and through the people who influence their decisions.

It's now our job to identify and recognize those influencers, trust agents, and tastemakers. With each new connection, businesses can appear in multiple, dispersed dashboards and timelines. Worthy social objects, combined with evangelism and clever promotion, will earn visibility and expanded syndication through retweets (RT), link shares, Diggs, Stumbles, bookmarks, tweetbacks, likes, and other forms of social recognition. With each new instance of sharing, content reverberates through extended social graphs.

The ability to provoke a response through the attention dashboard requires creativity, relevance, and a natural understanding of the nuances that trigger desirable action.

■ THE SOCIAL EFFECT: THE FUTURE OF BRANDING AND WORD OF MOUTH MARKETING

The responsibility is yours to create a dedicated tribe that supports, shares, and responds to your engagement. It's the only way to build a valuable community around you and what you represent.

The challenge, however, is first getting noticed. In the process, we gain awareness, reinforced by our actions and words to recruit peers, empower champions, and establish dedicated communities.

The ability to engage someone directly in the attention dashboard, incite a response, and hopefully have them share their experience with their network is what I termed *the social effect,* a modern adaptation of the network effect, driven by word of mouth across social and interest graphs.

To better define the network effect, it is the phenomenon that occurs when one user of a good or service affects the adoption and subsequent use of the product by other people.[6] In other words, the network effect dictates that a service becomes more valuable as more people use it, leading to an ever-increasing number of users. The most commonly used example of the network effect is the telephone. A more modern example would most definitely include the Internet. And just to stay on the social highway, we couldn't ignore Twitter, Facebook, or YouTube. While word of mouth is often influential in the beginning—for example, you may use something because someone you know uses it—eventually the masses will adopt a product or service because *everyone* uses it.[7]

The social effect is rooted in similar theory. It determines actual reach, resonance, and the course for social objects and relevant dialogue. The analysis and reverse engineering of the social effect visualizes behavior, conversation paths, and click patterns.

Connections with friends, followers, and their respective FoFs are constantly shifting and never duplicated. The conversations one maintains online produces a resulting expansion and contraction of the network at a particular point in time based on the topics of discussion. I refer to the state of the social graph characterized by time, theme, and connections as the interest graph, aka the relevant net, and, as we've discussed earlier, it is linked by context.

The social effect and its reach and resonance are defined by a series of gauges, measurements, and scales. Studying these elements and conditions contribute to the ability to distract activity in your favor, improving the resonance of your social objects (see Figure 13.1).

Disruption point: The place and moment when a social object is introduced into the attention dashboard. This is the point that I believe determines the potential reach.

The microdisruption theory therefore suggests that we study sharing and consuming behaviors within our relevant communities to help us establish the conditions associated with successful viewing and sharing activities. In the process, we learn more about the following social barometers: attention aperture, time, networks, and back channels.

Attention aperture: We are susceptible to diversion at specific intervals during our daily routine. The state of an individual's focus represented by the receptiveness to outside distraction based on circumstances defines the opening of the attention aperture. Identifying our influencers and also observing when they most often

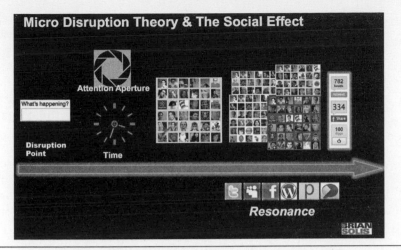

Figure 13.1 Microdisruption Theory and the Social Effect

share content or objects produced from others will help us define windows of opportunity to capture attention.

Time: Time is a major factor in determining interaction and sharing levels when new social objects are introduced into the timeline. Updates published in the early morning on a Monday will garner greater attention than a midday post on Wednesday. Time therefore suggests that we monitor activity immediately after each post to track responses, shares, and views to discover when our communities are most receptive. Try experimenting with the sharing of a series of intelligent and free URL shorteners such as bit.ly. You can immediately track the associated traffic and referring sources for each distinct URL you create to help you gauge immediacy in views, response, and momentum. This, however, provides only a cursory analysis. Deeper study in the form of Web analytics and conversation monitoring is required to eventually shape social activity.

Networks: Networks represent the interest graphs. For example, if we introduce the object in Twitter through our own syndication channel, we have the ability to potentially reach multiple individuals in various networks simultaneously. With a little help through engagement, social objects can then share, interact, and respond, thus triggering a social effect across multiple networks in unison.

Back channel: The back channel is among the most influential means for propelling social objects and sparking conversations within each social network. The back channel is defined as the conversations that occur outside of the public eye—private messages on Facebook, DMs on Twitter, traditional emails, and so on. This is where we introduce new content to influencers with whom we've already established relationships. It is through these direct connections that we can orchestrate the wide reach of objects. As these planned updates debut in the public timelines, connected friends and followers step in to further share the content, because it stems from a trusted source.

Understanding and mastering disruption theory and the social effect unveil the most important factors in making something go viral. Interest graphs and the relationships that define it are discoverable. Microdisruption theory visualizes the true opportunity for resonance and the potential course and reach for the social effect.

Remember, the secret to earning resonance is through relevance and engagement supported by a genuine intent to introduce value into the stream. This is how we build trust, establish authority, and earn significance over time. Brands, too, can become influencers.

■ NOTES

1. Brian Solis, "Coining the Statusphere: The Social Web's Next Big Thing," Channeling Brian Solis (March 9, 2009), http://briansolis.tumblr .com/post/85090914/coining-the-statusphere-the-social-webs-next-big.

2. "Attention economy," Wikipedia, http://en.wikipedia.org/wiki/Attention _economy.

3. Linda Stone, "Continuous Partial Attention—Not the Same as Multi-Tasking," *BusinessWeek* (July 24, 2008), www.businessweek.com/business_ at_work/time_management/archives/2008/07/continuous_part.html.

4. John Freeman, "A Manifesto for Slow Communication," *Wall Street Journal* (August 21, 2009), http://online.wsj.com/article/SB100014240529 7020355060457435864311740777 8.html.

5. "Rubicon," Dictionary.com, http://dictionary.reference.com/browse/ rubicon.

6. "Network effect," Wikipedia, http://en.wikipedia.org/wiki/Network_ effect.

7. "Network effect," Marketing Terms, www.marketingterms.com/dictionary/ network_effect/.

The New Media University 1101

Social Landscape and Initiatives

Scholastic institutions all over the world are preparing tomorrow's workforce for a new generation of careers. At the same time, we are all collectively learning and adapting to the new landscapes of media, business, and influence.

In the previous chapter, or, in keeping with our metaphor, in the first year of your MBA program, we studied the rise of the *statusphere*, the focus of awareness on attention dashboards, the thinning of attention span, and the competition for being a leading source of intellectual stimulation. We also discussed the fabric of the social effect and the influential factors that propel social objects across social graphs, thus making them legitimately viral.

I alluded to filtering earlier, and this is where we continue our higher learning. We'll then follow up with a study of how people currently populate the social landscape, to help us shape and fine-tune our social initiatives.

■ IMPROVING THE SIGNAL-TO-NOISE RATIO

Social media, for the most part, thrive on our excitement. We are part of a new (r)evolution that is defined through participation. However, our threshold for information processing is challenged. Part of this is due to what's referred to as *social network fatigue* (SNF) combined with the reality of information overload.

Social network fatigue is not well defined beyond its label. It refers to the phenomenon of user exhaustion, caused by too much interaction as well as spreading ourselves thin across multiple social networks. SNF also stems from burnout associated with the emotional, intellectual, and time commitments required to stay connected to peers in one or many social networks concurrently.

As a brand manager, your endurance must be greater than others of your tribe and interest graphs (also referred to as *nicheworks*). The future of human interaction and media consumption and production lies in our ability to focus and filter.

The best ways to engage, help, guide, and build communities are driven by anthropology, sociology, and psychology and are connected through technology. Technology will evolve, adapt, and pioneer new applications that help us in our mission to increase brand awareness through relevance, and resonance through engagement.

Chapter 15

Fusing the *Me* in Social Media and the *We* in the Social Web

The evolution of media and communications is timeless.

Once we put these lessons and insights into practice we truly graduate into apprentices of new media.

But before we do so, there's an important element in the socialization of media that can't go undisclosed: The socialization of media starts with not us, but specifically you and me. Let's spend one chapter together exploring and unraveling the butterfly effect.

The butterfly effect is an example made popular in the 1980s and taken from the chaos theory that describes how the fluttering of a butterfly's wings may be the initial source of events that result in a large storm. In reference to the Social Web, it is a potentially chaotic effect created by something seemingly insignificant, whereby a small change in one part of a complex system can have a large effect somewhere else.[1] That somewhere else could have devastating or wonderful effects on you or the brand you represent or both.

It sounds alarming, but this is not science fiction. I need your attention as we move forward together, as our journey is only just beginning.

■ CASTING A DIGITAL SHADOW: YOUR REPUTATION PRECEDES YOU

You will be googled. . . .

This couldn't be any truer. This might make you smirk, but go google yourself.

Figure 15.1   A Thought from George Bernard Shaw

View the results as if through the eyes of a stranger, a business prospect, a recruiter, an HR professional, your current or future boss—I'm leaving out BFFs and family, as it skews your perspective. We need an unbiased encounter with the results that return.

But also pay attention to what you don't see. Pay attention to how these results portray who you are and what you represent today and also discern how these pieces of the puzzle establish your potential for accomplishing your short- and long-term goals.

Truthfully, stop and think a bit about what it is you stand for, believe in, and aspire to become (see Figure 15.1). Let's expand the search. What do our tweets say about us? What does our Facebook activity reveal? Do they paint a desirable picture? Do these results represent you when you can't be there to explain them?

Everything starts with you. Your actions and words online are indeed extensions to how people interpret, perceive, and react to the brand you represent. At the same time, you also represent your personal brand—the digital identity that's established through the assembly of digital shadows you cast across the Web.

Our contributions to the Web are archived for years to come. When we tweet, upload videos and pictures, post on blogs and comments, and update our status on social networks, we cast a digital shadow that may or may not parallel our activities in real life. This digital shadow is cast across the Web only to be reassembled through the search pursuits of others—whether they're prospective partners, employers, employees, customers, influencers, or stakeholders.

■ DEFINING YOUR ONLINE PERSONA

The social economy is defined by the exchange of ideas and information online and in the real world, and is indexed by the dividends earned through interaction and alliances. Relationships, social objects, and engagement are the new currencies of the social economy. They fund valuable interaction, insight, and loyalty, and in turn, contribute to the social capital of the individuals who actively invest in their personal branding portfolio.

We are now defined by the size and shape of our social graph and our place within it. Size isn't the only thing that matters, however. In all seriousness, our experiences and resulting circumstances, possibilities, and options are defined by how we uniquely engage and participate throughout the Social Web. To put it another way, our interactions and contributions earn keys that unlock the doors to future opportunities.

In the workforce and in our personal lives, the things we share online define who we are—it's a fortunate or unfortunate reality (depending on how you look at it). Social profiles in Facebook for example, are showing up in search engines. What's in them can tell us everything about how you view yourself and therefore how you may wish others to view you. It's not only your profiles in the social networks where you participate, it's what you say and share everywhere, from blog posts and comments to wall posts, the music you listen to and the widgets you embed, as well as your status updates and even product or service reviews.

This is your digital identity and your real reputation and it's yours to define and nurture.

It's important to proactively weigh, factor, and contribute to the impression you want others to have when they stumble upon or intentionally find your profile(s). This is the first step in defining and shaping your online brand and it's necessary to master before you can represent the brands that will employ you.

■ YOUR BRAND VERSUS THE BRANDS YOU REPRESENT

Whether we believe it or not, everyone within an organization is at some level responsible for branding and public relations. Everything we do, online and offline, builds the public perception of not only our personal brand, but also that of the organization we represent. They must be symbiotic. And while many insist that a brand must be human, it must not act as just any ordinary human. It requires definition and also embodiment.

As an active participant in social media and also a professional working in any capacity within a company, eventually an important decision will determine your outward presence and whether or not your personal brand and your corporate responsibilities intersect, compete, or clash.

As many businesses are realizing, there is not only the possibility, but, in many cases, the requirement to engage with customers, peers, influencers, and prospects in their respective communities. New roles and responsibilities emerge for all employees.

■ MANAGING YOUR ONLINE REPUTATION

Everything starts with listening and observing where, how, and why these conversations are taking place and the tone and nature of the dialogue.

As part of the marketing process, companies employ (or should incorporate) a monitoring and online reputation management (ORM) program.

Typically, ORM focuses on company and product name(s), executives, or brands, and each of these services automate the process of searching and presenting the results in a manageable, easy-to-navigate dashboard. The differences between each lie under the hood, where the individual algorithms distinguish each service in how they discover, track, and present data. And none of these services are all-inclusive. There is still a manual element involved, requiring you to search specific communities directly.

Real-time search engines, alert systems such as Google Alerts, which scours News.Google.com, Blogsearch.google.com, and other media properties, are among the most effective free services available for tracking keywords and presenting them to you as they appear online. They give you, as the primary stakeholder, the opportunity to participate and respond immediately to help you better protect the integrity of your brands and stay connected to your community.

Emerging media will only continue to provide us with the opportunity to build and grow our brands and establish a position of authority based on our expertise and engagement. The more attention we devote to listening, participating, and contributing to related conversations over time the more our reputation matures. Feedback and criticism can offer value, even if they're incorrect in their assumptions and reactions.

■ WE ARE ALL BRAND MANAGERS

Organizing and managing a strategically posed brand is critical to how we are perceived in the real world.

Again, the comments we leave, the posts we publish, the pictures and videos we upload, the statuses we broadcast in social networks and streams, collectively contribute to disparate digital recreations of how people perceive us—as an individual, representative of a company, or the corporate brand we manage. While we can't control how people ultimately assemble these pieces and make judgments based on them, we can shape and steer perception by sharing the right content, the right way to invest in the brand we wish to portray.

We are all, at some level, becoming brand managers.

With social media comes great responsibility. . . .

■ NOTE

1. "Butterfly   Effect,"   http://dictionary.reference.com/browse/butterfly | effect.

Chapter

16

Learning and Experimentation Lead to Experience

In new media, we're frequently challenged to venture outside our lair of solace, and the more we live outside it, the more we begin to actually redefine our center of judgment, transforming how we process and act based on how new information reaches us.

Curiosity and experience reveal new, more effective, and more efficient ways to get from here to the ever elusive *there,* all while venturing into the unknown. It's what we implement that converts theory into practice, and practice into education and innovation.

Caution, however, isn't something we ought to carelessly throw to the wind. Within social networks and the blogosphere, the rules of engagement are being defined. There's much to learn, but we can't grasp or master anything by sitting idly and watching the world pass us by. Nor can we jump in with both feet and engage without observing how we effectively contribute value and earn the relationships that spark communities, associations, and ultimately action.

■ BECOMING THE EXPERT

Every day, you learn a great deal about your business and industry.

This is your moment, and it starts with becoming the type of person you would want to listen to, watch, read, and otherwise seek guidance. You are empowered to lead the way and employ the lessons and insights you absorb to always improve the state of the brand.

We are charting the specific steps necessary to accomplish new and great things. We do so by tying strategies and tactics to real-world business value, not because we can, but because we have to.

Sure, those responsible for green-lighting a new pilot, campaign, or program may or may not be qualified to do so. They may, instead, stand in the way, in a desperate bid for job security, and attempt to direct a social media project into oblivion, tangle innovation with a Web of process requirements and aging infrastructure, or, even worse, denounce new ideas.

Okay, so then what?

Thankfully, there are also gatekeepers who are never content with the status quo and recognize opportunity and their chance to not only adapt and evolve along with the market, but also help lead them to answers to make more informed decisions.

We're all learning.

We are the champions.... We are becoming the experts.

■ YOU'RE THE REAL THING

While many individuals can demonstrate the benefits of and processes for building and managing brands in social media, only those who have faced business-specific challenges, tested numerous initiatives, experienced buy and sell cycles, and lived through successes and failures related to their markets are eligible to become bona fide experts. But in all reality, we are forever students of new media.

It's not about the tools.

It's not about the ability to build profile pages within specific social networks and update them all day, every day.

It's not about creating a blog and populating it with content.

And it's definitely not about creating and polluting the Web with irrelevant social objects.

This is about social architecture, engineering, and the empathy required to build bridges between your company, its brand, and its audiences, customers, and peers. It's also about contributing value to the communities in which you wish to participate.

Want to master Twitter? Don't jump to purchase a book on Twitter. It's less important to know the history of Twitter or how to tweet and more important to use Twitter as an extension of who you are, what you stand for, and the value that you can add to the community.

The same is true for Facebook, YouTube, and LinkedIn, for that matter. At the end of the day, they're channels—albeit rich channels—for listening, learning, and engaging. Understanding the unique culture of each social network as it relates to your business and the corresponding behaviors that define desirable interest graphs is critical to establishing, implementing, and managing successful programs.

Tools are just that: tools. They will help you reach people. They'll adapt. They'll change. They'll emerge and merge. And many will simply vanish.

Think about it for a moment.

Your focus, no matter which tools you use, must be on assessing weaknesses and opportunities, defining goals and objectives, auditing the landscape and competitive activity, listening to where and how the community is speaking, and identifying concerns and challenges. We must take steps to create a governing and measurable strategy that will help us justify, refine, and improve our activity.

■ WHEN POV BECOMES A POINT OF VALIDATION

To best appeal to customers, peers, and other influencers, we need to embrace their point of view. This provides insight into their frame of mind. Doing so will lay the foundation that will allow us to learn from an educated position. From there, our experience and training builds upon itself in line with our markets.

We're usually missing the "day in the life of" viewpoint and the "why should I listen to you" perspective in our strategy and execution, yet it's supposed to serve as the core of everything we do and should be doing.

In my experience, we tend to broadcast, even when we are listening. We tend to communicate without regard for the bigger picture as it relates to participating parties, even if we're engaging.

The experience that's earned through the process of establishing a brand and building prominence, cultivating a vibrant community, earning trust and loyalty on behalf of a company brand, and inspiring measurable action and transactions, is immeasurable and critical.

You represent the future of your brand's connections, and resonance within emerging media. Don't get distracted. Get to work.

■ LET'S TALK ABOUT MEANINGFUL EXCHANGES

Any anthropologist or sociologist will tell you that before attempting to join any society, we must conduct initial fieldwork to observe and document the culture, behaviors, communication styles, customs, and traditions of its citizens. And before we can determine which networks we prioritize, we have to first listen to the conversations across multiple social networks to identify and distinguish relevant interaction from worthless chatter.

Use the conversation prism (see Chapter 18) to establish a conversation index.

Transformation begins with observation.

We need to spend more time listening and less time broadcasting or talking at people.

We must realize that there are benefits to monitoring, listening, communicating, and connecting.

■ WHO OWNS SOCIAL MEDIA?

It is essential to figure out who's in charge of the conversations for your brand. Is it advertising, PR, marketing communications, or customer service? Actually, it's all of these!

Perhaps CEOs, directors, and investors will read this and force change from the top down. But in most cases, change will be driven from the bottom up, and also will be influenced by middle management. As social media becomes accepted and practiced industrywide, change will also stem from outside pressure. Someone has to lead the discussions.

The easy answer is that no one owns the conversation and that each division and each person representing the company, inward and outward, will be responsible for contributing to it. Any division affected by outside behavior requires a social extension.

When you listen, categorize conversations by the department that each update was targeted. For example, could the comment have benefited product development or did the exchange require someone from customer service to respond. As you'll see, conversations will always map directly to specific departments within a company, thus requiring participation from everyone, including service and support, public relations, marketing communications, executives, product development, finance/investor (if applicable), and so forth.

The best companies will realize that the future of business is not created, it's co-created. As such, brands will share control associated with gatekeeping the brand and messages in social realms and trust their employees and customers to carry them forward. Don't get me wrong, traditional marketing can still run as it has; it simply now needs a complementary role with all the new media activities. There also needs to be a more cognizant process for understanding the people who compose the markets you're trying to reach.

■ GETTING DOWN TO BUSINESS

The primary metric for business success is measured in profitability and market share, not friends and followers. It is quantified in predefined and desired actions, not conversations. It is metered in presence and not chatter. The path to direct success is blocked by tollgates that are manned by influencers, who govern passage.

While basic communications and personal skills factor into engagement, they are technically responsible for defining perception, reach, and persona.

While many preach the importance of personality and voice and the humanization of the corporate brand in social networks, there's something to be said for mystique and there's definitely something to be said for creating perception.

Being yourself or simply being present isn't enough, and many times it can also take away from the persona that symbolizes the company and its products. We examined the need to define and personify the brand earlier.

Would Apple maintain its magic if everyday social media experts were actively engaging with people on Twitter? Would Steve Jobs preserve his charisma if we, as the public, could freely access him through social networks? Or would these prestigious brands lose their luster and charisma if they were absolutely accessible?

Think about it. Would simply having access to the company wherever, whenever, through the voices and personalities of John or Jane Doe change your perceptions of Apple or Mr. Jobs?

I remind you of this here because you are the first line of defense and offense.

In social media, the brands of participants will forever be at odds with the brands they represent. Who we are as an individual and who we are as a representative of a company aren't always in harmony. However, there is an attainable balance and it's this balance that inflates and steers the impression of all brands involved on both sides of the conversation—as it relates to the calculation of brand personality.

While we inject a human element into the image of the company to make it approachable and compassionate, we must also assess our intended role in the communities we wish to reach. Then, and only then, can we plot our bearing and trajectory.

It's a matter of being human versus humanizing the story, and there is a stark difference between them.

Humanizing the brand is necessary if, and only if, a human voice will reduce or eliminate potential friction between the customer and the company. Otherwise, social strategies must personify the greater purpose, significance, and symbolization of the brand, and reinforce those traits through everything we contribute. We do so by also humanizing our existing and potential customers, gaining empathy and sincerity in the process. But we must do so at a profound measure. It requires not only a deep-rooted comprehension of human nature and connections, but also comprehension of perception management and branding that leaves those you encounter more informed and fulfilled. We're instilling the attributes that engender awareness, affinity, and loyalty.

We look to you to act as the gatekeeper who protects the brand while serving the interests of those you're chartered to reach.

The shift from specialist to authority is driven specifically by experience and the activities that define your social portfolio. As a business professional seeking guidance and direction, become the person you're trying to reach by using the voice of the persona you wish to convey and fortify.

This is connectivity through inspiration. In the process, we become the very social media experts we sought to employ.

Be bullish.

Stand up and assume command.

You are the voice, spirit, and mind of the brand and only you can help the company connect with the people and culture that define it.

Chapter 17

Defining the Rules of Engagement

To prevent information leaks and other liabilities, companies are drafting guidelines for social media interaction. A rule of thumb: Don't be stupid.

—*BusinessWeek*[1]

With access to social tools, we are more influential than we realize, and that works both for us and against us.

Before we create and implement outbound social media programs, we must first educate employees on the benefits and hazards associated with social media and the workplace. However, this should not include banning access to these networks. I discuss that topic more thoroughly a bit later.

Without realizing the impact of a single update, employees are jeopardizing brand stature, reputation, and competitive edge. Also, employees are sharing candid and damaging thoughts and updates—intentionally and unintentionally—that possess an uncanny ability to surface when least expected and be discovered by people who were never supposed to see them in the first place.

And, perhaps accidentally, employees are sharing company secrets and information that should never see the light of day, and are doing so simply because they have access to the tools that personally connect them to their friends, family, and peers. Just because we have access to the tools doesn't mean we know how to use them.

Yet, heeding *BusinessWeek*'s advice is easier said than done. One might believe that common sense is pervasive and prevailing; I believe that common sense, however, is mostly uncommon. In a new media world where many of us are literally learning as we go, commonsensical behavior usually acquiesces to a resemblance to common nonsense, rather than sense and sensibility. Therefore, we need to proactively avert crises before they arise. Plus, it wouldn't hurt to have some direction in place so we know our role in this new business landscape.

■ INSIDE THE OUTSIDE: ASSESSING THREATS AND OPPORTUNITIES

Businesses are scrambling to understand the technologies and platforms associated with social computing and how to integrate them into the existing workflow. More so, information technology (IT), human resources, and executive management are also struggling with the impact of social networks on the culture and productivity within the company, as well as the resulting shifts in internal behavior.

Traditionally, new technology and policies were introduced to organizations in a top-down process once they were formally evaluated and ratified by IT and management. If new technologies, services, and applications were introduced by employees or outside influences, IT was responsible for assessing the benefits and risks from the perspective of improving and streamlining processes, and possibly cutting expenses.

Social computing has created a backdoor for many of these services that also introduces potential dangers to the existing infrastructure and to the systematic routines for ensuring productivity. For the first time, new technologies are permeating the enterprise and business infrastructures from the bottom up. And these technologies precipitate change, carrying the ability to significantly revolutionize business processes in every aspect of the business. In fact, social media starts to add new layers of process and responsibilities.

Some companies view social networks and blogs as a threat to productivity, network security, and company intelligence. They are therefore prohibiting access to these networks from within the firewall. Many studies have already concluded that there are indeed productivity decreases when employees have unregulated access to personal communications tools and distractions. But this isn't new. Distractions have long been debated, including smoke and coffee breaks, water cooler chats, and even cell phones, instant messaging services, and now social networks.

In August 2009, the United States Marines banned the use of Twitter, MySpace, Facebook, and other social networks for a period of one year, citing the risks to both personnel and network security.

The Marine Corps order attempted to explain the rationale:

These Internet sites in general are a proven haven for malicious actors and content and are particularly high risk due to information exposure, user-generated content and targeting by adversaries. . . . The very nature of SNS [social network sites] creates a larger attack and exploitation window, exposes unnecessary information to adversaries and provides an easy conduit for information leakage that puts OPSEC [operational security], COMSEC [communications security], and personnel . . . at an elevated risk of compromise.[2]

When news of this order initially surfaced, journalists and social media experts reacted in disbelief. However, understanding their concerns allows us to assess possibilities about how to deploy and guide usage as it relates to the business and mission of the armed forces, and any civilian organization for that matter.

On the other hand, before the Marines issued their ordinance, the Army had ordered bases to allow access to social networks, after a year-long banishment.

The Army public affairs managers shared the operations order publicly to clarify intentions and justify the command:

. . . the intent of senior Army leaders to leverage social media as a medium to allow soldiers to "tell the Army story" and to facilitate the dissemination of strategic, unclassified information. Therefore, the social media sites available from the Army homepage will be made accessible from all campus area networks. Additionally, all Web-based email will be made accessible.[3]

In an interview with *Wired*'s Danger Room, Price Floyd, the Pentagon's social media czar, shared his views of and vision for social media:[4]

OPSEC is paramount. We will have procedures in place. . . . What we can't do is let security concerns trump doing business. We have to do business. . . . We need to be everywhere men and women in uniform are and the public is. If that's MySpace and YouTube, that's where we need to be, too.

As such, the Pentagon ordered a review of social networks in the second half of 2009 to craft policies that dictate usage scenarios and goals for services such as Twitter, MySpace, and Facebook.

Officials acknowledged the potential influence within the military and also in the greater population for these networks. As a result, they developed rules that would allow the military to take advantage of the expedient communications inherent within social networks without exposing sensitive information, jeopardizing personnel, or placing computer networks at risk.

A number of top commanders and officers already maintain public profiles on social networks.

Admiral Michael G. Mullen,[5] chairman of the Joint Chiefs of Staff, and Army General Ray Odierno,[6] the top commander in Iraq, maintain Facebook profiles. Mullen also actively tweets.

Responding to questions on Twitter as to whether or not Mullen would continue to participate during times when the security, threats, and benefits of social networks are questioned, Mullen wrote, "Obviously we need to find the right balance between security and transparency. We are working on that. But am I still going to tweet? You bet."

In an interview with the *Los Angeles Times*, Navy Captain John Kirby, a spokesman for Mullen, acknowledged that the chairman had already seen the importance of using social media to communicate with the public. He stated,

> *The genie is out of the bottle. There is just such a power in it, we have to find a way to achieve this balance. No one wants to provide information to potential enemies, but this is a dialogue that we cannot afford not to be a part of.*[7]

Top generals are also are taking the initiative to reach troops and other constituents through personal blogs. For example, Major General Michael Oates,[8] a two-star general overseeing 19,000 U.S. soldiers in southern and central Iraq, maintains a blog and hosts chats to communicate within and to those defining the chain of command, as well as maintaining dialogues with troops who are scattered across Iraq.

So why am I sharing examples of social media bans and active communications in the military?

The answer is as simple as it is poignant. If the U.S. military is actively seeking guidelines for defining, regulating, and promoting the use of social media to improve communications and influence constituents, then it's safe to assume that your organization should follow suit.

Everything starts with assessment and the implementation of structure, followed by management and responsibility.

■ POLICIES AND GUIDELINES

Best Buy initially broke ground with its Blue Shirt Network, which fostered conversation, interaction, and content to improve employee communication and team spirit. The company also catalyzed customer support and participation when it introduced IdeaXchange, a dedicated feedback community designed to solicit feedback to help make Best Buy a better place to shop.

Among many other accomplishments, Best Buy again pioneered a new and controversial social program with the introduction of its @Twelpforce account on Twitter. The account is simple in design but radical in concept, deployment, and implications. Arguably one of the most outlandish social media mavens of its time, Best Buy leveraged the reach of mainstream traditional media in the form of television commercials to generate awareness for a specific new media initiative.

Twelpforce tapped the wisdom of its own crowds to assemble and deploy an armada of service professionals to help answer questions posed by everyday people on Twitter, and also to proactively share insights from their personal and professional accounts on the @twelpforce account directly (see Figure 17.1).

Without direction, training, and a supporting infrastructure, this program would most likely have imploded. However, Best Buy provided a set of guidelines and instructions to guide participants in the program to help them assist customers and ultimately engender goodwill and to inspire action in the process.

Risky?
Yes.
Creative?
Yes.
Another example of overusing "tw" in a name?

Figure 17.1   Twelpforce Tweet

Yes.
Effective?
Yes!

An excerpt from Best Buy Connect,[9] an internal network that serves as the voice of the Best Buy employee, offers guidance to participants of the @Twelpforce program:

The promise we're making starting in July is that you'll know all that we know as fast as we know it. That's an enormous promise. That means that customers will be able to ask us about the decisions they're trying to make, the products they're using, and look for the customer support that only we can give. And with Twitter, we can do that fast, with lots of opinions so they can make a decision after weighing all the input. It also lets others learn from it as they see our conversations unfold.

When you start, remember that the tone is important. Above all, the tone of the conversation has to be authentic and honest. Be conversational. Be yourself. Show respect. Expect respect. The goal is to help. If you don't know the answer, tell them you'll find out. Then find out and let them know.

To help you establish programs and policies, I've included the complete set of instructions, as I feel that they are indicative of a solid foundation for implementing and sharing guidelines.

APPROACH

Tell them you're from Best Buy—part of the Twelpforce. Be engaged, know what's going on out there but don't intrude or invade. If someone is talking about how they're looking for a product that we may sell, don't swoop in and tell them they'd be better off buying it from us. If they're looking for help, or opinions, they'll ask.

Don't talk about private company stuff even in direct messages. Don't ask for personal customer information even in direct message. Offer an email by direct message instead.

Connect people to outside sources or other Best Buy people when appropriate. Don't directly refer them to other customers on Twitter or elsewhere. If your answer requires more than 140 characters, create a blog on your local store page and refer customers to it. Or look in the Best Buy Community Support Forums—there are tons of great questions and answers there.

Above all, if you don't know or if you're not sure, ask. Always respond quickly and follow up quickly. Apologize for delays or misunderstandings.

What Do You Have to Do?

You don't need any special skills—you just have to be curious, proactive, and helpful—much of the same stuff you do every day.

The best thing you can do to start is to listen to what people are saying and asking on Twitter. Go to http://search.twitter.com and search for things you're interested in. Search for your favorite brand, your favorite category, for Best Buy. Find out what questions and problems people have. And figure out a way to help them. It all starts with a simple post.

Customer:

yoshimac: need to buy a new tv for bedroom so i can watch what i want no desprate housewives blaaaaaaaaaaaaaaa

You:

@yoshimac If you need some help figuring what to get, let me know. I work at Best Buy in the Home Theater Dept and could give you some opinions. If not, thats cool too.

What if someone else already answered her question? Have a different opinion? Let them know what you think. The goal of Twelpforce is to share our knowledge and give people the information they need to make a decision. When I look for a new home in a new city, I don't just ask one person, I get opinions from as many trusted sources as I can and then after weighing the input, I make a decision. But remember—if you engage, show respect. Expect respect. The goal is to help. Not to be creepy.

Other Tools for Searching for Twitter Questions or Customer Problems

Search @twelpforce on http://search.twitter.com after July 19th. Customers will be directed through the media support to ask questions directed at @twelpforce.

1. Twitter Search: It's the most basic and most obvious, but this tool now allows for RSS feeds as well as filtering based on language.

2. http:spy.appspot.com: Spy can listen in on the social media conversations you're interested in. What do you want to listen for?

3. www.monitter.com: It's a twitter monitor, it lets you *monitter* the twitter world for a set of keywords and watch what people are saying.

4. http://tweetbeep.com: Free Twitter alerts by e-mail.

5. Twist: Free site for Twitter visualizations over time.

6. Twitter Browser: Free application to see who is connected to whom. Good for relational analysis and velocity of a users' network.

7. Tweetstats: If you want to research a specific user, you can see how often he posts, when he posts, and who he retweets (that is, who influences him) and plan accordingly.

Assumptions have no business in business—especially when influential voices can sway the crowd for you or against you.

Policies and guidelines must be clear and explicit in intentions and implementation and leave nothing to chance. Training is absolutely required.

To help those who are unfamiliar with style guides, document and convey the brand essence and how to accurately display it in various forms of media. Usage scenarios, approved artwork, type treatments, and approved language should all be included. Conversational workflow should also be defined.

These new media style guides serve as the sheet music to ensure that we as brand representatives are singing the same song, in key, in unison, and beautifully.

Style guides are not new to business. They are staples in the world of advertising and branding, as they outline in great detail how, when, and where the brand is to be portrayed. We need a style guide for social media. As such, every company should create and distribute a style guide or handbook of guidelines, not only for social media, but specifically for each social network in which the company currently engages or expects to engage, as well as policies and instructions for discrete programs and campaigns. Instructions such as "don't be stupid" are not enough.

When I wrote the guidelines for Facebook use for a Fortune 500 company, it was 25 pages long. It was considered far too long for practical use, so we trimmed it so that it was easier to consume. The problem was, it left too much open to interpretation. As you could imagine, this is where common sense becomes help or hindrance. The company learned the hard way, as many of the employees took liberties with all that was missing from the final document.

While you may offer a quick-start guide to help you and your team kick-start programs, true success is defined by understanding, reinforced by practice and continued education. Therefore we cannot overlook the need for a detailed instruction manual complete with best practices, scenarios, pitfalls, objectives, rewards, and corresponding consequences.

■ EXAMPLE GUIDELINES AND POLICIES

Here are some additional examples to glean inspiration and direction. Please keep in mind, however, that these examples are representative of what is and not always what should be. As you read these, remember the lessons, stories, and advice that I've shared with you thus far. Source these for inspiration only, and create a social style guide that is representative of *your* world and the questions, concerns, capabilities, and opportunities that are present in your business.[10]

INTEL SOCIAL MEDIA GUIDELINES[11]

These are the official guidelines for social media at Intel. If you're an Intel employee or contractor creating or contributing to blogs, wikis, social networks, virtual worlds, or any other kind of social media both on and off intel.com—these guidelines are for you. We expect all who participate in social media on behalf of Intel to be trained, to understand, and to follow these guidelines. Failure to do so could put your future participation at risk. These guidelines will continually evolve as new technologies and social networking tools emerge—so check back once in a while to make sure you're up to date.

When You Engage

Emerging platforms for online collaboration are fundamentally changing the way we work, offering new ways to engage with customers, colleagues, and the world at large. It's a new model for interaction and we believe social computing can help you to build stronger, more successful business relationships. And it's a way for you to take part in global conversations

(continued)

related to the work we are doing at Intel and the things we care about.

If you participate in social media, please follow these guiding principles:

➤ Stick to your area of expertise and provide unique, individual perspectives on what's going on at Intel and in the world.

➤ Post meaningful, respectful comments—in other words, no spam and no remarks that are off-topic or offensive.

➤ Always pause and think before posting. That said, reply to comments in a timely manner, when a response is appropriate.

➤ Respect proprietary information and content, and confidentiality.

➤ When disagreeing with others' opinions, keep it appropriate and polite.

➤ Know and follow the Intel Code of Conduct and the Intel Privacy Policy

Rules of Engagement

Be transparent. Your honesty—or dishonesty—will be quickly noticed in the social media environment. If you are blogging about your work at Intel, use your real name, identify that you work for Intel, and be clear about your role. If you have a vested interest in something you are discussing, be the first to point it out.

Be judicious. Make sure your efforts to be transparent don't violate Intel's privacy, confidentiality, and legal guidelines for external commercial speech. Ask permission to publish or report on conversations that are meant to be private or internal to Intel. All statements must be true and not misleading and all claims must be substantiated and approved. Product benchmarks must be approved for external posting by the appropriate product benchmarking team. Please never comment on anything related to legal matters, litigation, or any parties we are in litigation with without the appropriate approval. If you want to write about the competition, make sure you know what you are talking about and that you have the appropriate permission. Also be smart about protecting yourself, your privacy, and Intel confidential information. What you publish is widely accessible and will be around for a long time, so consider the content carefully.

Write what you know. Make sure you write and post about your areas of expertise, especially as related to Intel and our technology. If you are writing about a topic that Intel is involved with but you are not the Intel expert on the topic, you should make this clear to your readers. And write in the first person. If you publish to a website outside Intel, please use a disclaimer, something like this: "The postings on this site are my own and don't necessarily represent Intel's positions, strategies, or opinions." Also, please respect brand, trademark, copyright, fair use, trade secrets (including our processes and methodologies), confidentiality, and financial disclosure laws. If you have any questions about these, see your Intel legal representative. Remember, you may be personally responsible for your content.

Perception is reality. In online social networks, the lines between public and private, personal and professional are blurred. Just by identifying yourself as an Intel employee, you are creating perceptions about your expertise and about Intel by our shareholders, customers, and the general public—and perceptions about you by your colleagues and managers. Do us all proud. Be sure that all content associated with you is consistent with your work and with Intel's values and professional standards.

It's a conversation. Talk to your readers like you would talk to real people in professional situations. In other words, avoid overly pedantic or composed language. Don't be afraid to bring in your own personality and say what's on your mind. Consider content that's open-ended and invites response. Encourage comments. You can also broaden the conversation by citing others who are blogging about the same topic and allowing your content to be shared or syndicated.

Are you adding value? There are millions of words out there. The best way to get yours read is to write things that people will value. Social communication from Intel should help our customers, partners, and co-workers. It should be thought-provoking and build a sense of community. If it helps people improve knowledge or skills, build their businesses, do their jobs, solve problems, or understand Intel better—then it's adding value.

(continued)

Your responsibility. What you write is ultimately your responsibility. Participation in social computing on behalf of Intel is not a right but an opportunity, so please treat it seriously and with respect. If you want to participate on behalf of Intel, take the Digital IQ training and contact the Social Media Center of Excellence. Please know and follow the Intel Code of Conduct. Failure to abide by these guidelines and the Intel Code of Conduct could put your participation at risk. Contact social.media@intel.com for more information. Please also follow the terms and conditions for any third-party sites.

Create some excitement. As a business and as a corporate citizen, Intel is making important contributions to the world, to the future of technology, and to public dialogue on a broad range of issues. Our business activities are increasingly focused on high-value innovation. Let's share with the world the exciting things we're learning and doing—and open up the channels to learn from others.

Be a leader. There can be a fine line between healthy debate and incendiary reaction. Do not denigrate our competitors or Intel. Nor do you need to respond to every criticism or barb. Try to frame what you write to invite differing points of view without inflaming others. Some topics—like politics or religion—slide more easily into sensitive territory. So be careful and considerate. Once the words are out there, you can't really get them back. And once an inflammatory discussion gets going, it's hard to stop.

Did you screw up? If you make a mistake, admit it. Be upfront and be quick with your correction. If you're posting to a blog, you may choose to modify an earlier post—just make it clear that you have done so.

If it gives you pause, pause. If you're about to publish something that makes you even the slightest bit uncomfortable, don't shrug it off and hit "send." Take a minute to review these guidelines and try to figure out what's bothering you, then fix it. If you're still unsure, you might want to discuss it with your manager or legal representative. Ultimately, what you publish is yours—as is the responsibility. So be sure.

Moderation Guidelines

Moderation is the act of reviewing and approving content before it's published on the site. Intel does not endorse or take responsibility for content posted by third parties. It is preferred that all content be posted by registered users of a site in accordance with accepted terms and conditions and a code of conduct.

Intel Content: We do not moderate content we publish. This means we allow our blog authors to post directly without approval, as long as they have taken the required trainings.

Anonymous Content: Anonymous content is defined as content submitted as a comment, reply, or post to an Intel site on which the user has not registered and is not logged in to the site. For anonymous content, we require moderation on all submissions. Authors of the originating content and space moderators are required to review the content for approval or deletion before the content can be published.

Registered Content: Registered content is content submitted as a comment, reply, or post to an Intel site on which the user has registered and is logged in to the site. We do not require moderation of registered content before the content is published to the site. Registered content is directly published and content is moderated post-publishing. Intel strives for a balanced online dialogue. When we do moderate content, we moderate using three guiding principles.

The Good, the Bad, but Not the Ugly. If the content is positive or negative and in context to the conversation, then we approve the content, regardless of whether it's favorable or unfavorable to Intel. However if the content is ugly, offensive, denigrating, and completely out of context, then we reject the content.

IBM SOCIAL COMPUTING GUIDELINES[12]

Responsible Engagement in Innovation and Dialogue

Whether or not an IBMer chooses to create or participate in a blog, wiki, online social network, or any other form of online publishing or discussion is one's own decision. However, emerging online collaboration platforms are fundamentally changing the way IBMers work and engage with each other, clients, and partners.

(continued)

IBM is increasingly exploring how online discourse through social computing can empower IBMers as global professionals, innovators, and citizens. These individual interactions represent a new model: not mass communications, but masses of communicators.

Therefore, it is very much in IBM's interest—and, we believe, in each IBMer's own—to be aware of and participate in this sphere of information, interaction, and idea exchange.

To learn: As an innovation-based company, we believe in the importance of open exchange and learning—between IBM and its clients, and among the many constituents of our emerging business and societal ecosystem. The rapidly growing phenomenon of user-generated Web content—blogging, Social Web applications, and networking—are emerging important arenas for that kind of engagement and learning.

To contribute: IBM—as a business, as an innovator, and as a corporate citizen—makes important contributions to the world, to the future of business and technology, and to public dialogue on a broad range of societal issues. As our business activities increasingly focus on the provision of transformational insight and high-value innovation—whether to business clients or those in the public, educational, or health sectors—it becomes increasingly important for IBM and IBMers to share with the world the exciting things we're learning and doing, and to learn from others.

In 1997, IBM recommended that its employees get out onto the Internet—at a time when many companies were seeking to restrict their employees' Internet access. In 2005, the company made a strategic decision to embrace the blogosphere and to encourage IBMers to participate. We continue to advocate IBMers' responsible involvement today in this rapidly growing space of relationship, learning, and collaboration.

IBM Social Computing Guidelines: Executive Summary

1. Know and follow IBM's business conduct guidelines.[13]

2. IBMers are personally responsible for the content they publish on blogs, wikis, or any other form of user-generated media. Be mindful that what you publish will be public for a long time—protect your privacy.

3. Identify yourself—name and, when relevant, role at IBM—when you discuss IBM or IBM-related matters.

And write in the first person. You must make it clear that you are speaking for yourself and not on behalf of IBM.

4. If you publish content to any website outside of IBM and it has something to do with work you do or subjects associated with IBM, use a disclaimer such as this: "The postings on this site are my own and don't necessarily represent IBM's positions, strategies, or opinions."

5. Respect copyright, fair use, and financial disclosure laws.

6. Don't provide IBM's or another's confidential or other proprietary information. Ask permission to publish or report on conversations that are meant to be private or internal to IBM.

7. Don't cite or reference clients, partners, or suppliers without their approval. When you do make a reference, link back to the source, if possible.

8. Respect your audience. Don't use ethnic slurs, personal insults, obscenity, or engage in any conduct that would not be acceptable in IDM's workplace. You should also show proper consideration for others' privacy and for topics that may be considered objectionable or inflammatory—such as politics and religion.

9. Find out who else is blogging or publishing on the topic, and cite them.

10. Be aware of your association with IBM in online social networks. If you identify yourself as an IBMer, ensure your profile and related content is consistent with how you wish to present yourself with colleagues and clients.

11. Don't pick fights, be the first to correct your own mistakes, and don't alter previous posts without indicating that you have done so.

12. Try to add value. Provide worthwhile information and perspective. IBM's brand is best represented by its people and what you publish may reflect on IBM's brand.

I've shared with you some of the most comprehensive examples available, and as you can see, they share many common attributes:

➤ Ensure a consistent, personable, and brand-enhancing tone or voice.

➤ Add value to each engagement—contribute to a stature and legacy.

➤ Respect those with whom you're engaging and also respect the forum in which you participate.

➤ Ensure that you honor copyrights and practice and promote fair use of applicable content.

➤ Protect confidential and proprietary information.

➤ Be transparent and be human (well, be believable and helpful).

➤ Represent what you should represent.

➤ Know and operate within the defined boundaries.

➤ Know when to fold 'em and don't engage trolls or fall into conversational traps.

➤ Keep things conversational as it applies to portraying and reinforcing the personality and value of your brand and the brand you represent.

➤ Stay on message, on point, and on track with the goals of your role and its impact on the real-world business to which you contribute.

➤ Don't trash the competition—not directly, anyway.

➤ Apologize when necessary.

➤ Be accountable for your actions and offer no excuses.

➤ Know whom you're talking to and what they're seeking.

➤ Disclose relationships, representations, affiliations, and intentions.

➤ Practice self-restraint; some things are not worth sharing.

Stop reading this book and establish or champion the development of personal guidelines in reference to the business and brand right now.

■ THE LOUISIANA PURCHASE AND THE GREAT BRAND GRAB

Okay, so you put down the book or your electronic reader to set guidelines for employee usage, right? Great. Glad to have you back. Let's continue.

Much like the early days of the Web, which eventually contributed to the chaos and madness of the dotcom era and its eventual financial fall, the Social Web is opening up a veritable land grab for social real estate at a fraction of the price that it will be worth to you tomorrow.

As in anything new and exciting, there's usually a rush to action. But for some reason, in social media the rush to relevance seemed subdued—at least initially. It was understandable, however. After all, depending on the organization, skepticism, procrastination, or lethargy were at play.

Part of the rules of engagement require that we establish a consistent presence across the social networks where we need to maintain a presence as well as plan for those where we might one day need to engage or simply protect our brand assets.

These usernames, pages, and profiles are instrumental in how we portray our brand and brand story. They also serve as the fabric for the greater social construct that links visitors to intended experiences through the channels that deliver our intended experience and help them obtain desired results.

> ➤ In every network, the brand and product name should be identical.

> ➤ The profile pages must reflect the aesthetics, information, and personality as determined by the social style guide in the spirit of the network in which they appear.

> ➤ Define the click paths to help visitors navigate your information network.

It should go without saying, but as you may or may not know, the landscape for social networks is vast and may be beyond our initial reach. However, excuses, ignorance, and ambivalence aside, we are responsible for attaining and managing our personal and professional brands, as well as those we represent, even if it simply implies that we secure the domain or username—including its derivatives, both positive and negative. For example, companyx, productx, companyxsucks, or companyxmustdie.

Create a standard naming convention that is simple, uncomplicated, concise (friendly to microblogs and other forms of micromedia), and easy to both remember and also to input on mobile devices. In addition to these guidelines, create a naming formula that is friendly and identifiable by the outside world. Too many organizations that I have worked with over the years forget that people outside the organization may not understand the significance of a unique department or division. Others attempt to inject more information than is necessary, embellished by quotes, underlines, and other symbols. This only leads to brand dilution and confusion.

This is true online as well. In 2008, FairWinds Partners[14] released a study that documented the power of Internet gripe sites. The *Wall Street Journal* explored the topic with an in-depth article, "How to Handle 'IHateYourCompany.com',"[15] which reviewed what some companies are doing, or not doing, to protect their brands online.

In its study, FairWinds researched the Web to identify gripe sites specifically containing "sucks.com." The study uncovered more than 20,000 domains with only 2,000 ending in the phrase "stinks.com." Of the major companies surveyed, only 35 percent owned the domain name for their brand followed by the word "sucks."

But domain names are only one of the many opportunities for customers to share their discontent, and in the emerging era of the two-way Web, communications, customer service, and brand and reputation management teams must not only collaborate to actively survey the landscape to detect and diagnose negative experiences, but also proactively plan for it. And part of that process is securing and establishing a uniform brand name in addition to its positive or negative variations and adaptations.

Service providers such as Knowem.com can not only scour the entire Web for available and taken usernames in social networks for you, but also acquire them and cost-effectively create profiles based on a template you create. One of the greatest value propositions of this service and others like it is that they automatically create profiles in emerging networks to prevent opportunists and angry customers from squatting on desired usernames. And if the username is unavailable (read *squatted*), Knowem provides helpful steps to retrieve domain ownership.

For example, when I worked with Anheuser-Busch, we initially discovered that the names associated with the premier corporate and product brands were already taken in key social networks. We were forced to manually contact each network to transfer ownership back, even if we weren't planning on deploying a strategy within each network immediately or in the near future. Produce and company names are, after all, brand assets.

■ RULES OF ENGAGEMENT

As the Social Web continues to emerge, establishing not only policies and guidelines but also defining the rules of engagement will help shape proactive and reactive dialogues to benefit the business, brand, employees, and customers. This is not the same as implementing and managing rules of conduct. Assessing the common traits found in the guidelines referred to previously, here is a suggested list of rules of engagement with which to compose your "sheet music."

➤ Unveil the communities of influence and discover their choices, challenges, impressions, and wants.

➤ Participate where your presence is advantageous and mandatory; don't just participate anywhere and everywhere.

➤ Consistently create, contribute to, and reinforce service and value.

➤ Concentrate participation where it will offer the greatest rewards for both sides.

➤ Assess pain points, frustrations, and also expressions of contentment, to establish emotional connections.

➤ Determine the brand identity, character, and personality you wish to portray—and match it to the individual persona of who's in front of it when online.

➤ Adapt predefined personalities with the voice of the community in which you engage.

➤ Observe the behavioral cultures within each network and adjust your outreach accordingly.

➤ Become a true participant in each community you wish to galvanize.

➤ Don't speak at audiences through messages.

➤ Dig deeper to connect what transpires in the Social Web to your business objectives.

➤ Learn from each engagement.

➤ Ensure that any external activities are supported by a comprehensive infrastructure to address situations and adapt to market conditions and demands.

➤ Establish a point of contact who is ultimately responsible for identifying, trafficking, or responding to all things that can affect brand perception.

➤ Act, don't just listen and placate—do something.

➤ Earn connections through collaboration.

➤ Empower advocacy.

➤ Embody the attributes you wish to portray and instill.

➤ Don't get lost in conversation or translation; ensure your involvement strategically maps to objectives specifically created for the Social Web.

➤ Establish and nurture beneficial relationships online and in the real world as long as public perception and action is important to your business.

➤ *Un-* campaign programs and ensure they're part of a day-to-day cause.

➤ Unmarket by offering solutions and becoming a resource to your communities.

➤ Give back, reciprocate, acknowledge, add value, and contribute where it makes sense.

■ INTEL'S DIGITAL IQ PROGRAM

While guidelines are critical, they are only as effective as the training, education, and implementation of that insight into day-to-day practice.

I serve as an advisor to Intel as part of the company's Intel Insider program, along with Frank Gruber, Tom Foremski, J. D. Lasica, Cathy Brooks, and other incredible people. I have enjoyed the opportunity to help instill these messages with the already forward-thinking people defining Intel's marketing, communications, and service teams. Ken Kaplan is responsible for the implementation of this educational program. But its reach is companywide, and thus carries a global impact.

I have also had the benefit of working with Intel's Bryan Rhodes on educational and organizational transformation projects (this is discussed in more depth later) and I believe that Rhodes's work and the corresponding new media educational programs that Intel has implemented and fostered should serve as the standard for all organizations.

Rhodes serves as the curriculum architect and senior digital strategist for the Intel Social Media Center of Excellence and chairs the Digital IQ program for all employees who already have or who will participate in new media on behalf of the company—for internal and external communications.

The goals of the Digital IQ program complement the company's shift of marketing investments from traditional to new media by increasing employee capabilities. The topics shared as part of this program provide insight into sales and marketing techniques, online retailing and reselling, and media, as well as search, analytics, and metrics. In all, Rhodes and his team have compiled a curriculum of more than 55 courses, complete with videos, supplementary

DIGIQ216	**Twitter Like You Mean It: The Right Way to Tweet Your Brand**	Launch
DIGIQ217	**Online Marketing Without Breaking the Bank New!**	Launch
DIGIQ219	**Importance of Brand Identity in Social Media**	Launch
DIGIQ221	**Timeless Marketing Practices in Digital Times**	Launch
DIGIQ301.1	**The Power of Search - Advanced**	Launch
DIGIQ301.2	**The Power of Search - Intro**	Launch
DIGIQ304.1	**Influencing WOM for Your Company**	Launch
DIGIQ304.2	**WOM: The Anatomy of Buzz**	Launch
DIGIQ304.3	**DWOM: Digital Word of Mouth Marketing Basics**	Launch
DIGIQ305	**Digital PR**	Launch
DIGIQ306	**Social Media Measurement**	Launch
DIGIQ307	**Advanced Search Engine Optimization**	Launch
DIGIQ308	**Digital Natives: Marketing to Youth Around the World**	Launch
DIGIQ309.1	**Case Study: China Social Media**	Launch
DIGIQ309.2	**Case Study: APAC Social Media Landscape New!**	Launch
DIGIQ309.3	**Case Study: EMEA Social Media Landscape**	Launch
DIGIQ309.4	**Case Study: IJKK Social Media Landscape**	Launch
DIGIQ310	**Mobile Marketing: The Wide Reach of the Small Screen**	Launch
DIGIQ311	**Marketing on Small Screen Mobile Devices**	Launch
DIGIQ312	**Introduction to Omniture Site Catalyst**	Launch
DIGIQ313	**Viral Marketing**	Launch
DIGIQ314	**End to End Marketing Online: A Fundamental Shift**	Launch

Figure 17.2   Digital IQ Partial Course Listing

materials, and a test at the end of each course. (See Figure 17.2 for a list of some of the courses.)

The aim of Digital IQ is to:

➤ Create a vast Intel digital force.

➤ Unlock digital genius.

➤ Capture digital sales and marketing best-known methods.

➤ Apply this knowledge on the job.

As such, Intel has instituted four role-based training levels:

1. Level IV is created for the digital marketing specialist, for whom the results of the program are intended to enhance and guide the creation of improved, relevant, and compelling content and social objects.

2. Level III is programmed for integrated marketing, communications managers, and internal bloggers, providing them with the tools, guidelines, lessons, and directions for integrating and distributing insight and information.

3. Level II serves as the blueprint for helping field account managers sell effectively, using social tools, networks, and services to reach their customers and prospects.

4. Level I is designed for everyone else, to help employees understand the landscape and promise of new media and how it affects their job and career, today and tomorrow.

The Digital IQ program mirrors university models in that its employees register for required courses as well as electives to earn a diploma. This certification allows employees to represent Intel in new media at the corresponding level.

To complete each level, participants are required to attend and pass as many as five courses to earn the desired certification. Each year, employees must complete courses in the continuing education program for recertification.

Perhaps the most common response to Intel's groundbreaking program is one of appreciation, followed quickly by skepticism about the ability to fund, design, and institute such a program within a particular part of the organization.

If the potential perils aren't enough to convey the need to do so, and induce a sense of urgency, think about Intel's results.

By the middle of 2009, Intel's then-10-month-old program had served more than 18,500 courses and delivered a total of 16,000 training hours. More than 68 percent of participants found it immediately applicable to their job, with even more attesting to the potential of their careers as they evolve. Funding for the program was overwhelmingly approved because of the buzz, improved morale, and company-wide engagement.

There is no choice. Employees must learn the art and science of content creation and distribution, engagement, and community development before they can lead conversations and the tribes that form around your brand, culture, and ideologies.

■ WITH SOCIAL MEDIA COMES GREAT RESPONSIBILITY

Please remember these words. . . .

Perhaps the biggest mistakes committed in social media occur when businesses jump in to social networks blindly, without establishing guidelines or a plan of action. What's really missing is a sense of what people are seeking and how and why they communicate, an understanding of where people are congregating, a definition of what they represent and how they will personify the brand online, and the goals, objectives, and metrics associated with participation.

Everything starts with education and the institution of policies to protect individuals and brands.

In addition to setting the guidelines and regulations for how and when employees should and shouldn't engage online, we must now teach our spokespersons, ambassadors, and advocates how to leverage the immediacy, extent, and potential of these powerful social tools. Our communities will follow by example.

Holding informal and infrequent workshops or publishing internal guidelines for self-consumption and interpretation is not nearly enough to satisfy the substantial requirements for an in-depth comprehension of the scenarios, circumstances, objectives, hazards, and nuances associated with engagement, influence, and community building.

This is more than publishing and it's far more important than empowering employees with the ability to chat online.

It's our responsibility to contribute to the increase of a significant, tuned, and strategic signal.

We are vested in the brands we represent—especially if we're on the front lines of emerging media. Enthusiasm, energy, spirit, and fervor are contagious, inspirational, and addictive.

■ NOTES

1. Douglas MacMillan, "A Twitter Code of Conduct," *BusinessWeek* (May 8, 2009), www.businessweek.com/managing/content/may2009/ca2009058 _089205.htm?chan=careers_special+report+-+social+media+2009_spe cial+report+-+social+media+2009.

2. "Immediate Ban on Internet Social Networking Sites on Marine Corps Enterprise Network NIPRNET," U.S. Marine Corps (August 3, 2009), www.marines.mil/news/messages/Pages/MARADMIN0458-09.aspx.

3. Noah Shachtman, "Army Orders Bases to Stop Blocking Twitter, Facebook, Flickr," *Wired* (June 10, 2009), www.wired.com/dangerroom/ 2009/06/army-orders-bases-stop-blocking-twitter-facebook-flickr/.

4. Noah Shachtman, "Marines Ban Twitter, MySpace, Facebook," *Wired* (August 3, 2009), www.wired.com/dangerroom/2009/08/marines-ban -twitter-myspace-facebook/.

5. www.facebook.com/admiralmikemullen.

6. www.facebook.com/RayOdierno.

7. Julian E. Barnes, "What's on the Pentagon's mind? Facebook," *Los Angeles Times* (August 5, 2009), www.latimes.com/news/nationworld/nation/la-na-pentagon-facebook5–2009aug05,0,3998956.story.

8. www.drum.army.mil/sites/tenants/division/CMDGRP/CG/CG.htm.

9. Best Buy Connect, http://bbyconnect.appspot.com/tips_and_expectations/.

10. "Guidelines," Best Buy, www.bestbuyinc.com/aggregator/our-guidelines.

11. "Intel Social Media Guidelines," Intel, www.intel.com/sites/sitewide/en_US/social-media.htm.

12. "IBM Social Computing Guidelines," IBM, www.ibm.com/blogs/zz/en/guidelines.html.

13. "Business Conduct Guidelines," IBM, www.ibm.com/investor/corpgovernance/cgbcg.phtml.

14. www.fairwindspartners.com/.

15. Emily Steel, "How to Handle 'IHateYourCompany.com'," *Wall Street Journal* (September 5, 2008), http://webreprints.djreprints.com/2022491227441.html.

Chapter 18

The Conversation Prism

Active listening and the resulting, informed engagement plants the seeds that flourish into meaningful conversations and relationships. Implementing engagement guidelines and best practices is a prerequisite for every business—that's the bottom line. But how do we know where to engage once these guidelines and directives are in place?

After all, we reviewed so many examples and will discuss many more over time, but how do we know what's right for us? Could practicing social media really be as easy as following the conversational template that seems so pervasive today?

While the tools businesses use may appear to weave a common thread, their implementation and, in turn, their usage are anything but ordinary.

Every company is responsible for charting its own course in the interactive Web and as such, each brand creates its own social DNA. It's distinctive in personality and uniquely reflected in the conversations and people who define and populate our online and offline landscapes.

The process of charting engagement strategies and routing our bearing ensures that we stay on course now and in the time to come.

■ I'M YOUR CUSTOMER . . . REMEMBER ME?

Be careful. You just might reinvent the wheel.

The wheel, after all, is an almost perfect example for reducing friction. To reinvent it is to go over ground that has been already thoroughly explored. However, the phrase itself is flawed. Many aspects of business require reinvention. Evolution is only as strong as its potential for improvement. Let's take customer service as an example.

For many years, businesses sought to reduce costs at the expense of customers by outsourcing support services to either domestic agencies or offshore organizations. Businesses also introduced automated front-ends to call centers, to practically eliminate any level of human or official employee interaction. While companies saved money, they created chasms between brand and consumer, diminishing opportunities for advocacy and referrals. Increasing profitability is smart business, but at some point smart decisions did not take into consideration the value of customers and the power of word of mouth. Outsourcing a critical business function that has the potential to reduce negativity in company or product experiences and win over positive sentiment is both a function of service and also strategic marketing. Placing this function in the hands of teams who may or may not understand the dynamics of the business environment and the true pains and challenges of customers can engender animosity rather than instill happiness and satisfaction. It's nearly impossible to serve as a brand evangelist if you're not vested or rewarded to do so. Customers can sense whether a representative is speaking from experience or reading from a script.

In 2008, the *Wall Street Journal* published a research survey authored by Jonathan Whitaker, assistant professor of management at the University of Richmond's Robins School of Business; M. S. Krishnan, professor of business information technology at the University of Michigan's Ross School of Business; and Claes Fornell, a professor of marketing at the University of Michigan's Ross School of Business.[1] The study analyzed offshoring and outsourcing activities of 150 North American companies and business units from 1998 and 2006. The results were not a surprise. According to the findings, this practice caused a significantly negative impact on customer satisfaction. And, when customer satisfaction degrades, it carries with it a financial impact that can affect sales or share value or both, over time.

Whether intentional or not, poor customer service can also affect the psychological experience of customers, introducing feelings of insignificance and a sense of being unappreciated. We've heard it many times, yet we are now just starting to acknowledge its meaning and implications: "A happy customer tells several friends and an unhappy customer tells many more."

The democratization of content publishing has only made this aphorism more applicable.

Psychological research indicates that positive reinforcement is most effective when introduced immediately after a negative experience, to affect conditioning.[2]

Bruce L. Katcher, Ph.D.,[3] an industrial and organizational psychologist with more than 20 years of experience in conducting customized employee opinion and customer satisfaction surveys for organizations, observed that the average business never hears from 96 percent of unhappy customers. And, for every complaint received, there are

26 customers with problems, 6 of which are considered serious. An average customer with a problem tells 9 to 10 other people, and 13 percent tell 20 or more.[4]

If we don't know that we're missing these opportunities, then we set the stage for a dramatic showdown that will almost always play out on a public stage.

Time to reinvent the wheel? Reinvention is already under way and it is driven by consumers offering and seeking answers and direction online, right now.

It's time for companies to reassess current practices and processes to proactively find and address issues with a human and empathetic voice. The role of engagement belongs with those who can effectively and genuinely represent the brand, its intentions, and promise in a brave and fledgling new world.

■ THE VALUE CYCLE: YOU, ME, AND MUTUAL VALUE

Before we are marketers, communicators, service agents, product architects, and human relations advisors, we are consumers. We purchase products. We share our experiences. We recommend and also complain about brands practically every day. Yet when we approach consumers as a company representative, we tend to forget the dynamics of relationship building and consumer behavior. We stop thinking and talking like consumers and start acting like employees.

In the interactive Web, people aren't lured into relationships simply because you cast the bait to reel them into a conversation.

Sincerity extends beyond the mere act of creating a profile on Twitter or forming a brand page on Facebook or a group in LinkedIn. Transparency carries a dual definition, see-through and genuine, with each separated by intent and action. Relationships are measured by the values, actions, and sentiments that others take away from each conversation. To talk at or to respond automatically without merit, intelligence, or quality is to grossly underestimate the people you're hoping to befriend and influence. It's the difference between a community and a halfway house; one will flourish, while the other will shelter transients, never growing into a thriving citizenry.

Identifying connected communities and observing the themes and culture of each provides entrée into the personification necessary to foster a genuine and equal ecosystem for dialogue.

It's about bringing information and solutions to people where they congregate before attempting to host their attention on our terms.

The art of conversations is mastered through the practice of both hearing *and* listening.

I'm listening to you.

I hear you.

I understand.

Action.

Identify opportunities to engage, but more importantly, experience the nature, dynamic, ambience, and emotion of the dialogue, all the better to sincerely and empathize and converse as a peer. Customers have been neglected long enough, don't you think? After all, we as consumers have experienced all we're talking about here.

■ THE CONVERSATION PRISM

Navigation is only as effective as the map we use to plot our course. As social media represents an uncharted world, the industry required a social cartographer to safely navigate its passages and accurately map the countless online continents, countries, and islands, and the rivers and oceans in between.

The map, as we would soon learn, exposed a vibrant and expansive new world that would only continue to materialize with every new discovery.

In 2007, I initially sketched a map for the social landscape that would later see a formal introduction, three iterative releases, and millions of views and downloads.

Working with Jesse Thomas of JESS3, we titled this social map, "The Conversation Prism"—see www.theconversationprism.com. Version 1 of the social map officially debuted in August 2008 and provided the first comprehensive and structured view of the Social Web and the networks and communities that defined it at the time. In October 2010, we introduced version 3.0, which evolved to document and organize the shifting landscape (see Figure 18.1).

What it also offered initially, besides an organized view of the new Web, was to demonstrate the sheer magnitude of the Social Web's potential, activity, and overall reach.

In the processing of mapping and arranging the conversation, I recognized that the act of categorizing social networks within a visually rich graphic would be temporary at best, demanding endless iterations for me to accurately document evolving and shifting online conversations as well as the communities that promote them.

Figure 18.1   The Conversation Prism
Source: Brian Solis and JESS3.

In the three years since its official introduction, the speed by which the landscape evolved only hastened and therefore required active cartography to better maintain relevance and structural integrity.

The goal was to observe, analyze, dissect, and present the dynamics of conversations, and how and where they transpired. It was driven by necessity, based on my work with many emerging and established brands looking to engage in the Social Web. The companies I would counsel required tangible evidence to support the notions that on-line conversations were thriving in less popular, but still relevant networks other than Facebook and Twitter. And, in many cases, after initial research, we would prove that the activity in these networks would validate the need for engagement.

The social map presented an organized view of social networks and communities categorized by usage, intent, and capabilities. Like the social networks that were forcing revisions of the conversation prism, top-level classifications for organizing them also continually transformed themselves. The prevailing framework for cataloging social properties was most effective when condensed and simplified.

➤ *Social bookmarks:* Sites and communities dedicated to allowing users to share, organize, and search relevant content from around the Web in one place.

➤ *Comment and reputation:* Networks and platforms that centralize the ability to assemble a view of an individual based on the conversational interaction in the Social Web (comments, ratings, and so forth).

➤ *Wisdom of the crowds:* Participatory sites that benefit from the crowdsourcing of content and intellect and in turn offer an aggregated, community-edited, and systematic index of relevant content.

➤ *Questions and answers:* Also fusing Web 1.0 and Web 2.0 sites, Q&A networks provide forums for asking and answering questions related to popular topics and companies, as well as highly specific subject matter.

➤ *Collaboration:* Networks and application platforms where invited or general visitors can collaborate on any given document or project.

➤ *Social Commerce:* Networks and communities where individuals connect with one another to find, research, and share purchased or desired products. Also where consumers can pool together to trigger deals.

➤ *Blog platforms:* Platforms that host the blogs or provide blog software for the creation and hosting of fully customized blogs elsewhere.

➤ *Blogs and conversations:* Search engines and networks that reveal activities occurring within the blogosphere.

➤ *Social curation:* Networks dedicated to curating relevant information or enabling the broadcasting of curated content across multiple networks

➤ *Crowdsourced news and content:* Networks that feature content and stories submitted by users, which are then open to voting and commenting.

➤ *Streams:* Networks that channel social objects and updates into one personalized stream.

➤ *Nicheworking:* Social networks dedicated to specific topics, activities, targets, and intentions.

➤ *Do-it-yourself and customer social networks:* White-label social network platforms that allow users to build their own custom, dedicated social network for hosting within a fixed community or on any website of their choosing.

➤ *Blog communities:* Communities dedicated to featuring blog content, conversations around blogs, and organizing blogs within an organized network or channel.

➤ *Micromedia:* Online communities that focus on brevity and short updates, including text, video, and audio.

➤ *Discussion boards and forums:* Message boards, groups, and discussion forums dedicated to topics, themes, projects, and purposes—this category represents sites and networks that are among the earliest examples of social media that are still pervasive today.

➤ *Social networks:* Networks that house our social graph and facilitate the ability to interact, share, respond, publish objects, and post updates in and around the activity of our contacts.

➤ *Listening and targeting:* Services that offer the ability to listen and organize conversations based on keywords and interest for insight, learning, and action.

➤ *Mobile devices:* Services, social networks, and communities that connect people, things, and content through mobile devices.

➤ *Attention dashboards:* Desktop and mobile clients used to stay connected to those who define your social graph.

➤ *Business networking:* Social networks where interaction is based on professions, professional networking, and business affiliations.

➤ *Reviews and ratings:* Sites that feature user-generated feedback, analysis, and experiences with products, brands, and services.

➤ *Location:* Social networks and communities that combine updates and posts while revolving around the physical location of the user and their contacts.

➤ *Video:* Sites that feature user-generated videos and host corresponding activity such as comments, ratings, and also the external embedding of videos in outside networks.

➤ *sCRM:* Communities that host user-generated or brand-hosted interactions that detail the experiences, challenges, problems, and recommendations for the improvement of products and services.

➤ *Documents and content:* Social networks that host interaction, embedding, as well as the connections between people and relevant content, such as docs, spreadsheets, and presentations that span a wide variety of subject matter.

➤ *Events:* Sites that feature events as the central point of conversations and activity.

➤ *Music:* Communities tethered by music and music-related dialogue and networking.

➤ *Wiki:* Hosted and white label wiki platforms for joining existing dialogue or creating new frameworks for collaborating on specific projects.

➤ *Virtual worlds:* Online communities in which users create avatars (virtual representations of themselves or favorite characters) and interact with one another within the constructs and missions of dedicated worlds.

➤ *Livecasting:* Online networks that offer the ability to stream audio or video in real time and host corresponding conversations and interaction during the broadcast.

➤ *Pictures:* Social networks where activity revolves around pictures as the social object.

■ THE ART AND SCIENCE OF LISTENING AND MONITORING

Using the Conversation Prism as our starting point for either venturing into the Social Web for the first time or changing our current course, we can effectively identify the coordinates necessary to create an accurate social map that's specific to our journey and destination.

The Conversation Prism is not the only means to discover critical conversations and the social networks where they dwell. But it is the cornerstone of the bigger discussion as to where, why, and how to engage. The purpose of the prism is to inspire research that leads to insight, which ultimately surfaces how brands can earn relevance.

The impetus behind the prism was derived from a consistent observation of top-down methodologies and practices of brands employed to create visibility in the Social Web. Simply stated, brands focused on building presences in the most popular communities without regard to relevance nor to how they would attract and captivate attention. Ultimately, it is the interactions with people within each network that will determine the success of the ensuing dialogues and outcomes.

The Conversation Prism also introduced lessons much more profound than simply listening to conversations in social networks to document activity.

It suggested a reversal in the traditional top-down approach to publishing and distributing messages through mass media, instead inspiring a bottom-up strategy that promoted intelligence through social research, mapping, and ethnography (the study and systematic recording of human cultures).[5]

For those so inclined, aware, and prepared, the process of listening encouraged in these pages also offers a window into the cultures and relative behaviors of the communities you're observing.

This sociological fieldwork is not only obligatory, it changes everything. At a minimum, it provides the insight necessary to develop an enlightened and culturally aware social media program that sets the stage to humanize the brand, foster relationships, engender emissaries to carry goodwill, and inspire action.

■ LISTENERS MAKE THE BEST CONVERSATIONALISTS

The Conversation Prism is a reference tool to start listening to the voices that define and steer your markets.

Tools and networks will come and go. Popularity will shift across existing networks, up-and-coming social sites, and not-yet-introduced websites. If you're not paying attention to when, where, and why conversations about your brand are taking place, then you're addressing only a small portion of a highly vocal contingent. And there are important conversations taking place without you right now.

The risk is that your customers and influential trendsetters could be misinterpreting your value proposition without dispute. Concurrently, they're also subject to the influences of your direct and indirect competitors.

Listening, learning, and participating in a measurable way any effective social program requires you to look beyond the usual suspects.

This is one of the reasons why being proactive and not necessarily driven by the corporate case study du jour can help you innovate and excel. Not doing so handicaps the overall reach and effectiveness of your marketing, communications, and service strategies.

In the current stage of social media, online conversations, along with real-world activity, cannot be ignored. Identifying these discussions is only the first step, however. It takes much more than simply running searches for listening systems. Casting a wide net to help you identify where your communities are thriving is the only way to truly identify which networks are important to your brand and business. It requires both a manual and automated approach. Once you understand where these conversations are transpiring, you can observe the cultures, climate, and basis for the dialogue and activity to create an intelligent engagement strategy while also justifying the participation of affected divisions throughout the organization.

■ CHARTING A SOCIAL MAP

Champions are defined not only by their enthusiasm, they are memorialized by their ability to always go above and beyond the call of duty. But as in anything we attempt in life and work, everything begins at the beginning.

Use the Conversation Prism as a perennial resource. It answers the very questions we wish to ask of others. With this as a guide, we're empowered with the tools, methodologies, and strategies that allow us to become the experts we sought to consult.

If you don't already have it, now's the time to create or access the list of keywords that are pivotal to your organization. This list should include brand, products, industry lingo and buzzwords, names of competitors and competitive products, and any subtle nuances specific to your world that we may miss here. But also, just for laughs (and for creating a sense of urgency), maintain a separate list of results for keywords associated with *name+sucks,* or variations with the word *hate* in it. To expedite the process, try using Boolean search techniques that include:

> ➤ NOT: Brand X NOT Brand Y
> ➤ AND: Keyword X AND Keyword Y
> ➤ OR: Keyword X OR Keyword Y

Many database searches are based on the principles of Boolean logic, named in honor of the British-born mathematician George Boole. It refers to the logical relationship among search terms.[6]

I review the results and how to package them specifically for usage by you and your team in just a few pages, but allow me to pave the way a bit here.

To best make the case for direction, focus, and applied resources, we are required to document important and relevant discussions by each network to form the foundation for what will ultimately serve as our brand-specific social map. A social map condenses the vastness of social networks presented in the Conversation Prism to visually communicate definitive communities in which important dialogue is materializing as chronicled by your research and observation. Suddenly, the social world becomes a much smaller place and a case can be made for how and where to focus.

■ CONVERSATION WORKFLOW

Conversations are increasingly distributed. This social distribution fragments our ability to connect with masses, but promotes a one-to-one approach that yields a one-to-many upside through the influence of social beacons.

Many companies that are actively engaging now are not actually reaching those social beacons through calculation and premeditation. They're either broadcasting to anyone or they're interacting with everyone. Reaching influential voices in social networks carries the ability to scale and extend your story across a multitude of social graphs.

The Conversation Prism offers instruction that details the initial steps to survey the entire social landscape and pinpoint relevant dialogue, prioritize participation strategies and direction, garner sentiment and feedback, and document volume, pitfalls, and also opportunities. The results populate a social map, yes, but also unearth a tremendous amount of answers to the questions you already had and didn't even know how to ask. Fundamentally, you're also able to design a detailed and precise conversational program as dictated by the words and actions of the people with whom we're trying to reach and connect. And, once we understand the implications and extent of activity and hotspots, we also can design an engagement hierarchy and organization chart that matches resources with activity. This process offers initial insight to the manpower, representation and corresponding budget required to participate at varying levels.

■ TAKING CENTER STAGE

At the center of the Conversation Prism is the brand. We visually document the conversational workflow in a hub-and-spoke model to garner insight for the umbrella brand as well as the individual business units as it turns.

The rotation of the concentric circles within the Conversation Prism assist in the conceptualization of the systematic processes and prompt the value-added engagement that rhythmically beats a drum for listening, publishing, and engagement.

To understand how to listen by using the Conversation Prism and to identify where and how to add value, let's dissect the meaning of each ring.

■ LEVEL ONE: THE EPICENTER

As a brand manager, you'll find yourself at the center of the prism—whether you're observing, listening, or engaging.

➤ Halo 1: The System

The next layer of circles is supported by the activities of learning and organizing engagement strategies.

1. *Observation:* Discovering the communities that are actively discussing your brand by using the search box within suspect and targeted social networks and communities.

2. *Listening:* Hearing the people, assessing volume, and documenting the underlying sentiment so as to more accurately craft response and participation programs, by assigned company representatives.

3. *Identification:* Recognizing and acknowledging the social beacons to potentially enlist as brand ambassadors, as well as the consumers who simply need a response or your attention.

4. *Internalization:* Not every bit of feedback will be beneficial to your organization, but you will recognize patterns or spots of brilliance that provide necessary insight to improve existing products and services over time. Remember that actions speak louder than words or intentions.

5. *Prioritization:* Assess and structure where and how your team should focus, who should respond, and how, based on the nature of the dialogue. Ensure that a conversation management system is in place, because it's easy to lose track of who responded to which person if documentation that shares status, required follow-up, or results is decentralized or nonexistent.

6. *Routing:* Serving as an extension to item 5, a system must be in place whereby delegates are assigned by topic and expertise. As such, we must introduce accountability and process for engaging, reporting, and communicating the outcome, conclusions, and any valuable wisdom or recommendations to consider. We review the lessons shared here and also in number 5 in the Chapter 23 discussion on social customer relations management, or sCRM.

➤ Halo 2: The Workforce

Social media represents the intersection of all departments that interface with the public and requires that each define a supporting infrastructure. Each division should operate under one master set of guidelines, but localized by department to guide assigned players and specific response and management strategies. Inward focus now must include outward contribution. Ideally, each organization will appoint a community or listening manager to monitor and also assign and manage the responses of each department. Over time, this process will be seamlessly integrated within the company's CRM infrastructure and, where applicable, will help establish an SRM (social relationship management) system for those departments not yet acclimated to social media and the technologies that support its scale and efficiency.

It's easy to see how this could quickly become overwhelming and unmanageable. One of the most fascinating aspects of listening, however, is that conversations always map to specific disciplines within the organization and authorities should therefore be appointed within each organization to provide a helpful response to steer conversations as necessary. These divisions usually include:

1. Customer or product support
2. Product and sales
3. Marketing and public relations
4. Community
5. Corporate communications
6. Crisis
7. Support

➤ Halo 3: Actualization

The outer ring completes the imagery of conversational workflow, but not the cycle itself. It is the representation of lessons we're learning through listening and participation that shape our future through introspection and adaptation. The process is powered by the continual rotation of listening, responding, and edification online and inside the company.

1. *Ongoing feedback and insight:* This is a necessary ingredient in portraying a socially aware and trusted brand. We must learn and demonstrate growth based on the feedback we receive. We must also continually share knowledge, provide resources, and communicate vision to earn trust, authority, and respect.

2. *Participation:* It's been said that participation is the new marketing. Perhaps it's better said that participation is a great well of knowledge that leads to more effective marketing *and* communications. The things we learn online practically serve as a free focus group. It takes humility within the culture of the company however, to genuinely inspire us to humanize our story. It's how we learn and improve.

3. *Online:* Effectively building online relations and relationships increases brand visibility and strengthens brand value. Embracing and empowering the community carries our brand personality across social graphs and interest graphs. Our engagement defines our status, stature, and capital within each network.

4. *Real world (or IRL, in real life):* The true metric for relationships is how well they carry from the Web to the real world. It's not about reaching customers using the latest shiny new object or jumping into the hottest new networks. It's about reaching stakeholders and influencers where they go to discover and share information. Engagement builds meaningful relationships that carry significant value, both online and offline.

■ CHARTING THE COURSE

This social map demonstrates the scope of missed opportunities to the team and decision makers and also unveils new possibilities.

While we can't control how our messages are internalized, we can surely shape perception at the point of discourse.

Remember, it's not what you say about your brand that reverberates as much as it is what your audience hears, how they share the story, and how you weave that insight into future conversations.

The Conversation Prism is a representation of social media and will evolve as services and conversation channels emerge, fuse, and dissipate.

In the social economy, engagement is a currency and relationships contribute to social capital. In social media, you will earn the relationships you deserve.

Transform the Conversation Prism into a brand prism specific to you.

■ ESTABLISHING A CONVERSATION INDEX

It's our job to identify the communities where our customers, peers, and influencers communicate with each other in a way that's transparent and frictionless. It's how we build relationships and how we establish our social capital while simultaneously increasing intellectual equity.

Social networks are magnets for marketers. But the people who define each online community are increasingly leery of hollow attempts at connecting.

True social marketing is not marketing at all. The new era of communications necessitates personalization through a genuine and humanized approach. It fuses marketing, service, sociology, psychology, creativity, influence, and a dedicated practice of relationship management. Human nature and the desire to connect, interact, and elevate is perpetual. It's our job to determine our role within the ecosystem.

■ THE COMMUNITY STARTS WITHIN

Before a company can collaborate with its extended community, businesses must first learn to collaborate internally. The greatest social network is the one that exemplifies the values, expertise, and capabilities of the organization.

We must operate as one or risk the appearance of operating alone. It takes a champion to bring everyone together. The champion's greatest weapons are data, analysis, and insight. This is how business leaders assess opportunities and make decisions.

➤ Step 1. Listening

The first step is to listen, by searching keywords and performing an initial audit within a given time frame. By assessing the volume, frequency, and tone of conversations throughout each network, we can establish the Conversation Index (CI), a benchmark to assess the state of our brand in the Social Web and also serve as a metric by which to compare our future activity.

Establish a Timeline

We cannot measure what we do not know and do not value. We need a baseline. This process begins with a social audit that reveals activity and the state of our brand and competition within each network. I recommend researching keywords, at least initially, for a fixed period of time, usually spanning 30 to 90 days. For example, begin and end the audit using a month or quarter that was uneventful as the research window. In months when a noteworthy or significant milestone occurred—for example, a product release, earnings report, or a shift in executive management—the results may offer a false impression of a sustained amount of activity.

Determine the Keywords

Before listening, formalize the initial keyword list. While it's important to create a comprehensive list, it's critical that we limit the short list to only a handful of terms so we can develop a top-level, organized review and analysis.

The Conversation Index is measured first for a baseline and then at regular intervals to draw comparisons and insight. The CI is also helpful to capture sentiment, reactions, visibility, action, and feedback surrounding specific events, leading up to, during, and following the landmark.

► Step 2. Documentation

Documenting the activity that you uncover is critical to establishing the Conversation Index. It is how you capture it for analysis and presentation that later determines how well management responds. The reaction you need is support. Beyond support, you must also surface insights that help you in the creative process. For example, how will your campaigns earn relevance, in which direction should they focus, and what's the strategy to earn attention and drive outcomes.

Many listening tools, such as ReSearch.ly, Spiral16, Sysomos, Radian6, and ScoutLabs, and so forth, offer a report template that captures activity and packages it in an easy-to-read format for analysis and presentation. I recommend that when you're initially listening to the Social Web, especially if you're following the principles and methodologies that define the Conversation Prism, that you also do so manually.

It's time consuming.

It's potentially tedious.

These points may be valid. However, the time and energy you save is directly linked to a loss of perspective ... and empathy. The process of establishing the Conversation Index serves two purposes:

documentation of activity and also the ability to feel what's really going on out there. No tool has proved that it can capture everything, and oftentimes, captured sentiment is off base. In fact, in many cases, tools can miss a significant portion of result-altering data. And as you manually digest the updates you're recording, you can't help but sense the underlying meanings in what you're reading. When we discuss the need to humanize our brand, we do so through an earned sense of compassion, concern, and caring.

As listening produces results that are unique to each brand, this template provides a framework for you to further customize.

Use a spreadsheet that includes our criteria to help you effectively capture and export our findings into reports, charts, and presentations. Assuming that we run a search over a 30 or 90-day period, the elements necessary to establish the Conversation Index includes, at a minimum, the following columns:

Network: The social network within which the conversation occurred.

Instance: The specific mention of the keyword and the supporting context.

Date: The specific date of the mention.

Sentiment: Assess whether the instance was negative, positive, or neutral.

Response candidacy: The assessment of whether the captured update required a response from a company representative and, if so, add an additional column that suggests the division most appropriate for engagement. In my research, I've noted that conversations can usually be handed over to finance, public relations, service, product development, marketing, and human resources.

Reach: Depending on the network, this input varies. Reach refers to the potential degree an update can range. For example, if the incident was on Twitter, document the number of followers that particular individual is connected with. If the mention is in a blog post or blog comment, note how many visitors the particular destination receives on any given day (determined by Alexa or Compete.com). While it's not intended to provide a total representation of influence, authority, or actual impressions, this information does give us a sense of scope, scale, and potential impact.

Competitive mentions: While it's time consuming to research this activity on behalf of your brand, it may be unrealistic to do so when measuring the volume of your competitors. Simply running through each network and documenting total numbers of mentions may suffice so as to establish a sense of the general share of voice and share of conversation. Share of voice is the percentage your brand is mentioned against competition. Share of conversation is the percentage of your brand mentions in the greater market discussion.

➤ Step 3. Presentation

When documenting the results during the listening exercise, it's absolutely critical to capture persuasive criteria in a way that's incontestable to decision makers. Exporting the numbers that dictate key findings as visual charts will establish a compelling case and benchmark for further endeavors as well as the ability to reference past status.

Packaging counts for everything because it visually demonstrates all that we've speculated. We either make or break our case with the information we've collected and the method for communicating our findings. Fundamentally, we must create a document or presentation that visualizes what we know and what decision makers and affected individuals need to know. I usually capture anything that creates a sense of urgency and present that separately. Ten categories to consider are:

1. Time frame.
2. Volume: Total number of "conversations" captured.
3. Active Networks: Organize the most active networks of relevance based on quantity of collective activity, justified by numbers, sorted by activity (for example, Facebook, 10 percent; Twitter 30, percent; blogs or blog comments, 30 percent; forums and groups, 10 percent; YouTube, 5 percent; Flickr, 5 percent; Digg, 5 percent; Delicious, 5 percent).
4. Sentiments: For example: 25 percent positive, 25 percent negative, 50 percent neutral. Provide examples of sentiment in cases of positive and negative.
5. Perception: Provide a general summary of how a brand is perceived through text or graph and share a few examples of each to hammer the point home.
6. Reach: Total potential impressions (however, this is not representative of a true audience).
7. Network reach: Potential reach by network (for example, Facebook reach = 125,000; Twitter = 175,000; Blogs = 250,000; YouTube views = 75,000; Flickr views = 5,000).

8. Responses required: Quantity of missed opportunities for responses.

9. Affected divisions: Divisions tagged to respond based on missed opportunities (for example, customer service, 35 percent; PR, 20 percent; marketing, 15 percent; product, 15 percent; HR, 5 percent; sales, 10 percent).

10. Share of voice or conversation: The share of conversations between your brand compared to that of your competition as established by the total quantity of mentions as well as the number of mentions by individual social network. Share of conversation usually demonstrates a sense of urgency, because it's much lower than SoV.

For extra credit, as you're reading through the instances that you're collecting, record trends that emerge and reappear related to potential topics, themes, areas for improvement, common questions, recommendations, and so forth. Provide these themes in an aggregate format that can be presented as a list or pie chart. For example, in the past 30 days, we observed the following themes: new product, 20 percent; earnings, 25 percent; comparison to competitive product, 15 percent; questions about the future, 10 percent; missed opportunities, 10 percent; requests for response in social networks, 20 percent. We can also analyze data to anticipate trends and possible scenarios over the next 30, 60, or 90 days.

Among the potential trends we're observing, we're also privy to honest feedback and product or brand experiences that will reveal a sampling of consumer satisfaction and recommendations. The data that you will possess serves as an indicator for market position and will also divulge potential ideas and supporting rationale for improving or developing new products and services.

Monitoring reveals the Conversation Index, the state of conversations and the networks and people behind the activity. This process also reveals potential calls to action that can be presented to demonstrate tangible next steps. Essentially all of the answers you need are contained within this research:

➤ Conversation state
➤ Active networks
➤ Brand awareness and resonance
➤ Business divisions and required resources
➤ Potential reach
➤ Framework for social media plan
➤ Rough estimates of required resources and costs

➤ Innovation

➤ Human touchpoints

It is imperative that we fold in a response mechanism to our social network programs while moving forward. Listening offers data. Hearing offers empathy and intelligence. Activity, action, and engagement steer perspective and encourage a sense of community and advocacy.

➤ **Step 4. Observation**

Communities support one another. Citizens actively help others make decisions, offer suggestions and referrals, proactively share negative experiences, and repeatedly ask questions—with or without our participation.

We are missing opportunities right now.

Once our target networks are identified and our Conversation Index is established, we must observe the conversational ecosystem to understand the corresponding culture and behavioral dynamics. We may have the answers now, but the disconnect between execution and collaboration is represented by the cultures, behavior, and personalities that define each community.

We need to ask and answer several new questions. For example, How are people communicating within network A versus network B? How are subgroups interacting within each network? What does the back channel look like? Who are the power users within our segment and are they connected to one another, and if so, how? Are people publishing, responding, asking, and answering questions? Who's answering them? How are other brands interacting with their stakeholders and prospects, and how is the community responding?

This information can be captured by employing ethnography, a branch of anthropology that studies and describes modern human cultures (rather than human behavior or physical attributes).[7] The goal of ethnography is to provide cultural interpretation to define "webs of meaning," the cultural constructions of our communities of interest.[8] Through case reports or field studies, our role as pseudo ethnographers is to capture and communicate the interworking of cultures through an emic[9] perspective. This gives us an insider's point of view. And, it is this perspective that is usually missing from our listening and monitoring analysis and will serve us invaluably as we forge our engagement strategies and tactics.

As ethnography captures data that defines cultures within our relevant nets, we must also document behavior to effectively interact within each. For example, many case studies in the Social Web are based on simple interactions on Twitter and the walls of Facebook brand pages. In many others, we see creative contests used as ways to trigger likes and new fans and followers. So what? We can do that in any medium. It is through observation, however, that we can also personify the communities that are active within our target markets and engage in ways that drive meaningful action.

Media unites people around topics and partisanship and therefore encourages an approach through which we also organize our potential stakeholders and advocates by behavior, interests, and preference. Each require different engagement strategies. Typically, brands have approached marketing and communications through the use of demographics to distinguish its audiences. Now we also embrace psychographics and behaviorgraphics to connect through personality and interests.

Demographics *are defined as the statistical characteristics of human populations used to identify markets.*[10]

Psychographics *are statistics that classify population groups according to psychological variables or trends.*[11]

Behaviorgraphics *is a classification of people organized by how they interact in the Social Web.*

The insight that we learn from observation reveals dedicated conversation ecosystems that spotlight real-world brand perception. It resets intentions, crystallizes engagement strategies, influences how we adapt our story to each community, humbles us, and introduces benevolence into the process.

We learn, earn credibility, and procure strategic intelligence through immersion—before we have an official agenda.

To excel in social media, we have to embrace modesty and refrain from egoism. We must not only build roads that pave the way for outward engagement, but also build paths back to our organizations so we can hear, respond, and learn from our interactions. Negativity is onerous. Unwelcome feedback is often painful to swallow. Whether or not it's right or wrong, it's nevertheless real-world perception, and it affects our bottom line.

We have to be open.

Let it touch us.

Change is part of instilling trust and earning confidence. Allowing outside stimulus, instead of deflecting or disregarding it demonstrates authenticity.

Adaptation will help you evolve and increase in relevance, both online and offline.

In the end, we are measured by our actions and our words.

■ NOTES

1. Jonathan Whitaker, M. S. Krishnan, and Claes Fornell, "How Offshore Outsourcing Affects Customer Satisfaction," *Wall Street Journal* (September 13, 2008), http://online.wsj.com/article/SB121441852405104029.html.

2. "Reinforcement," Wikipedia, http://en.wikipedia.org/wiki/Reinforcement.

3. www.dimihr.com/main-about-katcher.html.

4. Jodi R. R. Smith, "Customer Service Made Simple," *Huffington Post* (February 25, 2009), www.huffingtonpost.com/jodi-r-r-smith/customer-service-made-sim_b_169827.html.

5. "Ethnography," Merriam-Webster, www.merriam-webster.com/dictionary/ethnography.

6. "Boolean Searching on the Internet," Internet Tutorials, www.internettutorials.net/boolean.asp.

7. As defined by the Archaeological Institute of America, www.archaeological.org/webinfo.php?page=10299.

8. Brian A. Hoey, "What Is Ethnography?" www.brianhoey.com/General%20Site/general_defn-ethnography.htm.

9. "Emic," Merriam-Webster, www.merriam-webster.com/dictionary/emic.

10. "Demographics," Merriam-Webster, www.merriam-webster.com/dictionary/demographics.

11. "Psychographics," Merriam-Webster, www.merriam-webster.com/dictionary/psychographics.

Chapter

Unveiling the New Influencers

■ WE ARE MEDIA

Influence is not popularity and popularity is not influence. Influence is the ability to effect action. In social media, influence is our quest, as it can steer desirable outcomes.

We, the people, demanded recognition. We gained access to the tools and platforms that are putting the customer back into the spotlight. Our feedback now incites a more value-added circle of overall communications and product evolution. We have emerged influential and consequential to the bottom lines of businesses all over the world.

As consumers and publishers, we stormed these new platforms and staged a social revolution that forced the attention of those who so readily dismissed us—silence was no longer golden.

Social networks and platforms have expanded the roles of customers and peers from consumer to authorities, advocates, and critics. Those who master their domains are developing consequential communities around their areas of expertise, interests, and passions and now possess the authority to direct, instruct, and steer decision makers and actions.

We must now become much more than communicators, marketers, publishers, or service professionals. We too are consumers and this perspective must permeate our company culture. But when it's time to reach our peers and colleagues, we seem to regress. In short, we lose sight of how what we represent truly affects those whom we're trying to reach.

While we possess the ability to become the very people we wish to reach, we lose perspective in our methods and processes.

179

In the end, we earn the influence that our activities and shared experiences warrant. Our presence and participation affect the decisions and impressions of those around us.

Successful engagement is predicated on genuinely engaging and collaborating with people.

■ BUILDING A BRIDGE BETWEEN BRANDS AND MARKETS

Now, we're paying attention to social authorities and tastemakers, from technologists to mommy bloggers to lifestyle aficionados to political pundits and everything in between. Many times, the practice of reaching out to these individuals falls under the scope of public relations. But it's bigger than that. These information socialites represent the various roles of the social consumer—from customer to advocate to adversary. Thus, outreach depends on the intention and nature of the connection and could be run from any group where engagement is warranted.

These individuals are the new celebrities and their endorsements carry great weight. But are we blindly jumping in to social networks and engaging with the avatars instead of the people behind them? We identify them using keywords in tools such as Radian6, ReSearch.ly, mBlast, and even Klout. Ideally, we need to identify, engage, and recruit those who can help us create valuable, thriving communities that support the exchange of pertinent information and direction. This is not about avatar relations, or keyword association and this is most certainly greater than ordinary blogger relations. This is the era of consumer recognition and empowerment.

Tastemakers and trendsetters are recognized as the new influencers, but their roles in affecting consumer behavior are not derivative of the Social Web. Simply said, these individuals have always existed, just as conversations have always prevailed. Neither originated because of social media. Instead, these market makers individually contribute to a more influential public and are now readily discoverable. Social networks, blogs, microblogs, and all other forms of people-powered networks provide a looking glass into the interaction between consumers, as well as the ability to discern the level of authority each one possesses.

You've heard it time and time again: "People do business with people they like."

While that's true, they also spend money on products that help them do something that they couldn't do before, based on existing needs or frustrations with current experiences. They also buy things or spend money because their peers also do so. Therefore, people are looking for answers or trends, not necessarily friendly brands. They're seeking societies where they can learn, share, and contribute. And they're connecting with one another.

The lessons we learned in the last chapter teach us that listening and monitoring count for everything nowadays. It's by far the easiest step in identifying, potentially embracing, and ultimately leading the transition from an introverted organization into an extroverted, community-focused human network.

This is a privilege and an opportunity. We must remember this. . . .

It's the shift from top-down broadcasting to a more holistic methodology that embraces consumers directly with the tools and channels they use to communicate. The Conversation Prism is our blueprint. And effectively building a bridge between brand and markets requires the personification of the company and the ability to not only humanize its story, but also listen and respond to input through words and the adaptation of products and services.

Influential customers collectively create a network of information beacons that help others successfully navigate within their respective markets and industries. We're awakening to a new era of stature, in which groundswells of user-generated activity create leverage and cause impact. In the world of social media, brands can also earn influence, using the same tools and networks that have empowered bloggers and tastemakers alike.

While the direct-to-consumer (D2C) model might imply business-to-consumer interaction, this model works equally well for business-to-business, nonprofit, government, verticals, education, and, essentially, any market or industry where individuals and influencers are interacting, seeking guidance, or affected by the information they discover online.

Take a moment to identify your influencers and learn what moves them.

■ ENGAGE WITH PURPOSE

As I've said before, conversation is simply conversation, regardless of the tools. The qualifications to maintain dialogue are trivial. The task of simply showing up to the table is, honestly, child's play—the real question is about figuring out what we're trying to accomplish and then making it happen.

Those who pay attention to the dynamics, subtle nuances, and psyche of the words, tone, and nature of the dialogue can tell the differences between a simple response, withdrawal, reconciliation, and resolution.

When discussing social media and participatory protocol, let's no longer behave as though we were standing on top of a table during a cocktail party and obnoxiously yelling out messages at the crowd.

Actually monitoring, hearing, and internalizing the words of others inherently qualifies someone as worthy of engagement. Interaction, however, is measured by the exchanges that move things forward. The process of identifying influencers and monitoring relevant conversations is only as valuable as the steps we take to engage in ways that inspire desirable action.

Tastemakers and those who've earned the recognition of their peers are either dubious of corporate outreach or opportunistic in assessing its potential. Your approach counts for everything. Once influencers are identified, we must merge what we've learned through the Conversation Prism process with programs, stories, and meaningful motives that appeal to them and ultimately earn their participation. We must recognize their value and that they boast audiences that justify their position as an authority. If these bridges do not yet exist, we must construct them using only materials of relevance. I'm not talking about just giving away trips, free products, or simply paying influencers to form alliances with your organization. While buying alliances may be an option, thinking beyond giveaways and promotions keeps your brand sharp and relevant, now and in the long term.

A greater purpose is mandatory.

Identifying influencers is one thing. Engaging people and enticing not only their interest, but ultimately establishing an association and earning allegiance takes far more than interpersonal adeptness and a budget with which to purchase friendships.

We need to be acutely informed, open, and enlightened individuals who can engage others with both empathy and honesty.

■ THE SHIFT FROM MONITORING TO ACTION

Are you listening?

Are you really listening, or are you just monitoring dialogues or mining data?

The role of monitoring serves as the eyes, ears, and heart of the organization and deserves support from a comprehensive system that connects to every essential node in the corporate and human network.

There's a difference and we stand to gain or lose ground based on our intentions and follow-up activities. The type of listening I'm

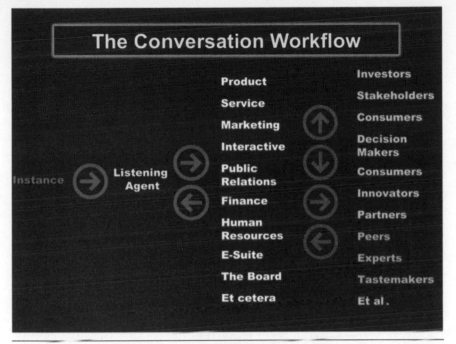

Figure 19.1   The Conversation Workflow

referring to here isn't simply identifying updates or threads tied to keywords. We did most of that work in the Conversation Prism chapter.

Listening requires a dedicated infrastructure and support system. It also requires hearing where we can make an impact.

As social architects and engineers, we are responsible for paving the roads for information to freely travel between listening agents, spokespersons, decision makers, and ultimately to consumers and influencers (see Figure 19.1). Officially establishing a conversational workflow and infrastructure is how we:

➤ Recognize strengths and weaknesses

➤ Improve products and services

➤ Analyze competitive advantages and disadvantages

➤ Maintain and improve existing and prospective employee relations and interactions

➤ Ensure customer satisfaction and foster loyalty

➤ Identify influencers and business prospects

➤ Enhance processes

➤ Warrant relevance

➤ Expand market share

➤ Strengthen valuation

➤ Earn credibility and trust

➤ Cultivate communities and encourage advocacy

➤ Learn

➤ Humanize

➤ Create and ideate

➤ Grow

Someone has to take responsibility for the process of listening to and channeling conversations. It requires more than one champion to truly harness the potential of the interactive Web and power of community. Without a complete working infrastructure that channels conversations and feedback, and the resources required to effectively channel, scrutinize, strategize, reply, or counter, or simply act, we are being negligent toward our company and its customers.

In some cases, a community or listening manager will act as the central hub to all, one, or more departments. Its construction depends on the culture and design of the company.

This is one of the most important roles in the transformation of any organization from an inward focus to an outward view. The intelligence and insight gathered during these exercises can tell us a great deal.

While jumping into social media is inevitable for many companies, the need to substantiate the effort to justify the shift in or creation of dedicated budget and personnel remains constant.

Before we can discuss return on investment (ROI), we first need to understand the proportions of the investment required.

■ X-RAY GLASSES AND BIONIC HEARING

We have the technology . . . we just need to know how to use it.

The list of tools to identify influencers, unearth and listen to online conversations, and track their paths is extensive, and the available services will only continue to multiply.

Automation is helpful in that it saves time and conserves precious resources, and, in some cases, provides us with answers to questions we never knew to ask. Initially, however, it's exposure as opposed to immersion.

To offer guidance on the next steps and to determine which tools to employ within your organization, I've developed a list of currently available solutions and services. Reviewing this list will enable you to start the process of uncovering the unknown and plotting your course of action. The decision about which solution to implement is yours to determine, as some will be more compatible with the infrastructure of your organization. I include an up-to-date list on the website for this book.

POWER TOOLS: WHAT BRANDS TO USE TO GET THE JOB DONE

Sure, we know that every organization has its unique needs, and we each need to select the tools and services that fit our infrastructure, processes, and teams, not to mention our budget. But, no doubt you're curious as to what's being employed now. What tools are the market leaders using to discover their tastemakers, trendsetters, and market makers? How are other companies listening and responding to the front lines?[1]

Southwest Airlines uses a search tool from TweetDeck to track the conversations and sentiments regarding its own brand and its competitors—searching for terms such as *bag fee* and *frontier*. As reported in the *Wall Street Journal*, a routine Twitter search uncovered a tweet referencing a Southwest Airlines flight that was preparing to make an emergency landing in Baltimore. The company had not yet released this information to its employees, including to Christi Day, the emerging-media specialist for the airline who discovered the tweet. Day investigated the matter at once, and continually posted updates to the company's Twitter page as the facts rolled in. According to Day, "The landing was uneventful, but Twitter followers appreciated the transparency and timely information."

Coca-Cola uses Scout (by Scout Labs) to monitor the comments on Twitter, as well as other platforms such as Facebook, MySpace, and even foreign language blogs. Scout rates each comment as positive or negative to help the beverage giant stay on top of public sentiment.

Whole Foods Market uses a tool from CoTweet to manage, track, and respond to the 300 to 500 tweets that are posted each day to the company's Twitter page. The tool tracks which tweets have been responded to, and which are still awaiting recognition and response. Whole Foods employees can also review any previous interaction and conversation threads with a customer to help them choose the most appropriate response. Likewise, Microsoft also uses CoTweet to manage its Twitter activity and ensure proper (and timely) responses to consumers.

■ SEARCHING THE SOCIAL WEB

➤ Conversational Dashboards

CoTweet: A Web-based collaboration platform that provides case management for Twitter exchanges with customers, task assignment and follow-up, keyword and trend monitoring, and conversation threading.

HootSuite: A professional Twitter client that manages the work-flow for multiple accounts. HootSuite's scheduling helps companies better control the pace of their outbound tweets to prevent exasperating their followers with tweet overload. HootSuite also offers brand monitoring and keyword tracking, Twitter search, and statistics.

PeopleBrowsr: A dashboard, and backend data analysis system, for managing communications across Twitter, Facebook, YouTube, FriendFeed, and other social networks. The service also doubles as an integrated search network for each network it connects and offers the ability to track and manage automated or customer responses to the results for keywords—providing an all-inclusive communications management platform.

Seesmic: A Web or desktop client that manages the social streams from Facebook, Twitter, and many other networks.

TweetDeck: Described as "air traffic control for Twitter," Tweet-Deck customizes and organizes the Twitter experience, manages multiple Twitter accounts, and offers search capabilities based on hashtag, brand, people, and so on.

➤ Blogsearch

Technorati: Considered the largest blog search engine in the world, Technorati tracks blog reactions (keywords) and blogs linking behavior.

Blogsearch.google.com: Similar to News.Google.com, Google Blog Search allows users to comb through blog posts for relevant discussions and identify authorities on any given subject. Google alerts are also available for blog search results.

Blogged.com: A community for identifying blogs and bloggers that cover particular topics from what's popular to the long tail. Blogs are rated by the community as well as by blogged.com editors to provide a human perspective.

BackType: Blog comments do not usually appear in traditional or blog search results. BackType is a conversational search engine that indexes and connects millions of conversations from blogs, social networks, and other social media so people can find, follow, and share comments.

➤ Forums and User Groups

BoardReader: Accurately finds and displays information within the Web's forums and message boards.

BoardTracker: A forum search engine, message tracking, and instant alerts system designed to provide relevant information contained in forum threads.

Go directly to the source:

- ➤ Google Groups
- ➤ Yahoo! Groups
- ➤ Ning
- ➤ Meetup

➤ Conversation, Visualization, and Metrics Management Systems

ReSearch.ly: Unlike the other listening and research tools, this is designed to specifically uncover interest graphs related to brands. Results display the degree of separation between the brand and individuals and allows for a variety of further segmentation by authority as well as full demographics and psychographics.

Spiral16: Unveils hidden patterns inside complex social media networks by providing a top-level view of data through visually rich, virtualized 3-D models. The platform also helps global brands monitor, manage, and analyze their social media presence to improve customer service, reputation, gather market intelligence, and understand conversations through sentiment.

Linkfluence: A research-based firm specializing in mapping, monitoring, and measuring trends and opinions on the Social Web. Linkfluence studies and offers solutions to visually map, monitor, and analyze social media activity and instances, and draws borders of conversational communities around brands and keywords to assess true impact on image and reputation.

PR Newswire Social Media Metrics: An intelligence tool powered by Sentiment Metrics that enables communications professionals and marketers to monitor, analyze, and measure the impact of what is being said about an organization, brand, spokesperson, or competitor. Social Media Metrics monitors over 20 million blogs, 5 million forum posts, and 30,000 online news sources, social networks, and microblogs, including Twitter. The system enables users to build customized searches to track keywords while simultaneously isolating specific geographic, demographic, and language parameters.

Scout Labs: A powerful, Web-based application that tracks social media activity and sorting through signals in the noise to help teams build better products and stronger customer relationships. The system provides a platform for monitoring, analyzing, and also managing follow-up and action.

DNA 13: Aimed at global enterprises, small agencies, and all sizes in between, DNA provides dashboard solutions that track and present reputation and visibility. It also organizes results and offers detailed analysis. Products include dnaMonitor and dnaEnterprise. Corporate positioning caters to communications and public relations professionals.

HowSociable: Provides a free look into brand visibility metrics by allowing a user to enter a keyword, name, or phrase, and identify the content transpiring in 22 networks.

WhosTalkin: WhosTalkin.com is a social media search tool that allows users to search for conversations surrounding important topics. It serves as a hub for search results on blogs, news networks, social networks, video networks, image networks, forums, and tags.

FiltrBox: Real-time social media and Web monitoring, FiltrBox monitors thousands of mainstream news outlets, blogs, and social media in one place. By consolidating results in one dashboard, users can eliminate redundant searches and alerts. Users can also import their Google Alerts to manage noise, remove duplicate results, and consolidate disparate results feeds.

Radian6: Radian6 is focused on building a complete monitoring and analysis solution for PR and advertising professionals. The Radian6 listening platform monitors the Social Web to uncover conversations related to specific brands on millions of blog posts, viral videos, reviews in forums, sharing of photos, and twitter updates. It also provides the ability to analyze buzz about a company, products, issues, competitors, and outcomes of specific marketing campaigns and social media investments.

BuzzMetrics: Now part of Nielsen, BuzzMetrics delivers trusted brand metrics, meaningful consumer insights, and real-time market intelligence to help clients apply the power of consumer-generated media (CGM) to their businesses. Nielsen BuzzMetrics uncovers and integrates data-driven insights culled from nearly 100 million blogs, social networks, groups, boards, and other CGM platforms. The services include brand monitoring, brand connections and customer relations, consumer insights, and brand campaign planning and measurement.

Trackur: A collection of online reputation monitoring and social media listening tools, Trackur scans hundreds of millions of Web pages—including news, blogs, video, images, and forums—and reports any discoveries that match relevant keywords.

Visible Technologies: Helps users listen to and learn what consumers are saying about their company or brand in the blogosphere and social media communities. It also fosters customer engagement by enabling users to effectively participate in these discussions by placing the right messages in front of the right audiences for a more direct connection.

Sentiment Metrics: Sentiment Metrics' social media measurement dashboard enables users to monitor and measure social media and gain a necessary level of business intelligence to develop more targeted marketing, improve products, and increase profits.

TNS Cymfony: Provides expert interpretation of how corporate messages are picked up across traditional and social media sources, enabling the ability to measure results and discover trends that affect the bottom line. Whether the goal is to influence the brand perception during a new product release, marketing campaign, or even through a crisis, TNS Cymfony's market influence analysis tracks consumer preferences across traditional and social media sources and provides the ability for listeners to act and engage quickly to keep public perceptions on track.

BrandsEye: Traces and assesses online presences and provides a real-time Reputation Score for both the user's brand as well as their competitors. This allows companies to monitor the sentiments and opinions of their own customers, while making educated judgments about how to respond to attacks on their own online reputation.

Cision Social Media: Social media monitoring of more than 100 million blogs, tens of thousands of online forums, more than 450 leading rich media sites, and a complete database of influential voices on the Web and in social media.

Alterian: SM2 is a software solution designed specifically for PR and marketing agencies to monitor and measure social media. It works with the company's Social Media Warehouse system, which tracks blogs, wikis, message boards and forums, video and photo sites, mainstream media, blogs, microblogs, and social networks.

Trendrr: Tracks the popularity and awareness of trends across a variety of inputs, ranging from social networks, to blog buzz and video views downloads, all in real time.

SocialMention: A social media search platform that aggregates user-generated content from across the universe into a single stream of information.

■ NOTE

1. The following examples are extracted from Sarah E. Needleman, "Relief for Twitter Headaches," *Wall Street Journal* (September 14, 2009), http://online.wsj.com/article_email/SB100014240529702046832045743 56441457884888-lMyQjAxMDA5MDEwNDExNDQyWj.html.

The Human Network

Discovering the new influencers through network and link analysis[1] allows us to see the very people who define our markets. While network analysis enables us to uncover local patterns within networks, link analysis extends these observations to determine the associations between objects. Ultimately, what we should start to see and feel is something truly more profound than any one social network. We now begin to see the genesis of a *human network,* a term that I have sprinkled throughout this book. The human network is representative of the connections that link us to one another across multiple social networks. This is the true social network, one without boundaries or limitations for collaboration and communication. The human network is also how Cisco Systems defines the intersection where technology meets humanity.[2]

Technology is facilitating the social effect and it is most certainly connecting us in ways that truly make the world a much smaller place, one in which we can participate in its definition and evolution—and also define our place within it.

■ BREATHING LIFE INTO THE HUMAN NETWORK

As individuals, our human network comprises both professional and personal connections and they differ from each other on the basis of shared interests as well as established relations.

The human network also illustrates the map of individuals with whom we can benefit from connecting. As a result of our research and observation, we can identify and discern tribes, tribal leaders, and specific individuals who can connect us with those individuals who can help us learn and motivate. We also garner perspective and empathy in the process. We also recognize various patterns of connectivity, influence, and hierarchy. These connections and rankings are different within each network and also in the context that governs our study. For example, if a communications or public relations group commissioned the examination, the resulting network will contrast with the outcome of reviews conducted by customer service or human resources. Therefore, the human network will vary on the basis of the nature of the dialogue.

I have studied mapping and influence in much of my work over the years. Analyzing contextual relationships in online media from blogs to social networks to traditional media properties dictates strategies and programming. In one such series, I observed how individuals establish conversational networks. For example, on Twitter, if I were to publish a tweet on the subject of green technology, the responses I'd receive would differ from those who may feel compelled to retort, should I publish an update concerning health care. As reviewed earlier, those responses would also differ based on time and the opening of the attention aperture. In Twitter, I employed two services (which are free) to help analyze this activity. First, I would monitor the Twitter stream of a particular individual based on a theme. I would then run the tests again as that theme changed, usually a few weeks later. Using Twitter-Friends[3] and Gravity, I could visually map the conversational network related to themes for both inbound and outbound activity, thus establishing a snapshot of influence and reach. Figure 20.1 shows a graphic of outbound conversations, and Figure 20.2 depicts inbound messages.

The inbound network represents the individuals who respond to us publicly, and the outbound network is representative of those to whom we reply. Removing ourselves from this picture and inserting an already recognized influencer, we can use these tools to establish inbound and outbound conversational networks, based on the interaction over a period of time. We can then assess the caliber of those responding to determine weight and authority for possible inclusion in our resulting influencer map.

In the process of analyzing conversational networks, I realized that I could also connect individuals across multiple networks and remove the barriers between them. For the most part, I did so manually, to ensure that my results were based on first-hand analysis and the qualification of individuals on the basis of preestablished authority, their published works, and the conversational and contextual networks they forged as a result.

■ THE HUMAN NETWORK: ALIVE AND CLICKING!

As a natural extension of work I was already performing at Cisco Systems, I was tasked with identifying digital and traditional

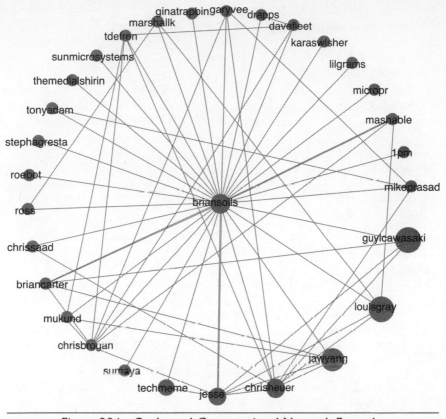

Figure 20.1   Outbound Conversational Network Example
Source: Twitter-Friends.

influencers on behalf of the corporate communications team and based on the company's priority business units. It provided me an opportunity to further study influence, linking behavior, as well as where and how these connections were forged and ranked. While this is part of influencer research in general, it should not go unsaid that no databases or preexisting lists were used in this process. We let influence stand on its own merits. If it wasn't discoverable, it wasn't influential.

Using the methodologies promoted by the Conversation Prism and the Conversation Index and also incorporating the systems for recognizing conversational networks, we pinpointed voices of authority, by subject, and analyzed how they connected to each other through their professional activity and interaction. In the process, we were able to reveal the human network. It was representative of blogs,

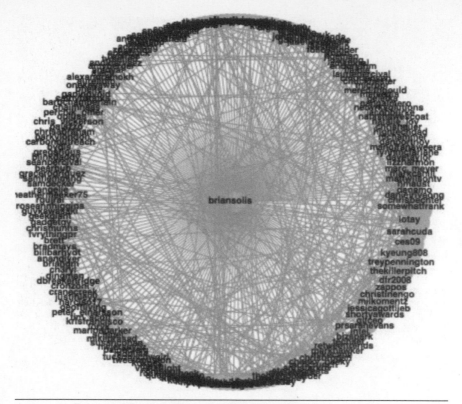

Figure 20.2   Inbound Conversational Network Example
Source: Twitter-Friends.

social networks, forums, and micronetworks, as well as corresponding inner networks that showcased tighter, yet distributed pockets of influence and collaboration.

We essentially applied the principles associated with network theory and envisioned through graph theory to humanize the landscape of influence.

Just for a bit of background, network theory,[4] as we applied it, represents the study of graphs that serve as a representation of relationships that are symmetrical, those symbolic of similar parts facing each other or arrayed around an axis.

To bring this human network to life, I turned to Pete Warden, creator of Mailana,[5] a social network analysis system. Warden was instrumental in the completion of this groundbreaking project, as he adapted his visual networking platform to integrate our research data into a visual and interactive map of influencers that spanned across

Figure 20.3   Visual Map of Influencers across Networks and Mediums

networks and mediums, organized by business units and the manual assembly of established relationships (see Figure 20.3).

The human network embodies social network analysis, the mapping of relationships with social networks, network theory, link analysis, and graph theory, all fused into one hyperconnected influencer network. Not only does this service provide a visual representation of relationships, it brings them to life. Contacts are clickable and the user can learn more about the individuals and their work. As each icon is clicked, it illuminates the connections that form distinct inner networks within the greater relevant net.

The mission of displaying the influencers and how they connect to each other was served. However, I continue to analyze network topology to learn more about centrality and the relative importance of nodes, edges, and hubs within each human network to better understand the influence of influence.

To further explore the behavior of hubs, nodes, hosts, intersections, connections, and distribution points, I contacted Stan Magniant, who at the time worked at Linkfluence.net, a relationship mapping service based in Washington, D.C., specializing in mapping, monitoring, and measuring trends and opinions on the Social Web.

Figure 20.4   Linkfluence

Magniant and team assembled a heat map based on its interpretation of graph theory to create a network topology that revealed
the inbound and outbound link behavior and also the corresponding
level of influence based on the quantity of nodes pointing back to
distribution points or hubs. After feeding data into the Linkfluence
system, both a network topology and hierarchy were immediately
apparent and, like the Mailana map, this too was alive and clicking
(see Figure 20.4).

Each node revealed inbound and outbound links and the intercon-
necting relationships and behavior they maintained. Influence and
reach were suddenly evident and ready for exploration. We could view
which outlets consistently received the bulk of inbound links based
on particular topics, while those linking back to primary sources.
Linkfluence revealed a hierarchical network structure that distin-
guished levels of influence and the corresponding networks of each.

Cisco's human network and its discernible structure introduced
a new landscape of influencers and paths of influence to individual
business units. These graphs were not only visualized, they were
reinforced by data. The data would later prove crucial in justifying the work and findings, as decision makers require conclusive

evidence and logical strategies to shift resources and attention in new directions.

■ VISUALIZING SOCIAL ORDER

Before we tackle the process of planning, I'd like to open a window onto the online behavior already observed and documented in social media to spark contemplation and creativity.

In social networks and online communities, the basis for cohesion, in its most simple interpretation, appears to be based on contextual exchanges and the viability of a mutually satisfactory reward system. We follow and connect with people we know, as well as those whom we admire, respect, and from whom we learn. We may also link to those we think will benefit from knowing us, and, in the process, take advantage of the networks they create for personal or professional gain. Based on perpetual interests and those that temporarily distract us, our networks will shift, expand, contract, and morph, based on the individuals we align with at any given moment. Applying social order to social networks, no matter which school of thought you subscribe to, reveals the structure and hierarchy, as well as the governing principles and culture. It is the social economy. And, it is the hierarchy that conveys the balance of power and the contributing roles of each defining class.

This recognition will allow you to prioritize focus and engagement. Not all friends, followers, and fans are created equally.

■ SOCIAL TECHNOGRAPHICS

Whereas much of the previous discussion has focused on participation behavior within specific social networks, Forrester Research created Social Technographics—a system for analyzing and classifying consumer participation in social technologies. For the past three years, Forrester documented this analysis in visual form, creating the Social Technographics Ladder to demonstrate and categorize individual activity across the Social Web.[6] Social Technographics Profiles places people who are online into overlapping groups on the basis of their level of participation.

The groups are segmented as follows:

Creators

➤ Publish a blog.
➤ Create and publish Web pages, video, audio, music.
➤ Write and publish articles or blog posts.

Critics

➤   Post ratings or reviews of products or services.

➤   Comment on the blogs of others.

➤   Contribute to online forums.

➤   Write or edit articles and entries in wikis.

Collectors

➤   Use RSS feeds.

➤   Vote for content online.

➤   Add tags to content.

Joiners

➤   Maintain profiles on social networks.

➤   Visit social networks.

Spectators

➤   Read blogs.

➤   Listen to podcasts.

➤   Watch videos.

➤   Read online forums.

➤   Read customer ratings and reviews.

Inactives

➤   None of these.

Along with the introduction of its most recent Technographics Ladder, Forrester published "The Broad Reach of Social Technologies,"[7] a report that found that more than four in five online adults in the United States now participate socially . The role of spectator, at the very least, is now practically universal and therefore should serve as the final straw for those executives who withheld attention, time, and resources from organizing and orchestrating a strategic social effort.

If social media were a scale or spectrum, we could simply divide it by elite content producers and consumers, contributing producers and consumers, consumers, and inactives. What's important to understand when analyzing the Social Technographics Ladder is to establish where on the ladder your consumers and audiences are placed and to what extent. As such, your content, programming, and approach require a highly tailored and customized focus, voice, intent, and infrastructure that match and appeal to individuals and the groups they represent, where, how, and when they consume and in turn respond.

To assist in this process, Forrester Research released an online Consumer Profile Tool that provides brands with Social Technographics, social profile information based on age group, country, and gender. Based on Forrester's survey data, you can view how participation varies globally among different groups of consumers.

■ TENETS OF COMMUNITY BUILDING

Ultimately, data is only as valuable as its incorporation into corresponding measures. This book is rich in research, information, theory, and experience and is intended to empower you to find your own answers and spark new ones. It is how the information in the book is applied that determines relevance in your world. The data that you gather is specifically relevant to your reality and what you discover, learn, and observe determines your next steps.

Applying Harold Lasswell's communication theory, which was originally introduced in 1949, we are to determine "who says what to whom in what channel with what effect."[8] As I introduced in my last book (*Putting the Public Back in Public Relations,* coauthored with Deirdre Breakenridge), in the Social Web we must analyze "Who says what, in which channel, to what effect; then ascertain who hears what, shares what, with what intent, where, to what effect."[9] This acknowledges that communication now continues after the initial introduction or encounter.

It is the connection between intelligence, intent, behavior, and people that explicitly and implicitly defines our community—ultimately determining our success. And it is the collaborations between business units in the social realm that ensure cohesion, balance, brand presence, perception, and resonance.

Therefore, our job is to learn. The insights we garner will reveal specifically how and where to engage. At that point, everything boils down to community cultivation.

The world of business is accustomed to using acronyms and letters of the alphabet in helping its leaders become proficient in particular areas of study.

For example, in communications, we're taught how to employ "The Seven Cs," which include:[10]

1. *Clear:* Ensure that your messages are clear, so that they are effective.

2. *Concise:* Through brevity, there's clarity. Speak through the words that your intended audience is comfortable with, no more or less than absolutely necessary. Eliminate buzzwords.

3. *Concrete:* You have a choice in your writing to use concrete (specific) or abstract (vague) words. While each has a place in business writing, concrete terms are typically more accurate and believable.

4. *Correct:* Accurate and correct content ranges in characteristics from the value and comprehensiveness of expertise shared on any given subject to spelling, grammar, punctuation, and format.

5. *Coherent:* Messages must make sense. They must be digestible. They must connect with those who come into contact with them. A message's flow and processing should be seamless.

6. *Complete:* Information must be complete and definitive, ensuring that more questions are answered than raised.

7. *Courteous:* Establishing goodwill is as much a function of delivery as it is format. Ensure that messages and stories are thoughtful and worthy of the intelligence and emotions of those whom we're trying to reach.

Moving along the alphabet, we're also presented with the Four Ps of Marketing, also known the marketing mix, which was originally introduced by Harvard professor Jerome McCarthy and Phil Kotler in the early 1960s.[11]

The Four Ps are:

1. *Product:* A tangible object or service.

2. *Price:* The price that the customer pays as determined by market factors such as market share, competition, material costs, product identity, and perceived value.

3. *Place:* Also referred to as the distribution channel, *place* is the location where a product can be purchased.

4. *Promotion:* Communications employed to promote the product in the marketplace, ranging from advertising, public relations, word of mouth, point of sale, direct mail, events, marketing, and now, social media.

In my work, I always approach the Four Ps with a fifth P. By recognizing the role of people in the marketing mix, it changes everything.

In 1997, Bob Lauterborn, professor of advertising at the University of North Carolina and co-author of *The New Marketing Paradigm: Integrated Marketing Communications*,[12] adapted the Four Ps and focused on the customer instead of on the product. His Four Cs of Service take into account that consumers are growing in influence and that companies need to determine how to send the right message at the right time in the right way to the right person. Instead of building and pushing products—for example, "build it and they will come"—the Four Cs champion the consumer's individual wants and needs.[13]

Attributes of the Four Cs of Service include:

1. Product evolves into *Commodity.*
2. Price becomes *Cost.*
3. Place becomes *Channel* or *Convenience.*
4. Promotion shifts to *Communication* (although one could argue now that the Social Web ushered in an era of conversations and collaboration over communication and promotion).

In 2004, Professor Koichi Shimizu of the Josai University Graduate School of Business Administration adapted Lauterborn's Four Cs into a framework for recognizing and leveraging the customer's role in business.[14] Shimizu introduced the world to the 7Cs Compass Model, which portrays customers as encircling companies and companies at the center of marketing activities, and also includes the role of consumers in addition to customers.

The 7Cs Compass Model includes:

1. Corporation and Competitor
2. Commodity
3. Cost
4. Communication
5. Channel
6. Consumer
7. Circumstances

The compass points in the model represent:

➤ *N* = *needs:* Analysis of customer needs—unsubstantiated opinions—some of which cannot be converted into concrete commodities.

➤ *W* = *wants:* The substantiated needs to expect commodities.

➤ *S* = *security:* The safety of commodities and production processes and the post-sale warranty.

➤ *E* = *education:* A consumer's right to know information about the commodities.

The compass points are balanced by navigational bearings that help businesses understand associated circumstances:

➤ *National and international:* Related to politics and law. I would add that consumer wants and needs and corresponding commodity relevance apply to the cultures in unique national and international circumstances.

➤ *Weather:* Weather and natural environments are still uncontrollable and worth proactive consideration. I suggest that weather can also represent socioeconomic environments and their supporting ecosystems and habitats (for example, individual social networks versus real-world societies).

➤ *Social and cultural circumstances:* Representative of the social system and problems of a nation. The following seven human cultural factors need to be included in marketing analyses:

1. Basic values and attitudes

2. Motivation

3. Learning capacity and achievement orientation

4. Technical know-how

5. Social discipline

6. Sense of responsibility for the common good and the community

7. Capacity for flexible adaptation to a changing environment.

➤ *Economic circumstances:* Related to national circumstances, but also including factors such as energy, resources, international income and expense, financial circumstances and economic growth, and so forth.

As interactive media earns prominence in today's society, the laws of marketing, customer service, product development, and ultimately, community cultivation recognized the roles of customers, consumers, influencers, peers, and competitors, among many other factors. Social media is the great equalizer and as such, we look again to the alphabet to help build a socially aware framework to serve as creative inspiration for finding people and establishing the relationships that will serve as the foundation for community building.

As in all forms of marketing and communications, principles and methodologies will continue to evolve. In the past several years alone, many social media pioneers have shared their views for documenting the ethos, governances, and ethics that serve as the undercurrent for community cultivation.

Chris Heuer, the founder of Social Media Club and new media innovator, discusses the Four Cs for a social framework:[15]

➤ *Context:* How we frame our stories.

➤ *Communications:* The practice of sharing our story as well as listening, responding, and growing.

➤ *Collaboration:* Working together to make things better and more efficient and effective.

➤ *Connections:* The relationships we forge and maintain.

Heuer binds together the Cs through a framework of values:

➤ Be human
➤ Be aware
➤ Be honest
➤ Be respectful
➤ Be a participant
➤ Be open
➤ Be courageous

In November 2008, social maven David Armano introduced his version of the Four Cs of Community:[16]

➤ *Content:* Quality content is ideal for attracting the audience necessary to build community.

➤ *Context:* Understanding how to meet people where they are; creating the right experience at the right time.

➤ *Connectivity:* Designing experiences to support microinteractions.

➤ *Continuity:* Providing an ongoing, valuable, and consistent user experience.

In July 2009, Gaurav Mishra, CEO of social media research and strategy company 20:20 WebTech, contributed a guest post to Beth Kanter's blog in which he proposed a 4 Cs Social Media Framework:

➤ *Content:* Social media transforms consumers into creators

➤ *Collaboration:* The facilitation and aggregation of individual actions into meaningful collective results through conversation, co-creation, and collective action

➤ *Community:* Social media enables sustained collaboration around shared ideas over time and across space

➤ *Collective intelligence:* The Social Web empowers us to aggregate individual actions and also run sophisticated algorithms to extract meaning

In his post, Mishra captured a core quality of community development that should not go overlooked, which also reinforces our initial discussions on social objects: "People don't build relationships with each other in a vacuum. A vibrant community is built around a social object that is meaningful for its members. The social object can be a person, a place, a thing or an idea."

One can conjure any order of Cs or Ps to further the dialogue. I've assembled these examples and theories for you because each represent intrinsic values that will improve our work in identifying individuals and groups and also the methods necessary to establish and foster flourishing and interactive communities. However, there are some gaps—some terminology was either inferred or absent, yet the concepts remain vital to growing a vibrant and dynamic community. Thus, I've assembled what I refer to as C^3.

C^3: The Code of Community Cultivation

➤ *Conversation:* Successful communities thrive on interaction.

➤ *Core values:* Philosophies and principles that guide our conduct and the relationships we forge.

➤ *Culture:* The behavior characteristics of the community we define and shape.

➤ *Cause:* Our conviction, our intent, our mission.... Without cause, we lose motivation and a supporting reward structure.

➤ *Credit:* Recognition, paying it forward, and attention are the attributes of empowerment and thus a stronger community.

➤ *Coalition:* Affinity and associations require liking, sympathy, commonalities, and compelling characteristics that compel someone to align with other people or with something else.

➤ *Conversion:* Change is paramount. The ability to shift someone from one state or place to another is powerful, transformative, and part of any ongoing community program.

➤ *Commitment:* Without resolve, passion, or drive we cannot expect to inspire others to join or remain part of our communities. We are the catalysts. We are contagious. We must establish and convey our conviction to ensure loyalty and camaraderie.

➤ *Compromise:* To grow and evolve, we must adapt, which requires us to listen and feel the feedback from our community. This is how we learn and innovate.

➤ *Champion:* Without champions, the ability to scale growth becomes difficult, if not impossible. We must instill enthusiasm and empower champions to help us extend our reach.

➤ *Compassion:* Empathy and sympathy are instrumental attributes for feeling the state, experience, and emotions of our peers and influencers for us to better understand the people we are trying to reach.

➤ *Confidence:* To convey expertise, insight, and passion authoritatively, confidence is the key to believability.

➤ Also includes the Cs from the previously mentioned examples: Content, Community, Continuity, Collaboration, Connectivity, Collective Intelligence, Context, Communication, Customer, and Consumer.

And of course, as in any business, the most important Cs to consider in any new media program include the C-Suite:

➤ CEO: Chief Executive Officer
➤ COO: Chief Operating Officer
➤ CMO: Chief Marketing Officer
➤ CTO: Chief Technology Officer
➤ CIO: Chief Information Officer

➤ CFO: Chief Financial Officer

➤ CSO: Chief Security, Strategy, or Social Officer

➤ And all other CxOs[17]

The underlying principle of any relationship-based program is that communities tend to reward selflessness, even if we are inconspicuously accomplishing our goals in the process of growing our networks and corresponding communities. Give your audience something to believe in.

■ NOTES

1. "Network theory," Wikipedia, http://en.wikipedia.org/wiki/Network_theory.

2. "The Human Network," Cisco.com, www.cisco.com/web/about/human network/index.html.

3. Twitter-Friends, http://twitter-friends.com.

4. NetWiki, http://netwiki.amath.unc.edu.

5. Mailana, http://twitter.mailana.com.

6. Josh Bernoff, "Social Technology Growth Marches On in 2009, Led by Social Network Sites," Groundswell, Forrester Blogs (August 25, 2009), http://blogs.forrester.com/groundswell/2009/08/social-technol ogy-growth-marches-on-in-2009-led-by-social-network-sites.html.

7. Sean Corcoran, "The Broad Reach of Social Technologies," Forrester Research (August 25, 2009), www.forrester.com/Research/Document/ Excerpt/0,7211,55132,00.html.

8. Theodore Levitt, "Exploit the Product Life Cycle," *Harvard Business Review* 43 (November–December, 1965), 81–94.

9. Brian Solis and Deirdre Breakenridge, *Putting the Public Back in Public Relations* (London: Pearson/Financial Times Press, 2009), 190.

10. James Stull and John W Baird, *Business Communication: A Classroom Simulation* (New York: Prentice-Hall, 1992).

11. William D. Perreault and E. Jerome McCarthy, *Basic Marketing* 14th ed. (New York: McGraw-Hill/Irwin, 2003).

12. Don E. Schultz, Stanley Tannenbaum, and Robert F. Lauterborn, *The New Marketing Paradigm: Integrated Marketing Communications* (New York: McGraw-Hill, 1996).

13. Roy McClean, "Marketing 101: 4 Cs versus the 4 Ps of Marketing," FOCUS Marketing Intelligence, www.customfitfocus.com/marketing-1.htm.

14. "Professor Koichi Shimizu's 7 Cs Compass Model," Josai University, www.josai.ac.jp/~shimizu/essence/Professor%20Koichi%20Shimizu%27 s%207Cs%20Compass%20Model.html.

15. Chris Heuer, "Social + Media: What's Needed Next," Drupalcon Keynote (September 3, 2009), Paris.

16. David Armano, "The 4 Cs of Community," Logic + Emotion (November 30, 2008), http://darmano.typepad.com/logic_emotion/2008/11/the-4 -cs-of-community.html.

17. "Corporate Title," Wikipedia, http://en.wikipedia.org/wiki/Corporate_ title.

Chapter 21

The Social Marketing Compass

Failing to plan is planning to fail.

—*Unknown*

■ THE CALM BEFORE THE STORM

Depending on the drivers for engagement and the state of adoption in the Social Web, our first steps might require a Day Zero approach. What if we could just start from scratch, what would we do differently? In most cases though, we have to recognize existing programs. Our work in the Conversation Prism and establishing the Conversation Index must prove complete and irrefutable. It serves as the social map for planning and defining our approach.

Now we have one more step to undertake before we are ready to draft a market-ready social media blueprint. For smaller companies, this process is straightforward. Nonetheless, we must conduct an audit that surveys the Social Web for any existing social profiles, objects, and accounts that are already in use or were created earlier and now remain dormant. This allows us to assemble the fragmented pieces that may exist and also assess the state of affairs, caliber of content, and relevance of accounts to evaluate and regroup. As a result, some accounts may remain, some may be reorganized, and others may become inactive or erased altogether. These actions will be determined by the results of the Conversation Prism research.

For intelligence purposes, we should also review the activity of our competitors. This deserves ongoing attention.

This step is designed to unearth any potential land mines or surprises to ensure that anything you do from this point forward is highly orchestrated. Contingent upon the specific results of this internal probe, our next steps may differ a bit. The risk that we're attempting to minimize right now is the dilution of the brand through rogue accounts created by individuals with good intentions, but not bound to a plan or centralized purpose. Without governance or organization, the brand's image can quickly spin out of control with each new unplanned profile or social object created and placed into practice. For larger enterprises, this threat may already be a reality, and the extent of the damage caused will vary.

Your job is to reel in everything that is already in play concerning your brand, or spark new programs for the uninitiated.

■ THE SOCIAL MARKETING COMPASS

Before we tackle the official process of creating a plan, here is one last exercise that will help us maintain focus and perspective. The fabric of our plan should be woven from threads of ethics, purpose, and principles and bound by salient business goals and objectives. Remember, social networks are emotional landscapes. As such, I'd like to introduce you to the Social Compass. Inspired by the term *moral compass,* I created the Social Compass (again with the artistic talents of JESS3), to serve as our value system when defining our program activities (see Figure 21.1).

A compass is a device for determining orientation and serves as a true indicator of physical direction. The Social Compass points a brand in a physical and experiential direction to genuinely connect with customers, peers, and influencers, using emotional hooks.

No infographic is complete without further explanation, and while its design may be extraordinary, it means nothing if we don't understand how to use it. When we listen and hear what's taking place in the conversational ecosystem, the compass works from the outside in, moving from the edge to the center. When we engage, we move from the center to the outside edge.

➤ The Brand

At the center of the compass is the brand; essentially, everything you do will revolve around it.

➤ The Players

Fundamental to any program, the players define how, when, why, and to what extent our activity is intermediated across the Social Web. They include:

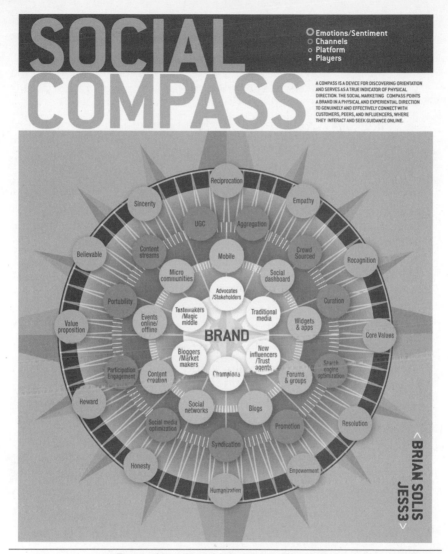

Figure 21.1   Social Marketing Compass

Source: Brian Solis and Jesse Thomas (http://Jess3.com).

➤   *Advocates and stakeholders:* Those individuals who maintain a stake in the brand and the success of the company, through emotional, strategic, or financial investment—and are usually among the first line of external champions.

➤ *Traditional media:* Reporters, journalists, analysts, and other forms of mainstream and vertical media who already reach our intended audiences.

➤ *New influencers and trust agents:* Individuals who focus a noteworthy portion of their updates, content, and voice on particular topics, industries, or markets.

➤ *Champions:* Whereas advocates and stakeholders have skin in the game to some extent, champions are merely inspired to share their experiences and views because they are passionate, compelled, or incentivized.

➤ *Bloggers and market makers:* Bloggers and market makers represent what some refer to as the *A-list*. This elite group can steer, shape, and galvanize activity that moves markets on the basis of their views.

➤ *Tastemakers and the magic middle:* Tastemakers and the magic middle are distinct from new influencers and trust agents, and, depending on the industry, serve as a subset of them. In their own way, they make markets and spark trends based on their activity. Tastemakers are the trendsetters and, in the Social Web, they usually boast notable followers and connections that emulate their behavior, whether it's explicit or implicit, on behalf of the tastemaker. The term *magic middle* was coined by David Sifry,[1] who at the time was CEO of Technorati, the world's largest blog network; he defined this group as bloggers who maintained an inbound link volume of between 20 and 1,000 links.

Now, I refer to the magic middle as any group of content creators who remain focused on a topic and have earned a substantial audience because of their experiences, views, and perspective.

➤ Platform

Every initiative, inclusive of those groups of individuals who define our markets and ensuing behavior, requires a platform upon which to connect, communicate, and congregate. These platforms represent existing and also emerging categories that are worthy of our attention today and tomorrow.

➤ *Mobile:* Any network that unites groups of targeted individuals through interaction on mobile devices.

➤ *Social dashboard, or microsites:* As discussed previously, social dashboards and microsites aggregate distributed social presences into one experience for channeling activity, providing information, fostering community, and guiding perception and impressions.

➤ *Widgets and applications:* Widgets and applications are portable services that spark interaction in a variety of networks, from mobile devices to Web-based social networks. They create an immersive experience designed to perform a dedicated function, including tasks, games, interaction, learning, and other forms of entertainment and engagement within a dedicated, embeddable environment, while branding or conveying messages in the process.

➤ *Forums and groups:* Web 1.0 still rules, and through research we learn that communication and influence is still widespread in forums and groups where people not only communicate with one another every day, they also organize events, manage projects, and teach and learn from one another on almost every topic imaginable and unimaginable.

➤ *Blogs:* Web-based blogs, in all of their shapes and sizes, deserve a tremendous amount of attention, as they are still among the most active and influential news sources besides traditional media. Not only do they hit mainstream audiences, they also focus on dedicated, vertical communities and nicheworks that equally contribute to your total market.

➤ *Social networks:* Of course social networks are a primary forum for today's social media interactions and therefore require a dedicated focus. As we've repeated so often in these pages, our attention is necessitated in popular networks as well as the nicheworks dedicated to our areas of interest.

➤ *Content creation:* The development and syndication of social objects carries the ability to reach people in almost every medium today, and will only continue to expand as technology advances. We are now in the content publishing and distribution business.

➤ *Events (offline and online):* The cultivation of communities is important online and also in the physical locales where we meet our customers, advocates, peers, and influencers. A fusion between online and offline communication is critical, and therefore mandatory.

➤ *Microcommunities:* While many refer to these services as microblogs, the truth is that they are not in any way, shape, or form reminiscent of blogs, nor is the behavior that they stimulate. We focus on them as dedicated platforms because of their unique interactions, communities, efficacy, and reach.

➤ **Emotions**

The socialization of the Web is powered by people, and it is a movement that is bound by the same natural laws that govern human behavior. Successful branding is made possible when individuals can establish a human and emotional connection. In social networks, the brand is represented by *you* and, for that reason, we must factor compassion, care, and feeling into our planning. Connect from the heart.

➤ *Reciprocation:* The gesture of a response is far more powerful than we perceive. It is the act of paying a good deed forward that actually contributes to the caliber, quality, and value of dialogue and interchanges. As influence is both democratized and equalized, giving back is a symbol of respect and gratitude.

➤ *Empathy:* Understanding the sentiment of another related to material interaction and experiences humanizes the context of an experience and conversation. You must *become* the very people you're trying to reach and to best do so, our understanding must extend beyond training, and embrace real-life exposure.

➤ *Recognition:* Identifying the contributions of others and promoting or responding to worthy individuals and instances are parts of how we cultivate communities and build relationships. From "thank you" to "I'm sorry," the symbolic deeds of acknowledgment, admittance, and identification serve as powerful forms of validation.

➤ *Core values:* The attributes that define the principles and standards of a brand are reinforced or diminished by its conduct. If we wish to attract influential peers, we must stand for something with which people can identify and associate. We must represent purpose. Our brand and our actions either encourage affinity or they don't.

➤ *Resolution:* The practice of solving problems, disputes, and other correlated issues is a focus and a mission that contribute to those actions that indeed speak louder than words. And if we're to be measured by them, then let our commitment to resolve impediments speak for itself.

➤ *Empowerment:* Providing the authority to achieve something not possible before the encounter instills confidence and advocacy and sets the foundation to scale community development. Empowerment alters the balance of engagement and transforms interactions into relationships.

➤ *Humanization:* Convey and embody a human voice and character in all we do in interactive media. From the creation and distribution of social objects to engagement with individuals, engagement is most effective when we personalize our approach. The Social Web is alive and powered by our ability to identify with others through direct interaction or by coming into contact with their personas, as attached to the content they interact with, share, or produce.

➤ *Honesty:* Be honest and virtuous in all interactions and not misleading whatsoever in any scenario so as to achieve your objective. Be truthful. If you don't have an answer or information, say so. If what you represent doesn't measure up in a particular setting, admit it. Focus on strengths and opportunities. Do not spin or market messages.

➤ *Reward:* Sometimes recognition isn't enough to satisfy someone for their contribution. The act of rewarding someone is a sign of appreciation. Rewards can span from monetary items to discounts to free products to access and special privileges. The consistent performance of rewarding community behavior fosters increased activity through positive conditioning.

➤ *Value proposition:* When humanizing our stories and interactions, it is the value proposition that speaks directly to specific markets. Many times marketing either attempts to generalize features or capabilities for the masses or simply reiterates the value propositions as dictated by internal management.

➤ *Be believable:* Words such as *transparency* and *authenticity* are overused in any discussion related to socialized outreach and therefore lose a good deal of their essence and meaning. It is more convincing and consequential in any encounter if you are *believable*. This can be passionate, exuberant, and contagious, unlike transparency or authenticity. Give me something to believe in.

➤ *Sincerity:* Your biggest objective moving forward is to earn and continue to gain trust. To do so, your actions must exclude pretense, and instead enrich interactions through the exchange of genuine feelings and intentions.

■ CREATING A PLAN: DEFINING THE FUTURE, NOW

To quote personal time management author and expert Alan Lakein, "Planning is bringing the future into the present so that you can do something about it now."

This may come as a shock, but a standard does not exist for drafting and implementing a targeted social media plan—and for good reason. Its content is unique to your brand, and therefore its documentation and output are also distinct. This section will offer the framework, but will require your perspective and insight to complete the design.

So far, we have assembled the content for this plan with most of the needed items residing in the data collection process that is used to listen and quantify the Conversation Index.

➤ Volume
➤ Relevant networks
➤ Sentiments
➤ Perceptions
➤ Reach
➤ Divisions currently affected
➤ Share of voice
➤ Themes or trends
➤ The state of social affairs
  ➤ Current accounts and activity
  ➤ Competitive intelligence

Now we need to place that relevant information into a plan of action. This sample template for defining marketing plans has been amended to serve our purposes. This example is intended to put into action our recommended programs, based on the strategies that match existing market behavior. Regardless of the size of the organization, this plan is designed to serve at the brand level. Dedicated social media programs will also require specific plans at the program and departmental levels.

■ SOCIAL MEDIA PLAN OUTLINE[2]

OUTLINE

I. Executive Summary

This is where we make our case. By providing a tight, organized, and high-level summary of intentions, tactics, and metrics supported by observations and analysis, we officially begin the process of gathering support.

The executive summary sets the stage through the documentation and communication of our research, insights, and discoveries, and the recommendations inspired by the very people we wish to reach.

II. Purpose

Based on the exercises performed through the Conversation Prism, the Conversation Index, the Brand and Personality Identity Cycle, the Social Audit, and the review of the Social Marketing Compass, we must distill our sense of purpose so that it resonates with our team. It deserves a spotlight here because it places the rest of the plan in context.

III. The Challenge and Opportunity

This section is used to communicate the specific challenges associated with engagement, based on existing data so as to set expectations and establish a frame of reference. No challenge is complete without also identifying and communicating the opportunities discovered in our studies.

IV. Relevant Networks

Include your findings from the listening exercises that stipulate which networks the company needs to pursue and why. Include data here as it justifies the rest of the plan.

V. Situation Analysis

Company Analysis
➤ Goals

➤ Mission

➤ Core values

➤ Culture

➤ Strengths

➤ Weaknesses

➤ Relevant networks (The Conversation Prism)

➤ Current activity and sentiment (Conversation Index)

➤ Share of voice (Conversation Index)

➤ The state of our digital footprint (Social Audit)

Competitor Analysis
➤ Market position

➤ Strengths

➤ Weaknesses
➤ Current activities and sentiment
➤ Digital footprint
➤ Share of voice

Divisions and Business Units Affected by Existing Conversations
➤ Service, marketing, product development, public relations, and so on.

Brand Personality
➤ Include brand attributes as related specifically to this program.

VI. Market Segmentation

Customer Analysis
➤ Types, or segments

Segment 1
➤ Description
➤ Challenges
➤ Value drivers
➤ Social networks and communities of interest
➤ Influential blogs
➤ Decision process
➤ Perception
➤ Sentiment

VII. Review the 5 Ps of the Social Marketing Mix

Based on the 4 Ps associated with the typical marketing mix (product, price, place, and promotion),[3] we can adapt these principles to our social marketing mix to document and communicate our assessment and corresponding strategy for each relevant network and recommended program.

➤ *People:* Who are we trying to reach, why, and to what extent? What is the desirable outcome based on our engagement and what is it that they're seeking or missing today?

➤ *Place (distribution):* Highlight the relevant networks and communities for participation or distribution of social objects or both.

➤ *Participation:* Refers to the social object, network, or engagement strategy you recommend, by network.

➤ *Purpose:* Much more than the goal for each program, purpose aligns the corresponding cause, value, and intent we bring to the conversation in each case.

➤ *Promotion:* Discuss how you will specifically promote each program within and around each network and object. Also communicate the logistics and budget required for each program.

VIII. A Click to Action

All plans should include desirable outcomes and defined experiences. State the goal of the program and work backward from there. Doing so allows you to integrate the click paths necessary that lead people, regardless of the source network, to a destination to convert clicks to outcomes. This is where we introduce milestones to measure in the form of KPIs.

IX. Strategies by Network, Community, and Blog Categories

Each relevant network will require a specialized strategy and approach based on our fieldwork. Demonstrate the plan for each network.

Network A
➤ Recommended activities
➤ Culture or social climate
➤ Social objects necessary
➤ Production schedule
➤ Time frame
➤ Resources required
➤ Roles and responsibilities
➤ Budget
➤ Goals and activity projections

Network B
➤ Same as Network A

Blog Group A
➤ Recommended storylines and engagement strategies
➤ Timeframe
➤ Resources and supporting information and content required

➤ Budget
➤ Goals and projections

Blog Group B
➤ Same as Blog Group A

X. Conclusion

This is where you can share realistic and creative ideas that get decision makers thinking about the possibilities and potential that emerging social media now holds, as supported by your diligent analysis and as presented through your creative and informed perspective. Use this section to also provide recommendations on the next steps for improving the social facade in general, as well as suggestions for business units not yet specifically included in this plan.

Remember this, however: with new ideas, new politics and dynamics unravel. You are essentially a change agent helping to solidify the company's ability to compete now and in the future. In the future, those around you will realize the latent advantages for not only the business, but for their individual careers. Stay strong and unswerving. This is your work.

As my good friend Hugh MacLeod says in his book, *Ignore Everybody,* "Good ideas alter the power balance in relationships. That is why good ideas are initially resisted."[4]

Once your idea garners acceptance and velocity, you will find yourself surrounded by supporters and back channel detractors. But make no mistake: It's because your ideas are substantial.

As we learn through success and failure, our nascent acceptance of champions and their creativity enable us to compete for the future and surpass those companies that don't.

■ NOTES

1. David Sifry, "State of the Blogosphere, February 2006, Part 2: Beyond Search," Sifry's Alerts (February 13, 2006), www.sifry.com/alerts/archives/000420.html.
2. "Marketing Plan Outline," Quick MBA, www.quickmba.com/marketing/plan/.
3. William D. Perreault and E. Jerome McCarthy, *Basic Marketing* 14th ed. (New York: McGraw-Hill/Irwin, 2003).
4. Hugh MacLeod, *Ignore Everybody* (New York: Penguin Group, 2009).

Facebook Is Your Home Page for the Social Web

Facebook is, at the moment, the most important social network in the world. Over 600 million people connect to one another in what would be the third-largest country in the world if it were a country. And, with the introduction of the Open Graph, we are interacting with our Facebook connections on our favorite websites where our social graph and the corresponding activity of likes, interaction, and commentary become the centerpiece for social curation and more importantly, our focused attention. We are putting our social network to work and we are learning how to share, discover, and collaborate in public.

Brands, regardless of size and focus, are converging on Facebook, where the idea of connecting with customers and prospects represents a potential boon for both earning relevance in a new domain as well as expanding overall reach. Facebook is a spark plug for word of mouth, and when engaged, contributes to the end of business as usual and the beginning of social commerce. In fact, the top 10 brands on Facebook today host more than 100 million likes there.

■ THE TOP 10 BRANDS BY POPULATION (ROUNDED OUT)

1. Starbucks—16 million
2. Coca-Cola—15 million
3. Oreo—12 million
4. Skittles—11.5 million
5. Red Bull—10.2 million
6. Victoria's Secret—8.4 million

7. Disney—8.3 million

8. Converse All Star—7.3 million

9. iTunes—7 million

10. Windows Live Messenger—6.8 million

Facebook and Twitter are unique in their design and their culture and each offer distinguishing opportunities for businesses. As such, they demand a dedicated focus, strategy, and approach.

Twitter is important and essential to learning, engaging, and cultivating customer communities. I believe that Twitter is your window to relevance, both understanding how to identify and to earn it.

Facebook, as both a network and a platform, is unlocking new and important connections between people, brands, content, and data. The technical and creative aspects of what Facebook is capable of facilitating on behalf of your business and the people who define your markets, requires indoctrination. And once we explore the culture and technical advantages of Facebook Connect, likes, and the scope and possibilities of the open graph, we get an idea of the deepening emphasis required to transform Facebook from a fan page to a bona fide brand page, creating nothing less than a social epicenter for business.

If Twitter is your window to relevance, Facebook is your focal point for the Social Web.

■ THE STATE OF THE FACEBOOK

With over 500 million active users, Facebook is by far one of the most important networks in the world. Fifty percent of those active users log on to Facebook in any given day. And in total, people spend more than 700 billion minutes per month posting, sharing, liking, commenting, poking, playing games, and interacting with one another as well as the content and applications that define the pervasive social ecosystem.

The average user is connected to 80 community pages, groups, and events and creates 90 pieces of content (social objects) each month. If you follow Zuckerberg's Law, then we will double the amount of content we share every year. When combined, the numbers are staggering. More than 30 billion social objects (web links, news stories, blog posts, notes, photo albums, and so forth) are shared each month. Facebook is a vortex for content.

Everyday individuals on Facebook maintain a social graph of 130 people, which is in line with Robin Dunbar's theory (Dunbar's number) of the maximum number of relationships we can effectively manage. However, with suggested friends, I believe that number will push us to expand our networks from relationships (strong ties) to relations (focused, weak, and temporary ties). I call this *Social Graph Theory*. And much like Zuckerberg's Law, social graph theory suggests that the size of our network will grow, but more importantly, become much more complex, yet focused. We will maintain relationships, but also expand into a thinner form of relations that include interest graphs, nicheworks (contextual networks) and temporary connections. What's important for businesses to realize is that individuals now maintain peer networks that resemble engaged audiences in which interests are the axis of conversational rotation.

Brands are increasingly globalizing and Facebook scales with the reach that they need. More than 70 translations are currently available and more than 70 percent of all Facebook denizens reside outside of the United States. And more than one million developers and entrepreneurs from more than 180 countries support Facebook as a platform with more than one million websites integrating Facebook sharing, liking, and visualized social graph features into content discovery and consumption. So what does that mean? Integrate Facebook functionality into your online properties (in addition to other relevant social presences, of course). Two-thirds of comScore's U.S. Top 100 websites and half of comScore's Global Top 100 websites have integrated with Facebook.

And what of mobile?

Smart phones are the new subtablet, so to speak. There are as many active users accessing Facebook on their mobile device as there are active users of Twitter. And that's a powerful statement. Today 150 million people access Facebook actively and they're twice as active on Facebook than nonmobile users.

■ IT'S NOT A FAN PAGE; IT'S A BRAND PAGE

Many brands underestimate Facebook and what's truly required to attract and captivate the social consumer. In my research, I find that a significant number of brands focus their efforts primarily on Twitter, treating Facebook as an afterthought. Rather than engage in each community with purpose and dedication, examples are abundant where companies are simply syndicating tweets to Facebook rather than updating each network individually. When people reply on Facebook, representatives are usually unaware, as they're mostly monitoring Twitter responses rather than Facebook. In these cases, Facebook becomes a graveyard for tweets instead of a community where likes are earned and conversations are fostered. After all, how do we expect to trigger the social effect without investing time and attention in the people who define the very social graphs we're hoping to engage and activate?

Facebook success is defined by our investment of time, resources, energy, and creativity. In other words, we get out of it what we put into it. In Facebook, it's not just about who we're connected to, it's about who we're not. What started as *fans* has evolved to likes and in that simple shift in phraseology comes something quite profound. Fans imply hierarchical relationships in which brands publish at will to a community that feels a bit more like a traditional audience. Likes beget a linear form of relationships through which we earn the endorsement of a social consumer, but to foster a community, we have to continue to do so. This introduces a peer-to-peer (P2P) dynamic in which rather than program our Facebook activity from a top-down perspective, we now have to consider an active participatory role in earning likes, attention, and hopefully advocacy much more frequently than we may have initially anticipated.

Success begins with a plan, which serves as a road map to reach customers and those who influence them. On the road to success, it is wise to refer to the map routinely to ensure that we stay on course. Doing so reminds us why we're here in the first place.

The roles of the social consumer are distinct and the reasons for connecting with a brand are equally diversified. It's our job to cater to each segment to earn their likes and attention now and over time.

Facebook is changing the way we think about business, customers and community and as such, there's much to learn. Everything begins at the beginning, and together, we will earn relevance and expand business opportunities in a new social marketplace one like at a time.

■ FROM E-COMMERCE TO F-COMMERCE

Mark Zuckerberg describes Facebook as a social utility that helps people communicate more efficiently with their friends, families, and co-workers. Indeed, Facebook is so much more than a social network. As a social utility, it changes the dynamics of relationships, how we communicate with one another, and how we discover, share, and learn. Facebook and social media are redesigning the information super-highway, forever altering how information travels and how people connect. The world is literally becoming a much smaller place and as a result, businesses are forced to compete for attention where it's focused. Otherwise, the concepts of digital darwinism and the need to engage or die most certainly become reality—out of sight, out of mind.

If Facebook is a social utility, then we can use it to engage, to foster a thriving community in which its denizens expect information to find them. The future of business is social and it's giving rise to a new genre of connected consumers, who are becoming influential in their own right.

As a platform, Facebook invites businesses to build a presence and design an engagement architecture that introduces a new opportunity to also grow in prominence and connections, thus defining, and socializing, the next chapter in business. A chapter in which commonplace terms such as *share, like, comment,* and *add* become the pillars for triggering a social tsunami of meaningful business touchpoints and outcomes.

It's not about simply having a presence, it's about fostering relationships with people and the varying contingents of consumerism they represent.

As such, Facebook brings to the life the need to integrate a fifth P into the marketing mix, People. And, with the rise of the social consumer, Facebook and social media in general, also introduce a new C into the Four Cs of community: Commerce.

While it may appear that we're progressing through the alphabet here, from E to F, Facebook represents an important platform to engage and activate the social consumer. F-commerce is the ability to execute transactions in Facebook without leaving the network or leveraging the open graph by integrating Facebook into traditional site-based e-commerce platforms. And more importantly, it ties each transaction to the social graph. With each exchange, an update is broadcast to the news feed of their contacts. This potentially sparks a social effect and may ultimately influence impressions and decisions over time.

Levi's, for example, introduced a Friends Store on its website that showcases the jeans that your friends have liked and also allows you to share the jeans you like. This introduces a peer-to-peer influence model through which we influence and are influenced by those we trust. Levi's is betting the denim that the more we interact within its Friends Store, the more people we will be introduced to it simply through our interaction. Doing so creates a bridge between the Web and Social Web, content and relationships, thus socializing the objects that move us.

The natural step for Levi's is to also recreate that experience within Facebook. With Facebook Tabs, the opportunity to create a Friends Store within Facebook exists now, as does the means to introduce a sophisticated, engaging, and fully functional storefront. There is debate as to why brands would willfully sacrifice traffic to its dot-com. In my experience, this comes down to the unique touchpoints that connect brands to traditional consumers and social consumers respectively. With the social consumer, attention comes at a premium and there are great advantages in capturing attention where and when it's focused.

1–800-Flowers.com hosts a shoplet within Facebook through which consumers can browse through arrangements and order without leaving Facebook.

Early in 2010, Procter & Gamble experimented with a storefront for Pantene, through which consumers could purchase products before they were introduced in stores. Not only did this approach integrate F-commerce into the social equation, it satisfied two of the top reasons consumers consistently report why they follow and like brands in social media: access to exclusive products and rewards or discounts as a benefit of the connection.

■ FACEBOOK TABS ARE THE NEW WEB PAGES

As in computing, hitting the keys ALT and TAB allows us to switch the windows we have open on the desktop. In Facebook, Tabs unlock Facebook's customization features. Whereas storefronts can take residence as a designated destination within the Facebook brand page, additional tabs can offer discrete engagement opportunities to appeal to the diverse roles of social consumers. Like traditional websites, tabs are the Social Web pages for dedicated experiences. And, not everything has to be related to marketing or promotions.

While we see many companies using tabs to increase likes through contests and promotions, the effect of tabs are limited only by vision, creativity, and execution. Most notably, each tab can assume the position of a landing page, which is intended to visualize the most current initiatives for each brand whether it's aimed at existing or new likes or both. This means tabs are assignable as landing pages, rather than sending people directly to The Wall, where specific content, stories, or programs are presented upon visiting the brand page.

The Facebook presence architected by Dunkin' Donuts is designed to serve a variety of business objectives. The current landing page is promoting the "Ultimate DD Coffee Fan Contest."

Just to the right of this tab, Dunkin' Donuts presents Marice, a creative application that brings an espresso bean to life and encourages you to customize messages to send to friends.

To encourage customer advocacy and loyalty, Dunkin' Donuts includes a landing page for its DDPerks program. Again, the experience is maintained within Facebook. This program can scale, should Dunkin' Donuts desire, to include an all-inclusive database that allows customers to access their Dunkin' Donuts' account in Facebook.

I should also note, that Dunkin' Donuts also uses the left side of the page to recognize its fan of the week. Spotlighting customers is among the most appreciated and effective social sparks that ignite beneficial sharing and conversations.

This is merely a small taste of what's possible with the structured customization Facebook supports. Perhaps one of the most understated aspects of tabs is that Facebook Markup Language supports website analytics code from major publishers. In my work, we often use Google Analytics to measure the activity of each page and how visitors interact and travel to and from the brand page.

■ MADISON AVE. IS MOVING TO CALIFORNIA AVE.

Contrary to popular opinion, Facebook ads do indeed work. In fact, when designed with relevance to specific social graphs and actively managed, Facebook ads perform extremely well. As in anything, there are best practices that one can follow, but in the end, it takes an intrinsic understanding of the people you're trying to reach and what compels them to click, understanding that in a network in which people are at the center of their own egosystem, personalization and incentives serve as pivotal social hooks. Remember, it's not about who likes you today, it's about reaching those individuals who represent tomorrow's likes. And, it's perpetual.

I'm currently running a diverse ad campaign for a client in which each of the pages on the brand page benefits from a series of ads designed to spark interest in designated content and experience inherent within each. For this program, we created a rotating campaign of 29 pieces of engaging creative that changes weekly or every other week—depending on performance. I might add that we are on a tight budget, so conversions are key to ensuring the longevity of the program. Thus, I monitor conversions not only from clicks to likes (C2L), but also conversions of likes to actions (L2A). Each page is intended to spur a unique action and is embedded in the experience. Using conversion science, we can change or enhance ads and each tab to improve performance.

Chapter 23

Divide and Conquer

Over the years, I've explored the drivers that propel businesses into the social world, analyzing their initial steps and planning and implementation processes, as well as how they assess and apply resources.

The most common motives to experiment with social media are spurred because of an internal champion or from a reaction-based set of circumstances that created a sense of urgency.

It's a moment characterized by "Ah-ha" or "Uh-oh. . . ."

■ SOCIAL MEDIA TAKES A COMMUNITY EFFORT

If we've learned anything in this book thus far, it's that any one person or group does not own the conversation; they simply map to them based on their nature and intent. In fact, your customers are among the most influential stakeholders present today, and without guidance or participation, they may aimlessly steer your brand in undesirable directions. The simple truth is that everyone owns socialized media, including *you*. Perhaps it's better said this way: The conversation is omnipresent and not defined, steered, or controlled by any one entity. We are merely participants in a greater production. We determine our role as an engaged organization as well as individuals in cooperation with the powers that be.

Truthfully, many departments will be forced to socialize, and therefore require social programs at the departmental level to be executed at the departmental level and perhaps managed by a centralized group that most likely oversees other areas of branding, marketing, or communications simultaneously.

In the meantime, without organization, unity, and direction, the risk and likelihood for social anarchy prevails. If we pay close attention, we don't need to look far to observe and pinpoint the disjointed efforts of even the best brands engaging online and the discontinuity and fragmentation in their use of social networks and participatory programs that seem only to muddle and dilute branding efforts and the state of existing equity and resonance.

■ DECENTRALIZATION AND CENTRALIZATION: ASSEMBLING AND CONDUCTING AN ORCHESTRA

Many of the cases that I'm reviewing these days demonstrate either a decentralized or centralized approach to social media. To give us clarity into the process of organizing teams and established hierarchy, think about an interactive media program as an orchestra. There are few, several, or many musicians who comprise an ensemble, representing a variety of different instruments arranged to perform particular pieces as designed.

Decentralized media is either intentional or simply the victim of an overambitious company tackling social media across the organization, without a hub or gravity. Using the orchestra analogy, this is less representative of a unified, structured group and more similar to a group of jazz improvisers. In some cases, the free flow and unscripted jam of these musicians fuses to create something truly incredible. They can riff on their own and come back to music without losing the flow. But in other cases, listeners are lost in the disarray and lack of structure of the music and the competing soloists. In jazz, however, musicians are usually virtuosos in their own right, in contrast to those new to social media. For the time being, very few are truly maestros.

Harmonious social media programs are the result of organization, rehearsal, and arrangement, and inspired by talent, leadership, and imagination. These groups are directed by an individual or team that coordinates the roles and contributions of those involved. Someone must assemble the players, synchronize their positions, and guide the flow of the production. It's the only way to strategically score and present an integrated performance. And each player is selected because they've proved their merit. Simply said, they have earned the right to represent the brand.

Even though the doctrines guiding the evolution of the Social Web profess democratization, within a business it's impossible to scale and perform harmoniously without instruction and administration. What's constant, however, is that without the establishment of structure from the onset, it's impossible to reel in existing efforts to redesign the social architecture or launch a Day Zero program.

■ THE SOCIETY AND CULTURE OF BUSINESS

The true value of a more socially aware mindset can positively affect every department within an organization to create a team that together nurtures a respected and trusted brand.

Our presence is requested in more than one channel and in more than one capacity.

Where new and emerging media is permeating the existing corporate culture, the behavior and culture of the workforce is also disrupted. Aside from the usual politics, lobbying, ambition, and ambivalence, the socialization of existing processes and systems is inevitable. However, the role of the workforce in its introduction, adoption, and success is crucial. Consequently, we must account for the human factor in anything we do while moving forward. It is they who will lead us into the future.

■ MEETING OF THE MINDS: CONSENSUS AD IDEM

The creation of a New Media Board of Advisors can help steer the evolution of change within the organization. This body is designed to help foster collaboration and cooperation, advise decision makers, and manage the division of labor.

The socialization of every department will lend support and direction to myriad important conversations taking place, currently without you, across the Web. Having representation from each is critical to organization, buy-in, and practice.

The Board of Advisors should be structured as any standard board used to advise businesses to help make critical decisions that have positive impacts on the bottom line.

The anatomy of the board should include the following representatives (where applicable):

- ➤ Legal
- ➤ Finance
- ➤ Product
- ➤ Service
- ➤ Marketing
- ➤ Communications
- ➤ Executive management (VP level or higher)
- ➤ Sales

➤ HR
➤ Web
➤ IT
➤ Research
➤ Interactive
➤ Advertising and branding
➤ Community manager

The list should also include any individual or individuals who are passionate about social media, either personally or professionally, to a certain extent. While their expertise may or may not add value to strategic discussions and calculations, their experience is invaluable and their energy is transmissible. We can all learn from one another.

■ OUTSIDE THE INSIDE: ESTABLISHING AN INSIDER PROGRAM

Internal advisors are instrumental in the definition of programming and also in the establishment of protocol. This specialized board also assists in the solidification of a chain of command required for the design, management, and execution of all things social. Once a program is in the process of creation or refinement, an outside point of view is helpful. In addition to the creation of an internal board of new media advisors, I also recommend either the addition of strategic partners to the team. The formation of an insider program counsels the team on ideas, activities, and performance. This program can either incentivize or reward its members through pay or products or services, or simply for credit and recognition.

For example, Intel Corporation inaugurated a group known as the Intel Insiders (now known as the Intel Advisors), of which I am an alumnus advisor. The advisory offers guidance on the company's new media events, initiatives, and objectives. Other board members include Tom Foremski, Frank Gruber, iJustine (Justine Ezarik), Cathy Brooks, Sarah Austin, and J. D. Lasica. We were specifically tasked with reviewing new product and program initiatives to offer input and suggestions before or following their introduction. I also was involved with the review and planning for the company's use of Twitter under the @Intel moniker. This advisory board has been in place for more than three years and its members serve voluntarily, without compensation. However, Intel is a household brand and a global brand, and therefore, association offers value for all involved. When reviewing smaller or emerging brands and businesses, insiders or outside advisors have been compensated with shares or a stake in the company, a percentage of revenues, with gifts or products, and or simply appreciation and recognition.

An insider program should feature the perspective of those who can affect perception, reach, and velocity, or those who are directly or indirectly affected by the actions of the company or its competition:

- ➤ Market partner
- ➤ Customer
- ➤ Investor
- ➤ Influencers, enthusiasts, and advocates
- ➤ Industry expert
- ➤ Delegates from any relevant external agencies

■ EXAMPLE: NEW MEDIA BOARD OF ADVISORS

➤ Governance

The role of a new media board of advisors offers value beyond its creativity, innovation, and resource and content management. The board regulates the strategy and activity from the creation of accounts and profiles, assigning responsibilities, and establishing conversational workflow and response processes (see Figure 23.1).

The board's strength lies in its ability to not only contribute to or define guidelines and policies, but to also enforce them when necessary.

For the board of advisors to run seamlessly, members would act wisely to elect an individual as its chairperson to oversee interaction, communicate status to executives, and also communicate direction back to the team, as well as to ensure productive collaboration. While much of this activity is brand new, and the rules are just now catching up to internal transformation. Sovereignty and jurisdiction is vital in these initial phases. I suppose that's the true essence of new media. It's always new. . . .

In the long term, though, as the company learns and adapts to emerging media, the board may no longer be necessary or of any consequence. Eventually, the teams persevere and master the art and science of new media and the corresponding methodologies. Eventually, everything folds back into the grind, or routine, however you may view it. For now, however, we have much to learn, and we're doing so, together.

Figure 23.1 New Media Board of Advisors

➤ The Mission

The charter of the new media board of advisors is to establish inbound and outbound processes and management protocol, answer questions, encourage inventiveness, educate, and assemble the teams responsible for engagement. Without a mission, we are bound to very little. And in this case, anarchy is not represented in the form of an overdue insurrection or revolution due to oppression. It is representative of the chaos of misdirected, competing, and potentially brand-damaging social networking and content creation.

We need a democratic parliament to act on behalf of the people in our markets and the people within our organization. Namely, the mission of the social board of advisors (sBoA) is to distinguish between hype and resolution or, as referred to in the geek world, shiny-object syndrome versus real-world applications. With the right team, the whole is better than the sum of its parts; hence, the first act of this governing body is to establish its mission.

The constitution of the sBoA is hereunder relegated to:

➤ Establishing guidelines and policies

➤ Auditing and documenting the state of the brand in the social realm

➤ Passing through an initial round of the Conversation Prism to establish a beta version of the Conversation Index

➤ Documenting the new media style guide

➤ Customizing and applying the principles and ethics of the Social Compass

➤ Overseeing and guiding content production and management

➤ Organizing the effort to discover and define the personality of the brand as well as the associated personal brands of those who represent it

➤ Ensuring that online and representative brands and associated personalities are in alignment

➤ Evaluating competitive and market behavior

➤ Constructing and introducing social architecture and workflow

➤ Identifying and recognizing capable and worthy representatives internally before scouting outside the fold, so as to assemble the most capable and exemplary teams

➤ Ensuring that resources are collaborating and performing as intended

➤ Maintaining a standard of education to ensure that all who are involved progress and develop over time

➤ Establishing metrics and key performance indicators

➤ Assembling a New Media Task Force

The board will help guide us, using our Social Compass in addition to the established guidelines and policies that serve as the foundation for everything we do moving forward.

The initial challenges are both similar and unique to each organization. Size, shape, and state of affairs determine where many begin and who joins the fray. Small businesses, for example, will have owners or employees or both who wear multiple hats so they can build a framework and engage. Larger organizations will have to recruit and progress at a pace that is compatible with their cultures and infrastructures.

What remains constant is the need for structure, organization, and thoughtful execution.

The task force works in concert with the board, but is unique in its mission. In my experience, the board is clear in its structure and goals, but it's not necessarily adept in the execution area of new media. Ideas and objectives aside, a specialized task force is also necessary to help transform corresponding strategies into functional reality across the organization.

Within every business, at least one person or persons emerge as either definitive champions or resident specialists. If this doesn't occur, hire a qualified individual immediately. This person or individuals will serve as the leaders of this new team (and, yes, I'm officially recommending that you add a new role and team to the organizational chart) and will serve as an internal new media agency, while the organization itself adapts to outside influences so it can better contribute to its direction in the market.

➤ Organizational Transformation: Redesigning the New Marketing Landscape

During these crucial stages in the organizational transformation process, an internal expert can provide direction, and in some cases support, to help each division begin the process of socialization or refresh its current approach, according to a logical and useful method.

Figure 23.2 illustrates this new media infrastructure. It is a representation of the realignment of organizational and resource structures that I have successfully architected and implemented within many companies. In this case, I spotlight a model used within a particular Fortune 500 business.

■ EXAMPLE: INTERNAL TASK FORCE

At the center of the chart is the brand. The board of new media advisors advises the brand and, in turn, feeds the business units and corporate teams dedicated to marketing, Web, communications, and service. Those divisions can then tap the internal wisdom of the internal new media task force for help as needed. The task force thus retains a team of experts and mavens either on staff or through consultant relationships. Note the areas of expertise and resources that could benefit the new media agency, such as digital librarians, architects and engineers, anthropologists, cartographers, and

Figure 23.2　Workflow Evolved

ethnographers (new roles and responsibilities are highlighted later in the chapter).

In this diagram, the community manager reports to the marketing function, providing the general team with information, data, and advice related to the corporate brand. Each business unit assigns a team member to the task of community management as it relates to their specific areas of focus to engage at the product or service level. This member would interact with the brand community manager to ensure collaboration and support. The project-level community manager may also serve another, specified role, such as project or product management, content creation, and so forth, and provide project community management support as needed or in a part-time capacity.

For example, if the public relations staff needs help identifying and mapping new influencers, the task force can help through direction, education, or execution. When the marketing team needs to reach trust agents or tastemakers through a direct marketing or sponsored tweeting initiative on Twitter, the resident experts will have access to best practices, partners, and most likely an idea of who these tastemakers are and where they communicate.

■ EXAMPLE: ORGANIZATIONAL TRANSFORMATION

In this example (see Figure 23.3), we visualize the new organizational landscape as it integrates the role of new media experts into the hierarchy of business processes. While off to the side in the image, the social media management function and its supporting resources serve as a central facility to provide cross-functional direction, support, and knowledge to all teams and divisions with a role tied to any outward or inward interaction through new media channels.

While the group reports to a high-level corporate function or the new media board of advisors or both, it is designed to serve almost every applicable division and discipline.

The social media agency maintains day-to-day responsibility for many core functions and is empowered to serve and also police its peers within the organization:

➤ Conversational alerts, channeled to the affected person or team

➤ Counsel on specific programs and initiatives specific to each unit or division

➤ Ongoing advice and best practices

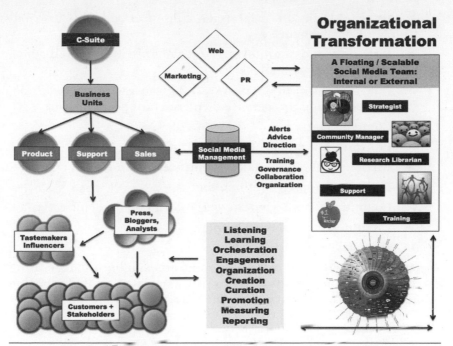

Figure 23.3   New Marketing Organizational Transformation

➤   Contributed content, personnel, and programming to the internal educational program

➤   Listening at the corporate level and assigning actions based on proactive or reactive scenarios

➤   The documentation of best practices

➤   Training based on specific initiatives

➤   Execution on behalf of business units and teams when applicable and necessary

➤   The creation of specialized teams around programs or the facilitation of external resources to help where appropriate

➤   Assessment of resources and associated costs per campaign

➤   The ability to identify influential communities and influencers

➤   The state and sentiment of the brand and competitors within the Social Web

➤   The culture of primary communities and the opportunities for immersion

➤   Trends

➤ Internal audits on social usage, content production, distribution, and engagement

➤ Listening and monitoring and documenting—intelligence gathering and trend analysis

➤ Engagement in the networks and groups within which relevant conversations are pervasive and warrant participation

➤ Content creation

➤ Conversation management and trafficking

➤ Influencer and tastemaker identification and networking

➤ Product and service refinement

➤ Community management, empowerment, and cultivation

➤ Event hosting and franchising

➤ Story development

➤ Humanizing company and product messaging and redefining the online journey and experience associated with the online presences associated with specific brands and products.

■ NEW ROLES AND RESPONSIBILITIES IN THE ERA OF EMERGING MEDIA

In February of 2006, Intel announced that it was in the process of hiring more than 100 anthropologists and other social scientists to work alongside its engineers.[1] Intel believes that to humanize its company, it must humanize its products. So much so, that the company placed three anthropologists as managers in business units: Eric Dishman in Digital Health, Genevieve Bell in Digital Home, and Tony Salvador in Emerging Markets. Pat Gelsinger, a senior vice president at Intel, in an interview with MIT's *Technology Review* magazine emphasized the impact of these new scientists having influence in more than just tactical product development: They're also playing a key role in long-term strategic planning.[2]

Nokia has also integrated the role of social sciences into its research and design. The company hired Jan Chipchase[3] to observe and understand how mobile design fits in to and affects lives, societies, and cultures.[4] In an interview with *New Scientist,* Chipchase shared insight into his mobile research in the emerging and rural markets around the globe: "We do research in such communities because these are the places in which we can best learn about the kinds of mobile use that will become mainstream in other parts of the world. We find these communities to be incredibly innovative in the way they use their mobile phones."[5] It's more than humanizing products. Social science can also humanize business processes to activate the fifth P. The following are other roles that social science can play, in which they will affect and benefit everything from marketing communications and public relations to product development and service programs to advertising and sales to company culture and management behavior.[6]

➤ *Content producers:* As brands become media companies in their creation of social objects, this role creates all necessary social content, including videos, images, Web pages, blog posts, policies and guidelines, tweets, wikis, comments, online experiences, profiles, and so forth. In many cases, connectors and industry experts and strategists wear this hat and assign the creation of important content to either content producers or other members on the team with direct experience, or simply produce it themselves.

➤ *Digital sociologists:* Observes the cultures, trends, and behaviors associated with communities, networks, and forums, and compares the interactivity around keywords and brands to contribute to engagement strategies, customer service policies, and improvements and product modifications.

➤ *Digital ethnographers:* Ethnography is the branch of anthropology that deals with the scientific description of specific human cultures. For those projects within which a deep study of online culture and communities is critical, an ethnographer is ideal for documenting a descriptive study of a particular human society.

➤ *Research librarians:* Complements or augments in-house or contract sociologists by analyzing relevant keywords used by customers, listening to and documenting conversations by content and sentiment, charting volume and frequency within social networks, identifying and analyzing true influencers and tastemakers across media, blogs, and social communities, and presenting data and charts for analysis by strategists.

➤ *Community managers:* Listens to conversations in social networks, forums, and the blogosphere documented by research librarians or through their own process; assigns relevant dialogue to appropriate team leads; manages the workflow and response status; and in most cases is the first line of response.

➤ *Digital or social architects:* Digital or social architects are responsible for building the online bridges between the company brand and consumers through widgets, sites, online dashboards, blogs, social newsrooms, social media releases, wikis, social networks, fan pages, forums, groups, and any other application, platform, or group responsible for hosting content, conversations, and interactivity.

➤ *Social engineers:* Engineering can create the roads and highways that connect a brand to its audiences and communities. Engineers can also observe behavior and trends within communities to better inspire new product designs, programs, and corporate initiatives to align more closely with the needs and desires of its consumers.

➤ *Connectors:* Informed individuals and teams that can connect stories to influencers and inspire activity, direction, and conversations. Connectors act based on intelligence, empathy, sincerity, and the ability to truly bridge a story to someone else in a way that's specific and compelling to them as an individual and also as it relates to their audience and social graph.

➤ *Industry experts and strategists:* Someone has to act as the conductor to this all-star orchestra. Qualified individuals have mastered the art and science of attaching new and traditional media to the bottom line of their business and also possess a deep understanding of and experiences with customer empathy, market trends, and the governing technology that connects the people within desired market places.

➤ *Cartographers:* Those responsible for visually mapping relationships, linking patterns and influences in social maps of relevance (through the Conversation Prism) and interaction, among other ties.

These new job functions create a new level of services that complement existing, traditional, and emerging corporate activities. The opportunities are limited only by the imagination of those responsible for engendering change from within.

■ NOTES

1. Michael Fitzgerald, "Intel's Hiring Spree," *Technology Review* (February 14, 2006), www.technologyreview.com/InfoTech/wtr_16340,294,p1.html.
2. Ibid.
3. See www.janchipchase.com/.
4. "Meet the Mobile Anthropologist," *Nokia Conversations* (July 2, 2008), www .conversations.nokia.com/2008/07/02/meet-the-mobile-anthropologist/.

5. Jason Palmer, "Interview: The Cellphone Anthropologist," *New Scientist* (June 11, 2008), www.newscientist.com/article/mg19826602.000-interview-the-cellphone-anthropologist.html.

6. Brian Solis, "The State of PR, Marketing, and Communications: You Are the Future," PR 2.0 (June 8, 2009), www.briansolis.com/2009/06/state-of-pr-marketing-and/.

Chapter 24

A Tale of Two Cities

■ WEB 2.0 AND THE EVOLUTION OF CRM 2.0

As in Charles Dickens's novel, *A Tale of Two Cities,* this chapter is set amidst a revolution that depicts the quandary facing individuals who stand for something more significant than the status quo. While not as dramatic or profound as the experiences depicted in Dickens's book, a tale of two cities exists between the current state of affairs in customer relationship management and the idea of what relationships should symbolize for today's businesses amidst this social mutiny.

The foundation for CRM, customer relationship management, was set in the 1980s and was traditionally viewed as the technology and doctrines governing marketing automation, sales automation, and customer service.

As Web 2.0 gave rise to a genre of social computing and collaboration, the enterprise infrastructure, business paradigm, value chain, and workflow were forever transformed. Processes and methodologies were suddenly placed under the microscope finding the search for new opportunities for efficiencies and innovation, and thus Web 2.0 spawned an era of Enterprise 2.0. In the process, CRM experienced a renaissance and was ripe for a new name to reflect the impact of Enterprise 2.0 and Web 2.0 on customer management. While many suggestions were introduced, this new generation of CRM was captured most effectively as CRM 2.0. Led by Paul Greenberg (author of the best-selling book *CRM at the Speed of Light*), Axel Schultze, Christopher Carfi, Mei Lin Fun, Brent Leary, and Andrew Boyd, among others, CRM 2.0 would rise alongside Enterprise 2.0, reaching its apex in innovation and visibility in 2007 and 2008.[1]

But while CRM 2.0 was gaining support, social media was rewriting the playbook for customer influence and interaction.

Social media emerged in parallel as a sprawling ecosystem for breeding influence among customers and set the stage for something more significant than CRM 2.0.

While CRM defined an era and captured the processes, systems, and ideologies that promoted streamlined relationship management, CRM in and of itself didn't imply social interaction or internal adaptation. And although CRM 2.0 was rooted in thoughtful intentions and efforts, its lifespan was finite.

It just didn't meet the demands and ongoing requirements of a more socially aware society of influencers.

Starting in 2007 and 2008, Social CRM gathered momentum. Brent Leary,[2] Paul Greenberg, Filiberto Selvas,[3] Ross Mayfield,[4] Jeremiah Owyang,[5] and I,[6] along with among many others, rallied support for a more social form of customer relationship management.

In July 2009, Paul Greenberg officially shifted focus from CRM 2.0 to Social CRM in his post, "Time to Put a Stake in the Ground on Social CRM":[7]

> *The debate and discussion about what defines Social CRM, aka CRM 2.0, vs. its traditional parent has been going on for about 2 years pretty regularly, and started, according to thought leader Graham Hill, almost a decade before that.*
>
> *Personally, I'm done defining it and am moving on. I think enough time has been spent trying to decide what we're calling it and what it is. I think that we've reached the point that though there is no one point of view, there is a general idea of what we have. So this post, which will be on ZDNET and PGreenblog is my stake in the ground for the definition of Social CRM.*

The focus was now on socializing the infrastructure of CRM. Thus Social CRM (sCRM) focused on creating an infrastructure that recognized the value and input of customers and the systems and processes required to connect with them now and over time. sCRM also introduced new feedback loops to process outside intelligence.

sCRM represents a shift from managing customers to listening to and engaging with them across the organization. It includes:

- ➤ Methodologies
- ➤ Business strategy
- ➤ Technology platforms
- ➤ Collaboration, internally and externally
- ➤ Conversation
- ➤ Human interaction
- ➤ Human culture
- ➤ Customer

➤ Experience
➤ Influence
➤ Relationships

Social CRM reflects the maxim of social democracy and forged a decree that crowdsourced governing principles and innovation. It helps companies take heed and adapt to the will and influence of its peers and customers through public forums and networks.

The customer is now recognized as the social consumer.

The shift in the outward focus and inward adaptation of organizations that recognize the power and extent of online conversations will soon discover that the C in sCRM slowly disappears.

■ TWITTER AND SOCIAL NETWORKS USHER IN A NEW ERA OF RELATIONSHIPS

My foray into the Social Web and D2C (direct to customer) engagement as a complement to traditional media harkens back to the early days of bulletin boards, which would later evolve into communities such as Yahoo! Groups and, ultimately, social networks. I also paid great attention to the early era of websites created by HTML-savvy enthusiasts who shared news, thoughts, rants, and observations related to their passions and interests. These influential sites would serve as the precursor to blogs.

But here we are, many years later, and mainstream brands are finally starting to pay attention. We're waking up to a new world of opportunity that changes nothing less than how, what, where, to what extent, and with whom we communicate.

The Internet was the harbinger for individuals to establish authority and control and the Social Web would forever transform business dynamics.

Even though millions of consumers active in the Social Web beckoned for participation from brands, it would take Twitter, and a couple of years of incredible growth, to serve as a great catalyst for the reinvention of CRM and how we identify, track, respond to, and manage online conversations. Twitter essentially made everyone in the world of CRM and CRM 2.0 pay attention. It sparked the change for how brands truly engage across the Conversation Prism, aka the Social Web, and served as the guiding concepts for the formalization of sCRM.

Online discussions, rants, and observations are either alarming and motivating brand managers or luring them into entrapment scenarios. But the reality is that real-time dialogue fuels connections and perceptions in the statusphere, blogosphere, and online communities. It's this swelling tsunami of chatter that will only intensify.

As we discussed, this swelling activity necessitates brand involvement from almost every outward facing department, not only marketing, sales, channel, and service, to proactively share answers, solve problems, establish authority, and build relationships and loyalty, and to do so one tweet, blog post, update, and like at a time.

In the world of business, social media forces companies to augment the offshoring of reactive customer service with the nearshoring of proactive engagement. The conversations that power social media spark a sense of urgency for brands to identify influential voices and talk to customers where and when relevant conversations are transpiring.

In an interview with Jon Swartz of *USA Today*, Bill Tolany, global coordinator of integrated media at Whole Foods Market, shared his views on the new service landscape, "Social media is a natural extension of customer service."[8]

Whole Foods has more than 50 Twitter accounts and growing—tweeting on topics as specialized as cheese, wine, and specific items, with each participant trained through the integrated media department.

In the same article, Swartz interviewed Elissa Fink, vice president of marketing at Tableau Software, to discuss how Twitter was improving the experience for users of the company's business software: "The more ways you provide customers to contact you, you're more likely to satisfy them. It shows you're listening to them."

And as Salesforce.com CEO Marc Benioff observed in *USA Today*, "Brands aren't about messages anymore. Brands today are conversations—and today the most important conversations are happening through social media such as Twitter and Facebook."

Dion Hinchcliffe documented in his blog at ZDNet the rise of sCRM and the advantages of using social software to reinvent customer relationships.[9] He observed that in sCRM "the elimination of decades of inadequate communication channels will suddenly unleash a tide of many opportunities, as well as challenges, for most organizations." Hinchcliffe also observed four key aspects of Social CRM:

1. *A social environment:* Customers must be able to create an identity and perceive other customers, as well as individual workers, and be able to interact with both types of parties in a Social CRM environment.

2. *Customer participation mechanisms:* While discussion forums are very open-ended and can be used for many types of participation, Social CRM becomes more strategic when there are participation mechanisms that are driven by the specific needs of the organization or its customers. These might include social customer support, competitive contests, innovation or prediction markets, or joint product design, perhaps with finely tuned controls (such as Kluster).[10]

3. *Shared collective intelligence:* Web 2.0 applications are most successful when they create a shared repository of information created by the joint participation of their users. Good social CRM tools will make sure that the directed activities of a social CRM environment are accumulated, discoverable, and reusable. The artifacts of these activities are likely customer problem resolutions, product improvements, sales opportunities, and so forth. In other words, "Relationships that get better the more people use them" would be a good way to paraphrase one of the key mantras of 2.0 applications in a CRM context.

4. *Mechanisms to deal with conversational scale:* There is still a fear that deploying social tools to interact with online customers en masse will create unexpected costs or increased overhead as thousands—and in some organizations' cases—millions of customers try to engage with them.

To help us visualize the sCRM architecture, Hinchliffe created a helpful infographic titled "The Social Business Front Line: Customer Relationship Management."

In this graph, he places the sCRM management network between businesses and customers, where partnerships are forged and cultivated. Also connected to the sCRM network are workers who oversee and participate in relevant interactions and also a silo that captures collective intelligence through community-generated activity.

With sCRM, the focus is on people placing the onus on the company's front line to ensure that productive collaboration and the brand resonate. Hinchcliffe marks this through five Key Attributes of the Social Business Front Line:

1. Social environment
2. Crowdsourced results
3. Community-driven
4. Joint accumulated value
5. Scalable relationships

■ WHEN THE *S* IN sCRM STANDS FOR *SELF–SERVING*

I'd be remiss if I didn't at least share with you some of the more controversial ways that sCRM is channeling its inner CRM through the automation of consumer and prospect engagement. Not unlike many of the direct marketing initiatives, spanning from e-mail to snail mail, sCRM is already emulating the one-way broadcast systems that new media missionaries have so diligently rallied to socialize (see Figure 24.1). If we think that for one minute marketers, executives, and salespersons will forget all that they've learned through their years of profiteering, we're highly mistaken. New media doesn't affect us, until it does.

In one such example, a television network used Twitter and an sCRM system (described in the tool section) to promote a new series. In this case, the back channel proved lucrative to the promotional campaign. Using a Twitter-based framework similar to systems employed by e-mail marketers, this freely available sCRM Twitter application enabled network marketers to search Twitter for all tweets related to the actors of the program. The software automatically followed each person using the branded Twitter account (the show), sorted the tens of thousands of reciprocating follows by influence and relevant keywords, and then automatically sent prescripted messages by DM (direct message) to each person—without human intervention. The promotion of the show was deemed a success, with more than 100,000 individuals qualified and more than 20,000 DMs sent in a single push.

This particular initiative was solely focused on one-way promotion. None of the responses from the back channel effort were ever read, acknowledged, or addressed. It's the difference between broadcasting and engagement.

But imagine if they were one and the same. Imagine what could have grown from this interaction? The system actually accommodates both outbound and inbound sCRM—remember, most tools should embody technology and the supporting ethos of relationship management. As responses arrive, the system, along with a program manager, could have easily assigned conversations to the appropriate individuals representing designated groups.

To embrace inbound conversations is truly what the s represents in sCRM. It's a shift in mindset and purpose—all it takes is a plan and a supporting process or team. This is *social* media!

For example, on any given day on Twitter, movies, music artists, TV shows, and products literally become the talk of the town—well, of Twitterville,[11] at least—with many actually earning enough momentum to become trending topics (roughly 4,000 tweets per hour). These priceless conversations represent one part of an sCRM

Figure 24.1   The Social Business Front Line: Customer Relationship
Management

Source: From http://blogs.zdnet.com/Hinchcliffe.

process. We know their level of interest on the subject. Basically, we have the tools right now to capture that dialogue, gather intelligence, and channel the data into databases for immediate response and engagement programs or future campaigns or both. Yes, we can create social databases that are organized by relevant interest graphs. But right now, most businesses are missing this opportunity to capture this vital input. These invaluable opportunities are fleeing into the digital horizon.

■ VENDOR RELATIONSHIP MANAGEMENT (VRM)

In December of 2006, Christopher Carfi wrote about vendor relationships management on his blog, The Social Customer Manifesto, and offered a simple, but important message, "This [VRM] needs to be on your radar."[12]

Carfi documented the history and development of VRM, tracing back to its roots in 1999 when the concept of vendor relationship management was referred to as *tekram* (*market* spelled backward).

Doc Searls made the case[13] for consumer-powered influence in respect to vendor management, and Mike Vizard coined VRM in response during a Gillmor Gang podcast in September 2006.[14]

Paul Greenberg responded to Carfi's hosted discussion on VRM with an observation that would serve as one of the movement's credos: "The vendor and customer have to collaborate to optimize the relationship. It is no longer one-sided. That means that the customer's management of the relationship is the recognition of the partnership that successful implementation demands and there has to be skin in the game on both sides."[15]

VRM at its core is reciprocal to CRM, capsizing the concept of talking at or marketing to customers and shifting the balance of power in relationships from vendors to consumers—preferably somewhere in the middle. Like sCRM, VRM is representative of a greater mission. While sCRM is focused inside out, VRM focuses on outside in. Using tools and a technology ecosystem as examples of VRM, think Priceline and Lending Tree from a product perspective and Get Satisfaction from a service angle.

As described by VRMLabs, VRM is a customer-vendor locked seesaw: "Customers and vendors are a locked see-saw [sic] with one hugely outweighing the former. Like with a real world see-saw, the fun is spoiled for both. Giving individuals tools to redress the balance, the pressure from customers should level the players."[16]

VRM is the symmetry of customer and vendor collaboration, and the implementation of the relationship into relationship management.

As such, Project VRM was established by industry champions to ensure that the oscillation between customer and vendor is uniform. Project VRM is a development effort at the Berkman Center for Internet and Society at Harvard University, and is led by Doc Searls, a fellow with the Center. It is a community-powered wiki with real-world sources, extensions, and implications that foster discussion, participation, and partnerships between technologists, market experts, customers, and vendors to establish guidelines and platforms to improve the relationships between vendors and customers. As noted in the "About the Author" page of Project VRM, "It is Doc's [Searls'] belief . . . that VRM is required to bring a useful and productive balance of power between vendors and customers, supply and demand—for the good of both—in the marketplace."[17]

When reviewing the progression of CRM and its supporting categories and descriptions, the word *automation* was omnipresent. As we've learned from our time together, automation is a word that's usually absent from the descriptions of social media and sCRM—this is especially true in reference to engagement.

In the end, the goal of VRM seeks to enhance the relationship and interaction between demand and supply by providing more efficient and mutually beneficial solutions for demand to partner with supply.[18]

As in any relationship, for VRM to have a positive impact, vendors must find compelling incentives, while customers seek solutions through newfound empowerment.

VRM represents hope and challenges so as to define paths to resolution and coalition.

■ THE VALUE OF SOCIAL CUSTOMERS

In Paul Greenberg's *CRM at the Speed of Light: Social CRM Strategies, Tools, and Techniques for Engaging Your Customers*,[19] he discusses the correlation between advocacy (evangelism) and loyalty.

One way to measure advocacy is through a *net promoter score* (NPS), a trademarked metric system developed by Fred Reichheld, Bain & Company, and Satmetrix. Introduced by Reichheld in a 2003 *Harvard Business Review* article "One Number You Need to Grow,"[20] the NPS analyzes how businesses can create more promoters and fewer detractors. Reichheld expounded on this idea in his 2006 best seller, *The Ultimate Question: Driving Good Profits and True Growth*.[21]

The key to NPS is evaluating the value inherent in the answer to a very simple question, "How likely is it that you would recommend our company [or product] to a friend or colleague?"

The answer is rated between 0 and 10 and, based on the score, the respondents are grouped into one of three categories, detractors (0–6), passives (7–8), and promoters (9–10). The next step is to then get feedback on why they scored as such in the attempt to empower advocacy.

In 2003, Werner Reinartz and Dr. V. Kumar published the "Mismanagement of Customer Loyalty," a pioneering study on the connection between customer profitability and loyalty.[22] Their findings concluded that *not all loyal customers are profitable, and not all profitable customers are loyal.*

Did you catch that part?

If anything, the social customer is, at the very least, becoming much more prominent and influential than ever before.

In 2008's *Managing Customers for Profit: Strategies to Increase Profits and Build Loyalty,*[23] Dr. Kumar introduced a series of new equations and ideologies. Among them, customer brand value (CBV) and customer referral value (CRV) extend customer lifetime value to anticipate customer behavior and quantify social value and potential profitability. For the purpose of this discussion, and the book in general, let's examine CRV for a moment. Dr. Kumar defines CRV as the ability of managers "to measure and manage each customer based on his ability to generate indirect profit to the firm."

Like Reichheld, Dr. Kumar studied the alacrity of consumer referrals. However, the difference between the work of Reichheld and the work of Kumar is the extent to which the original question, "Would you refer this to someone you know" is asked and answered. Dr. Kumar believes that the true value lies in the answer to the question, "Did you actually make the referral?" and what happened next: "Did they actually become a customer?"

We need to measure the click to action!

While businesses analyze the breakdown in activities to improve sCRM, we can identify active voices online, whether or not they're customers or prospects, because the social customer isn't the only catalyst for advocacy and action. The true promise and future of relationship management lies among "The Social."

■ VRM + sCRM = SRM

Ross Mayfield, founder of SocialText, developed a versatile dashboard for enterprises seeking to collaborate internally with co-workers and externally with customers and stakeholders. He often refers to the engagement iceberg,[24] in which only a small portion of customer conversations and engagement are truly visible, while most occur beneath the water line and thus, out of view. Mayfield also notes that the nature of the dialogue and how conversations progress throughout the Web usually require more than one person or department to engage.

As we've covered practically everywhere in this book, each online conversation worthy of response can be directly matched to specific divisions within an organization and usually rank in this order:

1. Support
2. Sales

3. Public relations
4. Marketing, or brand
5. Product development
6. Human resources

As already discussed, in listening, we find conversations inevitably map to specific departments. Thus, the nature and sentiment tied to the social ID and response mechanisms require workflow to introduce resolve by the specific disciplines they affect. As a result, when we view conversations as they map interdepartmentally, the C in sCRM begins to disappear (see Figure 24.2).

Thus, the observations tied to real-time activity demonstrate the reality that every department eventually needs to socialize. Much like the divergence between CRM and CRM 2.0 and that of CRM 2.0 and sCRM, sCRM now starts to represent something much bigger than just social customer relationship management.

Customers are now merely part of a larger equation that also balances vendors, experts, partners, and other influencers.

sCRM and CRM look at the value of a customer using a variety of tools and methodologies such as customer lifetime value (CLV) and customer life cycle management and the value of commerce that can be attributed to the customer relationship over time.

We're moving away from an era of simple listening, monitoring, and responding to an age of direct engagement (reactive and proactive) in concert with the management of this activity. It's rooted in our ability to essentially become the *person*, not just the *customer*, whom we want to embrace and inspire. As such, existing customers and prospects are only part of a much more sophisticated equation. Or said another way, customers are now playing one of the leading roles in a more elaborate production, sharing the stage with other cast members that represent all facets of business workflow and governing channels of influence.

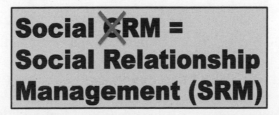

Figure 24.2 Social Relationship Management

■ NO BRAND IS AN ISLAND

Social relationships management (SRM) is a credo aligned with a humanized business strategy and supporting technology infrastructure and platform. SRM recognizes that all people, no matter what system they use, are worthy of our attention—even if it's just listening.

SRM adopts a doctrine that champions:

➤ Collaboration over conversation
➤ Listening over intermittent searching and research
➤ Action and resolution instead of monitoring
➤ Personalization over automation
➤ Adaptation over ignorance

Relationships management or SRM is much more than engagement strategies and tactics. It requires completely revamped tenets and infrastructure to support relationships and empowerment. We can't expect people to always come to us. We must build bridges that also go directly to them.

■ SOCIAL BUSINESS TAKES A HUMAN TOUCH; NO, REALLY

The socialization of media is the undercurrent for the Industrial Revolution of our time. Yet, here we are today, forcing social media into the aging paradigms that the social revolution set out to upset in the first place.

Businesses still weigh the return on investment of participation. Teams debate over who owns the company's social presences. The parochial in middle and upper management see it as either a playground or an extension of existing broadcast channels. Champions believe it is a time to engage and improve experiences. Visionaries recognize its ability to socialize the entire business. Yet, almost every example we see today of successful social media endeavors is, in reality, siloed and disconnected from the rest of the organization.

Marketing runs a creative contest on Facebook, but the rest of the business is unaware of the campaign.

Customer service reacts to customer problems, yet product development is unaware of the recurring problems and themes.

Representatives are unwittingly diluting the brand they represent with unguided tweets, updates, posts, comments, and videos.

Human resources monitors the mistakes made by employees, but no one guides them through training, guidelines, or branding.

Customers ask questions about products and services, and while these updates show up on the monitoring reports of community managers, they do not receive a response from the sales team.

The list goes on and on with little resolution, as we are focused on real time versus the real world. We need not only champions, but we now need leaders to help us cut through the red tape and unite the organization behind a flag of relevance and evolution.

Everything starts with recognizing that we must cater to an audience whose parts are, in fact, greater than its sum. We must partition our social strategy to engage the diversity of the social consumer and address the unique requirements and attention of each (see Figure 24.3).

Figure 24.3   The Roles of the Social Consumer

This is about humanizing not only the brand, but also the methodologies that govern customer relations and adapting the systems that support it.

► Socializing CRM

sCRM is the hot ticket in Enterprise 2.0 at the moment, yet its champions are mired in technology as are the champions for social media in general. We're blinded in many ways by the networks and our need to listen, respond, and update. But we miss the intimacy necessary to learn, adapt, and earn relevance. And now, we're consumed with wiring Twitter, Facebook, LinkedIn, Foursquare, and Yelp into our existing CRM infrastructure to help us automate enlightenment and engagement. While we close gaps caused by the distribution and scale of the Social Web and the people who define it, we fail to see the human touch points to connect with the right people in the right places at the right time. That is, after all, where scalability resides: the ability to engage influential consumers in a one-to-one-to-many practice to amplify intention, purpose, and value.

$$1 + 1 = \text{Many}$$

In essence, we're practically fooled into a belief that we should not overthink social, but not doing so, we trivialize the opportunity, ultimately investing in a program that at the end of the day, falls short of meeting the needs of the social consumer.

What's the value of a like?

What is a Twitter follower worth?

What is the significance of a tweet, check-in, or comment?

How do we reduce the costs of support through social?

To answer these questions, we must have a vision of the experience and actions we wish to introduce into these rich and active social ecosystems. Yes, this is a *click to action,* and for businesses to socialize CRM, they must socialize the entire business. Not all of the three Fs (friends, fans, followers) are created equally. Individually, rarely collectively, they are looking for substance, direction, recognition, and even empowerment. To activate the Social Web and unlock meaningful conversations, we must look beyond customers. We must *officially recognize* all those who influence their actions and introduce a conversational workflow that traverses the business chasms to learn and lead—in public (see Figure 24.4).

Figure 24.4 The Social Consumer

■ SOCIAL SCIENCE IS THE CENTER OF SOCIAL BUSINESS

Customer Relationship Management > Social CRM > SRM
> Relationships > Relevance

One of the celebrated companies renowned for its innovation in social customer service is actually a lesson in how social anything becomes great PR. When you look behind the scenes, you actually see more duct tape and rubber bands than fluidity and polish. Business units are still siloed and even the chief executives have gone on record saying that the acts of engagement do more for the company's image than it does for the improvement of products and services. Just look at your favorite social media source and you'll see an endless array of examples of how brands are succeeding in social media. Again, most of them are basking in the brilliance of individual victories, some are actually breaking through the internal barriers that prevent collaboration, and others are simply stunts designed to spike conversations, sales, and a good public image. Nothing wrong with it . . . especially if it works as intended.

You and I are here together, right now, to do something greater. It's up to us to lead the way for the socialization of business, understanding that it's an uphill journey for the foreseeable future. But in the end, our experience and triumphs are unparalleled.

Social media is the gold mines of anthropology, sociology, and ethnography. To excel here, we must embrace social science to create and earn relevance. Some businesses already get this. For example, Intel employs anthropologists such as Genevieve Bell to understand how certain cultures adopt technology and also how products should be designed with humans represented in every step of the process. I challenge businesses seeking to socialize their business to hire social scientists to not only understand culture and its role in consumerism, but also to humanize the processes and systems erecting to facilitate engagement and social CRM. It takes a human touch to embrace and inspire the social consumer, build communities, and activate advocacy. If we can hear, see, and feel the customer and all those who influence them, then why would we think social is where we can excel. Surely, it's not because we show up. It's only because we earn and deserve our place within each network.

We must humanize our brand, our products, and our processes to improve and influence experiences. Doing so will help us find our voice, our mission, and our purpose . . . our cadence. Give people a reason to connect with us, trust us, and represent us.

■ NOTES

1. Bob Thompson, "Social CRM: Strategy, Technology or Passing Fad?" Customer Think (September 16, 2009), www.customerthink.com/blog/social_crm_strategy_technology_or_passing_fad.

2. Brent Leary, "Social CRM: Not Your Father's Customer Relationship Management," Small Business Trends (May 14, 2008), http://smallbiztrends.com/2008/05/social-crm.html.

3. Filiberto Selvas, "Are the Cool Kids Leaving Facebook? So What?" www.socialcrm.net/.

4. Ross Mayfield, "The Social C.R.M Iceberg," Ross Mayfield's Weblog (August 11, 2009), http://ross.typepad.com/blog/2009/08/crm-iceberg.html.

5. Jeremiah Owyang, "The Future of Twitter: Social CRM," Web Strategy by Jeremiah Owyang (March 22, 2009), www.web-strategist.com/blog/2009/03/22/the-future-of-twitter-social-crm/.

6. Brian Solis, "Twitter and Social Networks Usher in a New Era of Social CRM," PR 2.0 (March 20, 2009), www.briansolis.com/2009/03/twitter-and-social-networks-usher-in/.

7. Paul Greenberg, "Time to Put a Stake in the Ground on Social CRM," PGreenblog (July 6, 2009), http://the56group.typepad.com/pgreenblog/2009/07/time-to-put-a-stake-in-the-ground-on-social-crm.html.

8. Jon Swartz, "Businesses Use Twitter to Communicate with Customers," *USA Today* (June 26, 2009), www.usatoday.com/tech/news/2009–06–25-twitter-businesses-consumers_N.htm.

9. Dion Hinchcliffe, "Using Social Software to Reinvent the Customer Relationship," ZDNet (August 18, 2009), http://blogs.zdnet.com/Hinchcliffe/?p=699.

10. See www.kluster.com/.

11. Shel Israel, "Twitterville: How Businesses Can Thrive in the New Global Neighborhoods," *Portfolio* (September 2009), http://redcouch.typepad.com/weblog/twitterville.html.

12. Christopher Carfi, "VRM: Vendor Relationship Management," *The Social Customer Manifesto* (December 18, 2006), www.socialcustomer.com/2006/12/vrm_vendor_rela.html.

13. Doc Searls, comment to Christopher Carfi's post, "Vendor Relationships Management" (Dec 19, 2006), www.socialcustomer.com/2006/12/vrm_vendor_rela.html.

14. Gillmor Gang, http://cyber.law.harvard.edu/projectvrm/VRM_discussion_in_podcasts.

15. Paul Greenberg, comment to Christopher Carfi's post, "Vendor Relationships Management" (Dec 18, 2006), www.socialcustomer.com/2006/12/vrm_vendor_rela.html.

16. About VRM Labs, www.vrmlabs.net/about/.

17. About Project VRM, http://cyber.law.harvard.edu/projectvrm/About.

18. Project VRM Main Page, http://cyber.law.harvard.edu/projectvrm/Main_Page.

19. Paul Greenberg, *CRM at the Speed of Light: Social CRM 2.0 Strategies, Tools, and Techniques for Engaging Your Customers* 4th ed. (New York: McGraw-Hill Osborne Media, 2009).

20. Frederick F. Reichheld, "One Number You Need to Grow," *Harvard Business Review* (December 1, 2003), http://harvardbusiness.org/product/one-number-you-need-to-grow/an/R0312C-PDF-ENG.

21. Frederick F. Reichheld, *The Ultimate Question* (Cambridge, MA: Harvard Business Press, 2006).

22. Werner Reinartz and V. Kumar, "Mismanagement of Customer Loyalty," *Harvard Business Review* (July 1, 2002), http://harvardbusiness.org/product/mismanagement-of-customer-loyalty/an/R0207F-PDF-ENG.

23. V. Kumar, *Managing Customers for Profit: Strategies to Increase Profits and Build Loyalty*, (Upper Saddle River, NJ: Wharton School Publishing, 2008).

24. Joshua Weinberger, "Social Media Maturity Model: 30 Posts, 30 People, 30 Days," Destination CRM Blog (June 1, 2009), www.destination crmblog.com/2009/06/01/social-media-maturity-model-30-posts-30-peo ple-30-days/.

Chapter
25

We Earn the Relationships We Deserve

Twitter and social networks in general are luring users into a Web of both interconnected and extended connections—forging potentially valuable relationships with the individuals we know and those we admire, respect, and one day hope to know.

The race to extend one's social graph across the statusphere is laying the groundwork for a more formidable platform to share one's thoughts, opinions, observations, messages, and agenda. This is as true for individuals as it is for marketers, sales organizations, and brands.

■ EARNING THE THREE Fs: FRIENDS, FANS, AND FOLLOWERS

As Twitter's civilization personifies the natural tendency to extend the connections that strengthen the network, individuals also share the desire to participate in the expansion. As such, we, as a dedicated online society, grow in prominence.

As personalities, the path between where we are and where we would like to be is defined by our actions and the practices we embody. We have a choice to increase our congregation organically or through prescribed measures. Brands too, face the same crossroads.

Trend and keyword marketing or hashtag exploitation are two very different tactics that attempt to yield similar results. Trend and keyword marketing are usually reactive in their composition.

Reactive campaigns are rooted in the discovery of online conversations related to particular keywords, for example:

"I'm looking for help with HDTVs."

"I am so upset with X company; their service is absolutely horrible."

"I'm in the market for a new hybrid car."

"Can anyone recommend a great place for pizza around Brighton?"

Someone within the marketing or service departments for related or competitive organizations invests a portion of the day identifying these target conversations and then replies to them in the public timeline with a response aimed at providing resolution, answers, or direction. This practice aims at generating goodwill, advocacy, and, hopefully, new followers and customers.

Companies who do this extremely well include Dell, Comcast, Southwest Air, JetBlue, Virgin America, H&R Block, Wells Fargo, Bank of America, Sprint, Home Depot, Cisco, Panasonic LiHD, and many, many others.

However, there is a dark side to this practice and it is usually driven by shortsightedness, underestimation, greed, lack of respect, or naïveté.

■ #HASHTAGS

Hashtag marketing can assume either a proactive or reactive model.

Hashtags or tags are keywords or terms assigned to a piece of information. This type of metadata helps describe an item and allows it to be found again by browsing or searching. Tags are chosen informally and personally by the item's creator or by its viewer, depending on the system.[1] Hashtags are also used for forming groups, such as #engage-bookclub, or for expressing a state of mind, thought, or observation, such as "I am so tired after work, what to do? #timetorelax."

Similar to the reactive nature of conversational or response marketing, reactive hashtag marketing seeks to solve or uncover dialogue related to user-defined topics. While keywords are somewhat similar, #hashtags are user-introduced subjects specifically tied to a theme. For example, if you are having an issue with your cable service, you could tweet, "Ugh, my cable service is out again in Providence. #nameofprovidersucks." If others who are experiencing similar issues see your tweet or update, they could also express frustration and include the same hashtag at the end of their post.

As we've seen over the last two years, @comcastcares has actively monitored conversations related to keywords tied to or around Comcast, with priority given to those keywords and hashtags such as #comcastsucks or "hate Comcast," to help them solve problems and ultimately convert negative experiences into neutral or positive results. It's this shift in perception that quite possibly converts antagonists into advocates.

■ HASHTAGS: A PROACTIVE APPROACH

Hashtag marketing can also assume a proactive approach when brands deploy campaigns designed to trigger word of mouth around a keyword in the attempt to garner rapid and extensive momentum that earns a spot in Twitter's coveted list of Trending Topics.

Moonfruit, a free website creator, stirred things up on Twitter and the blogosphere when it announced a Twitter promotion to celebrate its tenth anniversary. The company announced that it would give away 10 Macbook Pro laptops in 10 days to selected individuals who either retweeted the suggested message proposed by Moonfruit, "Celebrate 10 years of Moonfruit and win a MacBook Pro http://bit.ly/96bxC #moonfruit," or creatively used the #moonfruit hashtag in a tweet. All entrants were encouraged to tweet often to increase their chances of winning. The caveat? They had to follow @moontweet to find out if they won.

This program is referred to as a "Tweet to Win" campaign and it's straddling the line between spam and fair game.

Not only did Moonfruit become a trending topic, the account skyrocketed to more than 40,000 followers almost immediately and ultimately increased visibility for its Web design services. Did it also increase sales? Yes, it did. The account now hovers just under 30,000.

According to an article in ClickZ,[2] a news and expert advice resource for digital marketers, Moonfruit founder Wendy White was overwhelmed by its success. The promotion resulted in a 600 percent lift in site traffic and doubled user sign-up for service trials in just a few days. "The response has been beyond belief, far more effective than other marketing channels," White reported.

In this case, the company not only amplified its community and potential reach today and in the future, it also extended its value proposition across the social graphs of trusted individuals who opted to tweet as part of the contest. Friends become a powerful catalyst for extending the reach by applying a filter to content. But they can tarnish friendships and potentially erode confidence if their tweeting is misused. This is something for both brands and individuals to consider—as their participation in these campaigns can have negative impacts on their connections, inadvertently straining relationships by causing an imbalance in the routine that defines an acceptable signal-to-noise ratio.

No matter if it's a "tweet to win" or a "tweet to *insert action here,*" campaign, gaining friends and followers through a public timeline strategy is a finite strategy without a long-term strategy in place.

■ OFFERS AND SPECIALS

When it comes to earning friends and followers by offering specials through Twitter, no one leads the way quite like @Delloutlet. In June 2009, the company reported more than $3 million in sales directly tied to tweets promoting specials available solely on Twitter.

@delloutlet currently boasts more than 1.4 million followers seeking exclusive deals available only on the microcommunity.

However, it's not just the big boys who can brandish authority on Twitter to the tune of tens or even hundreds of thousands of new followers and millions in new sales. Small businesses are demonstrating the power of Twitter and the rewards for giving back to the community as a way of earning friends and followers.

One of the most often-cited examples of a small business cultivating relationships on Twitter and building a vocal and loyal community is @NAKEDpizza. Backed by Mark Cuban, Naked Pizza is an all natural and "good for you" pizza joint in New Orleans that bears the motto: "Doing it one day at a time. We care. We really do."

Naked Pizza has earned each and every one of its roughly 5,000 followers on Twitter by tweeting interesting information (related and unrelated to pizza), recognizing customers, answering questions, and listening to local conversations relevant to their business. Based on listening exercises, Naked Pizza followed the right people and, in turn, many followed them back.

In an interview with *Advertising Age* magazine, Jeff Leach, Naked Pizza co-founder, explained, "Every phone call was tracked, every order was measured by where it came from, and it told us very quickly that Twitter is useful. Sure, there's the brand marketing and getting-to-know-you stuff. . . . But we wanted to know: Can it make the cash register ring?"[3]

Indeed, it did. On April 23, 2009, the company reported that Twitter accounted for 15 percent of total sales that day.

When Naked Pizza is discussed as a small business that's blazing the trail on Twitter, Berry Chill (@YogiJones) isn't far behind.

Berry Chill has three locations in the Chicago area and uses Twitter to send out "sweet tweets" to draw new and existing customers in the door. Typically, the special requires the recipient to show that they're followers on Twitter, and as a reward they can receive discounts or even a free yogurt. One such promotion recorded more than 1,100 yogurt giveaways.

Michael Farah, founder and CEO of Berry Chill, attested that Twitter was increasing the customer base and attested to Twitter's use as an inexpensive acquisition tool: "Our last big promotion gave away $5,500 worth of product—but sales were the same as the day before. The people who were existing customers standing in line attracted people who hadn't tried it."

■ PAY PER TWEET

Izea debuted to both accolades and controversy its Sponsoredtwts (@spontwts), a Twitter advertising/pay-for-tweet service that complements its other sponsored conversation, Pay Per Post blog offering. Izea is credited with creating the sponsored conversation market in 2006 with nearly one million conversations funded to date. The company defines sponsored conversations as a social media marketing technique in which brands provide financial or material compensation to bloggers in exchange for posting related content about a product, service, or website on their blog, and now on Twitter, too.

Sponsoredtwts has effectively experimented with several public campaigns that have achieved the goals set forth by the brands that sponsored conversations on Twitter and has helped many companies achieve their objectives and happily serve as referrals to other businesses.

If it's anything similar to its blog program, Izea plans to recruit Twitter users in droves and reward them with monetary compensations or product incentives.

Brands that have successfully used the pay-per-post service include 1-800-Flowers, Beaches Resort, Black and Decker, Bumble Bee Tuna, Disney, Ford, Hamilton Beach, Hewlett-Packard, Kmart, Microsoft, MTV, Overstock, Paramount Pictures, and Universal Music.

Izea is not alone in this market. Twittad connects peers and friends of friends with advertisers through creative ad campaigns rooted in paid tweets.

In one campaign, Craftsman Tools turned to Twittad to drive sign-ups and buzz for its NASCAR VIP Pass Giveaway. Craftsman ran the giveaway through multiple advertising channels, and even James

Eliason, president and CEO of Twittad, is the first to remind people that the pay-per-tweet model should always be used in conjunction with other forms of online and offline advertising.

Twittad came up with 15 different tweet messages that users could select. This number helped ensure variation in the messages, so that followers wouldn't see the exact same message from multiple users. Each Twittad user sent three tweets during the week-long campaign. Twittad and Craftsman saw multiple retweets and sharing among friends who were fans of NASCAR. Click-throughs were fast and furious for the first five minutes after a tweet was sent and then tapered off from there (as a result, Twittad wisely spaced out accepting users into the campaign, to smooth out the traffic pattern over the seven days).

As for hard results, the numbers are impressive. The Twittad campaign reached 1,575,000 followers on Twitter. And Craftsman saw approximately 4,000 sign-ups as a direct result of the Twitter campaign, as well as growth in followers to their @Craftsmanclub account.

Another pay-per-tweet solution is Ad.ly, a self-service platform for celebrities, including Kim Kardashian, Brooke Burke, Nicole Richie, and Dr. Drew. It helps advertisers and marketers looking to leverage the social graph of these celebrities connect brands with fandoms. Tweets range from the low hundreds to several thousand per tweet. Ad.ly CEO Sean Rad is quick to stress the importance of matching the right publisher with the right advertiser. By selectively targeting appropriate celebrities (and their audiences), Ad.ly tweets can successfully tread the line between advertisement and relevant content (although they're always disclosed as paid advertisements).

There are risks involved here that any brand manager should consider before being lured by the promise of word of mouth, celebrity association, and prosperity. It's the differences between visibility and presence, hype and realization, and earned versus paid. Granted, as in any celebrity endorsement campaign, including Weblebrities, a product and brand benefit from the value of association. But since we're referring to words, we must choose them carefully—as well as the voice used to share them, regardless of the stature.

The Federal Trade Commission is monitoring this activity closely to ensure that disclosure is readily visible and comprehensible, whether it's a post or a tweet. The penalties for not properly disclosing that these conversations are sponsored is not only damaging, it's very public.

As a result of the evolving level of influence inherent in the Social Web, the notice incorporates several amendments to the FTC's guidelines concerning the use of endorsements and testimonials in advertising and blogging, which address endorsements by consumers, experts, organizations, and celebrities, as well as the disclosure of important connections between advertisers and endorsers.

In October 2009, the Federal Trade Commission released its final revisions to the guidance it gives advertisers on how to keep their endorsement and testimonial ads in line with the FTC Act. The guides were last updated in 1980.[4]

In the end, we earn the relationships we deserve.

■ NOTES

1. "Hashtags," Twitter Fan Wiki, http://twitter.pbworks.com/Hashtags.
2. Douglas Quenqua, "MTV Plays Telephone with Twitter," ClickZ (May 1, 2009), www.clickz.com/3633603.
3. Abbey Klaassen, "Twitter Proves Its Worth as a Killer App for Local Businesses," *Advertising Age* (May 18, 2009), http://adage.com/digital/article?article_id=136662.
4. "FTC Publishes Final Guides Governing Endorsements, Testimonials," Federal Trade Commission (October 5, 2009), www.ftc.gov/opa/2009/10/endortest.shtm.

Chapter 26

The New Media Scorecard

One of the most fascinating aspects of socialized media is its ability to track and measure almost anything that matters to your business—as it unfolds. With the right tools, we can peel back the layers between the digital and real worlds to reveal actions and outcomes.

Whether you realize it or not, you are already making progress. To ease us into this complex and diverse discussion, I've peppered the materials needed to build a framework for relevant business metrics throughout this book.

In the Social CRM chapter (Chapter 23), we learned how to measure customer value and influence. Earlier in the book we examined the processes associated with identifying and establishing authority. We also reviewed methods for discovering communities of influence and capturing relevant activity so as to institute a measurable Conversation Index. We also learned how to define experiences, establish desired click paths, and track and measure activity and outcomes. Each step forms a foundation of metrics that serve as benchmarks moving forward—focused specifically on the programs and goals as implemented at program and brand levels. After all, while the need to measure initiatives is pervasive, we have no basis for comparison without benchmarks.

There are several schools of thought when it comes to measuring the effectiveness of new media. In this chapter, we explore the tools and methodologies that translate activity into tangible value for your business and its management infrastructure.

Our first step, however, is to understand who within the organization is already measuring Web activity and immediately become part of the process. The Web team or data analyst(s) typically maintain control of valuable online performance information, usually sourced from Web analytic tools such as Omniture or Google Analytics. Those on the e-commerce team are already examining how, when, and where customers are making purchases online. Advertising and marketing are familiar with click conversions and impression on digital ads and

271

other programs. Much of what each of these teams do is aligned with your work. Working together, your roles will adapt to more effectively translate social data into business value. This analysis will affect and shape current and future campaigns.

■ THE DISPARITY BETWEEN SOCIAL MEDIA ADOPTION AND MEASUREMENT

While the allure of new media is hypnotizing, bewitching us to leap before looking or fire before aiming, its value is truly revealed in the behavior and ensuing analysis that stems from engagement.

We now have the ability to incite change directly and indirectly and track the resulting actions and responses as they travel from community to community and person to person, transcending the boundaries between the digital and real worlds.

Engaging without analysis is akin to driving aimlessly, without direction or purpose.

Measurement is the key to relevance and future successes.

Here are just a few ways that change agents are measuring the return on investment (ROI) of social media:[1]

➤ Best Buy measures the ROI of its internal "Blue Shirts Nation" community in terms of lower turnover rates.

➤ The National Association of Manufacturers measures the ROI of its blog in terms of greater access to the halls of Capitol Hill.

➤ Dell measures the success of its IdeaStorm community both in terms of lower support costs and in the number of new ideas generated.

➤ SeaWorld reached out to roller coaster enthusiasts with its social media program and measured its ROI in terms of lower outreach costs as well as tickets sold.

■ ROA: RETURN ON ACRONYMS

One of the most commonly asked questions in new media marketing is often voiced by someone who is usually unqualified to appreciate the response.

You know the question. We hear it all the time.

"What's the ROI of this?"

While many think it, the initial answer is usually suppressed: "I dunno, what's the ROI of anything we do? What's the ROI of customer service? What's the ROI of PR? What's the ROI of branding? What's the return on human resources? While we're at it . . . what's the ROI of research?"

I'm only partially kidding.

What if we asked the question this way: "How can we measure ROI if the I stands for ignorance?"

As I always say, ignorance is bliss until it's not.

The truth is that we need to have answers. The good news is that the answers are available. If we don't know them, we must seek them. We just need to know what to look for and where.

In traditional businesses, return on investment is calculated by dividing net profits after taxes by total assets.[2] For example, if you invested $50,000 and the investment was worth $75,000 after two years, your annual return on investment would be 25 percent. To get that result, you divide the $25,000 gain by your $50,000 investment, and then divide the 50 percent gain by 2.

In new media, ROI can work similarly, but the acronym is also morphing to make way for new metrics, including:

➤ *Return on participation, return on engagement, or return on involvement:* The review of activities, patterns, reactions, and results associated with direct interaction or through social objects.

➤ *Return on experience:* The analysis of the effects of experience through design aesthetics, engagement, and words.

➤ *Return on influence:* The study of the impact of influence as it reverberates across communities and resulting behavior.

While experts play with the I in ROI or x in ROx to reflect other measurement scenarios, to truly garner insight and value from the gauging of our activities, we must first define the R, or return. Defining the R allows us to analyze behavior and activity as it applies to the business. Return on investment is a bona fide analysis related to business finances. Its value is indisputable—even in the seemingly elusive world of social media.

This is done initially by asking a handful of simple questions to surface the return we seek:

➤ What are we measuring and why?

➤ What does success look like?

➤ How will we know when we get there?

➤ Are there incremental milestones worth noting?

➤ Who else within the organization benefits from our work and how would they measure meaningful results?

Observing the literal translation of the I as investment, we must also factor in the corporate assets that power any and all business initiatives:

➤ Intellectual capital

➤ Resources

➤ Finances

➤ Campaign costs

As inexpensive as social media is considered to be in comparison to traditional programs, there are always fixed costs associated with any activity.

In June 2008, I published an early formula for calculating the I in ROI based on the research results from the Conversation Prism and Index studies.[3]

■ THE ESSENTIAL GUIDE TO SOCIAL MEDIA: RESOURCES—PERSONNEL AND BUDGETS

➤ Activities to Meter

➤ The average frequency of relevant conversations

➤ Identify the more active hubs and communities

➤ The context of the conversations to better determine the time and variety of resources required

➤ Resource Assessment Formula

Number of average relevant conversations per day per community.

Multiplied by the quantity of relevant communities.

Multiplied by 20 (average minutes required to research and respond and also monitor for additional responses), variable plus or minus, and depending on the case, usually plus.

Divided by 60 (minutes).

Equals the amount of time required and, in turn, the resources and associated costs required depending on internal labor (salaries or hourly rates), external consulting fees, plus the cost of equipment and other necessary resources.

■ THE SOCIAL BAROMETER

Over the years, I have established the criterion to measure my work as it specifically relates to the companies and the business units each customized initiative was designed to benefit. Along the way, I have also maintained a spectator perspective, as I've documented the evolution of the interactive media landscape. Much of this is so new and exciting that businesses are diving in out of perceived urgency without investing resources in acquiring or embracing existing techniques for evaluating participatory programs.

However, there are best practices tied to soft and explicit metrics that we can implement to justify and judge our work. Depending on the level of sophistication and also primary focus and purpose of your business, the combination of these calculations will vary in importance.

As we assess the methodologies, formulas, and criteria required for creating a system for measurement, we must identify the attributes that are important to the organization as well as those that will receive buy-in at the departmental and executive level.

Don Bartholomew, a social media research and measurement consultant, observed that communications professionals, for example, often confuse outputs with outtakes or outcomes—basically confusing exposure with action.

He proposed a metrics taxonomy to help us truly understand our mission for measurement:[4]

Exposure: To what degree have we created exposure to content and message?

Engagement: Who, how, and where are people interacting or engaging with our content?

Influence: The degree to which exposure and engagement have influenced perceptions and attitudes.

Action: As a result of the effort, what actions, if any, has the target taken?

Bartholomew also defined three zones of measurement: websites on the left side (measured by Web analytics), social networks in the center (measured by content and behavior analysis) and offline on the right side (captured by audience research).

From the left, companies or brands control, own, or manage websites—corporate sites, Facebook pages, Twitter accounts, LinkedIn pages, and blogs, by way of example—and create content to lure consumers toward engagement. This zone is measured primarily by Web analytics. In the middle are the actual social networks and conversations between individuals. We are interested in this zone in data sets that cannot be gathered solely using Web analytics packages. How often is the brand being mentioned in conversation? What is the sentiment of the comments? How often is the brand being recommended and by whom? Content and behavior analysis, including tracking technologies, are the primary measurement tools in this zone. The third zone represents all the real-world, offline transactions that may be of interest. Did someone visit the store or attend an event? Did he buy a product? Did he recommend the brand or product to a friend over coffee?

■ START WITH THE RESULTS, THEN WORK BACKWARD: DEFINING GOALS AND OBJECTIVES

We can't measure what we do not recognize as value. We cannot measure success if we don't know what success looks like. It is for these very reasons that we must first establish our day-to-day programs and incremental campaigns around the end result—as shaped by the research work performed in the listening and observation stages of the Conversation Prism.

This is important, as I'm often asked to reveal a formula or template that reveals the secret to measurement. The metrics are as diverse as the roles of the social consumer. Charting growth among the three Fs (friends, fans, and followers), views, or traffic to a blog or website or likes, comments, and retweets are representative of entry-level metrics. Growth here is not a reflection of key performance indicators, (KPIs), ROI, or any other measurement acronym, for that matter. Define the outcome and work backward from there. For example, in customer service, one of the key metrics for social media is the noticeable reduction in trouble tickets and inbound calls and email around common subjects. Sales organizations, of course, track leads, foot traffic (if applicable), sales, and referrals. Brand managers use the Conversation Index as a way of documenting progress showing growth in share of voice and share of conversation, an increase in positive sentiment, and boost in advocacy. Marketers focus on conversion ratios and the rate individuals clicked through to the next stage of the campaign.

Clicks to action, including the experience and the click path, must get tied to measurable outcomes.

K. D. Paine (Katie Delahaye Paine) is recognized as "the queen of measurement." She observed that the importance value of social media is what happens because of it. She therefore suggests that we actually consider dropping *media* from social media when it comes to measuring its effects.[5]

While I partially agree, K. D. recognizes that the metrics required for measuring the effectiveness of social media are new and different from anything currently used in marketing: "We need to be working closely with the data geeks and the market research folks and measure the things that happen faster and better because of social networking."

K. D. outlined a change in business habits and efficiency as a foundation for metrics:

➤ Process improvement
➤ Time to market
➤ Number of new product ideas
➤ Number of suggestions
➤ Length of time it takes to find a solution to a problem
➤ Efficiency with which a product is launched
➤ Level of social capital
➤ Churn rates among your customers or employees or both
➤ Cost of recruitment

Therefore, establishing objectives and tying activity back to the results we desire require both planning and calculation.

To help, K. D. Paine created an immensely helpful measurement program checklist (edited to reflect the lessons shared in this book).[6]

MEASUREMENT PROGRAM CHECKLIST BY K. D. PAINE

Step 1: What Are Your Objectives?

1. What are your organization's key goals for this year?
2. What are your department's key goals for this year?
3. What do you hope to accomplish with your measurement report?
   ➤ Get budget approved
   ➤ Increase budget
   ➤ Increase head count
   ➤ Get more internal support
   ➤ Get more external support

➤ Justify my existence
➤ Get a raise
➤ Get promoted

Step 2: What Audiences Are You Targeting?

List all that apply, not just the following common ones. (If in doubt, put all the executives and marketing people in your organization in a room and ask them.)

➤ Media
➤ Prospects
➤ Customers
➤ Partners
➤ Employees
➤ Governments
➤ NGOs
➤ Communities
➤ Investors
➤ Thought leaders
➤ International community
➤ Other

How does a good relationship with your various target audiences benefit your organization?

1. Increases sales
2. Increases attendance
3. Increases donations
4. Increases likelihood of desirable legislation passing
5. Increases preference
6. Increases awareness
7. Improves employee retention
8. Improves employee loyalty
9. Improves customer retention
10. Improves customer loyalty
11. Improves likelihood of purchase
12. Attracts new customers
13. Attracts new prospects (lead generation)

14. Attracts new or potential donors
15. Increases amount of purchase
16. Increases frequency of purchase
17. Boosts stock price
18. Increases profitability
19. Reduces turnover
20. Decreases time to market
21. Decreases number of complaints
22. Decreases absenteeism

Step 3: Set Priorities

Prioritize your audiences with this exercise: You have a total of 100 points to allocate. Award those points to the audiences that you have identified in order of their importance to your organization, based on your answers to questions in Step 2.

Step 4: Determine a Benchmark

Who or what keeps your boss or client up at night? In other words, what are the competitive threats or perceived competitive threats to your organization? Select from the following list to determine what you will be comparing your results to.

➤ Competitor(s) or peer companies
➤ Industry benchmarks
➤ Yourself over time
➤ Last year's results
➤ Last quarter's sales or Web or commerce metrics

Step 5: Select the Right Measurement Tool

If your objectives (see Step 1) include "increase awareness," improve products or service, "attitude change," or "education," you will need to conduct an online audit in social media to determine the current state of affairs and establish a benchmark.

If you are seeking to measure sales and leads, you should be tracking website traffic and conferring with the sales team to document numbers, referring sources, and existing hurdles.

➤ Sentiment
➤ Share of voice versus the competition

➤ Share of discussion versus the competition
➤ Audience reached
➤ Important trust agents and tastemakers

Pat LaPointe at *Marketing Measurement Today* developed a framework for approaching social measurement in response to one of the most common questions he faced: "How should I measure the value of all the social marketing things we're doing, like Twitter, Linked-in, Facebook, and so forth?"

LaPointe's answer was as commonsensical as it was poignant, "*Why* are you doing them in the first place? If you can't answer that, you're wasting your time and the company's money."[7]

SOCIAL MEASUREMENT FRAMEWORK BY PAT LAPOINTE

1. Fill in the blanks: "Adding or swapping in social media initiatives will affect _____ by _____ extent over _____ time frame. And when that happens, the added value for the business will be $_____, which will give me an ROI of _____. This forms your hypotheses about what you might achieve, and why the rest of the business should care.

2. Identify all the assumptions implicit in your hypotheses and flex each assumption up or down by 50 percent to 100 percent to see under which circumstances your assumptions become unprofitable.

3. Identify the most sensitive assumption variables—those that tend to dramatically change the hypothesized payback by the greatest degree based on small changes in the assumption. These are your key uncertainties.

4. Enhance your understanding of the sensitive assumptions through small-scale experiments constructed across broad ranges of the sensitive variables. Plan your experiments in ways you can safely *fail*, but mostly in ways to help you understand clearly what it would take to *succeed*—even if that turns out to be unprofitable upon further analysis. That way, you will at least know what won't work, and change your hypotheses in Step 1 accordingly.

5. Repeat Steps 1 through 4 until you have a model that seems to work.

6. In the process, the drivers of program success will become very obvious. Those become your key metrics to monitor.

The frameworks proposed by K. D. Paine and Pat LaPointe represent methodical approaches to help us assess performance as compared to expectations with tangible business performance metrics.

■ AUTHORITY: THE ABILITY TO GALVANIZE ACTION AND QUANTIFY IT

Revisiting influence as I define it (the ability to inspire desired and measurable action), the world of metrics essentially opens up new opportunities well beyond traditional analytics. Measuring traffic, views, and referring sources requires purpose, a front end in which we can engage, define, and capture measurable activity, monitor, assess, and adapt. It is important to focus on performance and establish our key performance indicators in advance, which will allow us to track the progress and execution of our programs.

In social media, performance data is typically organized as follows (whether intentionally or unintentionally):

➤ Volume
➤ Engagement
➤ Action

Remember, no matter how many formulas you review or trends you observe, for metrics to be accurate and meaningful, they have to apply to your world. Therefore any combination of volume, engagement, and action can define success and failure, which ultimately determines your level of authority and influence.

➤ Volume

Volume is symbolic of brand presence, the frequency with which it appears, its amplification, and its reach across the Web. It represents the extent to which your brand appears and resonates online, as defined by the communities, conversations, and people behind the surrounding activity.

To better understand how to recognize and quantify volume, we must define the characteristics and associated attributes with defining individual value:

➤ *Dialogue:* The quantity of discussions transpiring in the front and back channels, taking the shape of questions, answers, suggestions, and general interaction around the brand, as documented by networks and the Social Web as a whole.

➤ *Themes and memes:* Trends, topics, and discussion threads related to the brand, without direct influence from the brand.

➤ *SEO and SMO:* Linkbacks and links to the brand site, page, or a branded social object with value symbolized in the form of page rank, relevance, and authority.

➤ *Sentiment:* The perception of the state of the brand at any moment in time—the process of attempting to shift sentiment in the conversion section is the difference between volume and action.

➤ *Customer satisfaction:* The state of customer fulfillment and gratification (see details in Chapter 23).

➤ *Audience:* The size of individual communities, networks, and social graphs, measured independently as well as in the aggregate.

➤ **Engagement**

One of the most compelling aspects of interactive media is represented in the moniker that I just used: interactive media. It's indicative of two-way exchanges and it's measurable as such. I describe engagement as the time spent with the brand, either individually, in a community environment, or through direct interaction. Engagement metrics are captured through the impact garnered from conversations with brand representatives, time spent viewing or taking action around social objects, as well as browsing, viewing, and interfacing with branded online content.

Engagement can include:

➤ *Conversations:* Direct exchanges tied to the brand, represented through comments, blog posts, tweets, and retweets, wall posts, and shares—as eConsultancy says, "An engaged customer is a highly valuable one."[8]

➤ *Time:* The duration spent viewing or interacting with the brand, a social object, or content, from widgets to pages to profiles to conversations.

➤ *Social graph and relationships:* The size and shape of a social network tied to a person or a brand, measured by quality and quantity.

➤ *Fans and followers:* The number of individuals subscribed to receive the updates in social networks and communities.

➤ *Interaction:* The level in which people contribute information, social objects, and other content to brand hosted communities and networks.

➤ *Registrations:* Individuals who proactively register or subscribe to information, content, offers, and so forth.

➤ *Curation:* The process of publicly sharing favorite content through social bookmarks, retweets, reposts, favorites, and likes (which are all discoverable and calculable).

➤ *Traffic:* The cumulative activity directly at or around a site, page, profile, or social object.

➤ *Views:* Less about Web pages or more specifically tied to the viewing of specific social objects, such as videos, images, and widgets.

➤ *Shares:* The act of sharing content and objects across the Social Web.

➤ *Immersion:* The depth of interaction or engagement with online content, applications, conversations, or social objects.

➤ *Impressions:* The potential reach of the engagement or social object as determined by connections and traffic.

➤ Conversion

Action is profound in both its value to the bottom line and in its ability to convey discernible statistics. The ability to capture and measure action, if tied to calculated social programs, and meaningful business metrics is among the most salient forms of assessing return on investment as a true performance equation. Whereas volume and engagement capture the state of brand perception and presence, action reveals the activities that directly contribute to business health and profitability. This is why social media programs should feature carefully designed calls to action combined with the ability to capture and analyze the data on the back end—in real time.

Quantifiable data points and key performance indicators and measurable tactics can include:

➤ *Conversions:* The process of transforming individuals from one state to something of greater value, such as prospects and visitors into customers, or customers into advocates.

➤ *Click-throughs:* Crossing the chasm between social presences and objects to branded sites and microsites rife with calls to action—transcending from the virtual into real-world customers and users.

➤ *Offers:* Social media is expected to be a tremendous catalyst for individualized deals, discounts, exclusive offers, specials for products, services, and also local transactions. Airlines are measuring the response for special fares they offer in social networks; local businesses are documenting responses tied to specialized programs designed to lure prospects and transform them into customers; these efforts link to sales as a metric.

➤ *Ratings:* Customer review sites are repositories for brand experiences and sentiment. Without Astroturfing these sites, customers can be encouraged and directed to share positive thoughts.

➤ *Increased sales:* If @delloutlet can attribute approximately $3 million directly to its Twitter stream, Blendtec can recognize a 500 percent increase in sales, and other brands can realize increased revenue through its engagement specifically in the Social Web, integrating social programs and barometers designed to trigger and capture sales is within your grasp.

➤ *Data capture or registrations:* Growing lists of targeted prospects and customers is ideal for increasing relationships as well as direct communications channels—the number of individuals who share information either goes up or down on the basis of your activity.

➤ *Conversations or share of voice:* As discussed previously, conversations and share of voice are identifiable and measurable, providing a lens and revealing the state of presence and sentiment as a solitary number or in comparison to competition at any point in time, over time.

➤ *Sentiment conversion:* While sentiment is a reflection of volume and state, the act of shifting sentiment is a strategy and tactic that is both identifiable and measurable.

➤ *Customer/acquisition/retention/referrals/loyalty:* Customer interaction and recognition improves satisfaction, loyalty, and future revenue—assessing the cost of customer acquisition and retention using other forms of marketing and service programs and media compared to the costs associated with your social programs. As a metric, Zappos.com (a wholly owned subsidiary of Amazon.com) reports that 75 percent of its annual $1 billion in sales are from repeat customers.[9]

➤ *Lead generation:* The number of new prospects acquired through specific new media initiatives compared to other programs and dedicated performance.

➤ *Feedback and change:* Capturing thoughts and feedback through online voting and survey initiatives can be measured in change and interaction—the value of a brilliant idea is priceless.

➤ *Visitors and traffic:* Whether we're pointing people to a particular place or steering activity and responses based on our interaction, traffic is measurable and indicative of interest and movement.

➤ *Downloads:* The number of people who get something in exchange for something, for example, a downloaded widget, custom wallpaper, a white paper, coupon upon completion of registration, following, becoming a fan, and so forth.

➤ *New markets:* The establishment of new markets and channels based on engagement in nicheworks.

➤ *Participation or membership:* Capturing affinity is instantaneous in its results and value, designing programs around membership drives (such as a fan page, group, and so on) reveals the growth rate of a community (dialogue and interaction also become factors).

➤ *Cost savings or avoidance:* What did the company save by applying feedback and insight gleaned from the Social Web, solicited through either feedback or direct interaction.

■ THE Cs OF MEASURING ACTION THROUGH COST

Yes, more Cs! For those in the online marketing and advertising world, this section will be remedial. However, since social methodologies and programs are transforming many disciplines within the business, we are creating hybrids of professionals who now need to become a jack of all trades as well as a master of some.

The Cs in this case refer to cost, which can represent the I in ROI, as it serves as a benchmark for measuring the true price associated with activity—taking the form of monetary and resource assets. Their meaning and value in the era of interactive media is often debated, but using the law of "it depends," any one or combination of these Cs can help you measure what specifically matters to your business.

Cost per impression (CPM): The cost of acquiring eyeballs through impressions. Payment is often triggered by mutually agreeing upon activities such as a click-through, registration, sale, and so on.

The CPM deal is calculated by multiplying the CPM rate by the number of CPM units. For example, one million impressions at $10 CPM equals a total price of $10,000. The amount paid per impression is calculated by dividing the CPM by 1,000—for example, $10 CPM/1,000 impressions = $.01 per impression.[10]

Cost per click (CPC): The cost or cost-equivalent paid per click-through or a campaign in which payment is based on impressions, not clicks. For example, impressions are sold for $10 CPM with a click-through rate (CTR) of 2 percent. One thousand impressions × 2 percent CTR = 20 click-throughs. $10 CPM/20 click-throughs = $.50 per click.[11]

Click-through rate (CTR): The analysis of activity that sends a viewer from one place to a place of designation. It is the average number of click-throughs per hundred ad impressions, usually expressed as a percentage. The CTR measures the percentage of people who clicked through a media asset to arrive at a destination site. It is used as a measure of immediate response, but not to show the overall response.

Click to Action (CTA): The introduction of an outcome into the equation and the conversion ratios associated with impression to click-through. Many professionals track CTA in real time to improve imagery, messages, and venues to experiment and improve conversion ratios.

Social media is encouraging metrics that identify real business value, resulting in less interest in click-through rates and more interest in conversion and CTA rates. Active and high click-through rates don't necessarily guarantee good conversion rates, with the two rates often sharing an inverse relationship.[12] But with desirable and beneficial outcomes, everything improves.

Eric Von Coelln, who evaluates the numbers behind social media marketing and gaming, assessed the click-through rates after tweets to benchmark engagement. Von Coelln analyzed tweets that contained links from powerhouse brands, including @Zappos, @JetBlue, @SouthwestAir, and @ZyngaPoker. His study found that 1 to 3 percent of active followers actually click through to view the content.[13] Hence, CTR in this case didn't necessarily amount to much more than a benchmark number, but if we explored the activity that transpired after the click-through, we could assess conversion rates or, as you see next, the ability to recognize the effects of social actions.

Cost per action (CPA): A model in which payment is based solely on qualifying actions such as sales or registrations. The actions defined in a CPA agreement are tied to conversion, with sales and registrations representing the most common transactions. The CPA model resides at the opposite end of the C spectrum from CPM, with the CPC somewhere in the middle.[14] Affiliate marketing, for example, is one of the most-often-referred-to performance-based models, in which merchants and advertisers determine what actions they choose to reward and how much they are willing to pay for that activity.

Cost per engagement (CPE): CPE is a performance-based metric that assumes advertising impressions are free. Advertisers and marketers pay only on the basis of user engagement, wherein a prospect interacts with the content. Examples include polling, games, rollovers, tours, downloads, and so forth.

Another form of CPE is analyzing the fixed costs associated with existing resources such as employees, contractors, and services. We can measure time associated with an activity designed to produce results or drive action. Knowing the cost of time spent to yield an outcome gives us the ability to capture and assess engagement over time as it relates to specific goals.

■ THE ENGAGEMENT PHASE

Social media is equalizing. As such, the social objects and engagement strategies that are introduced through online communities provide much more value than exposure and branding.

In one such case, David Berkowitz, senior director of emerging media and innovation at 360i, proposed CPSA,[15] a new pricing model for social media that factors the cost per social action. CPSA is connected to distinct social qualities that lead to either new relationships (such as through viral referrals or acquiring new followers and fans) or deepening existing relationships (such as through likes, comments, responses, and ratings). Berkowitz proposed that the primary benefit of CPSA is that it offers marketers a program where they know that they are paying specifically for social and relationship-oriented programs.

Engagement value and presence differ from network to network and from community to community. For example, the rate at which people are exposed to and thus interact with an object or person in Twitter is different from the rate in Facebook, which is different from YouTube or blogs. Embedding calculated and productive action within any existing framework allows you to capture a cost per social action, not as a standard industry metric, but as a form of tailored measurement within predefined and understood paradigms. That activity can be measured within each network regardless of the C program mentioned previously, as well as in the free programs we pursue through direct engagement—responding, interacting, sharing content, introducing objects, and so on.

Procter & Gamble became one of the first companies to launch a results-based online ad model that rewards publishers for consumer engagement.[16] P&G, which owns brands such as Gillette, Pampers, and Pantene, will offer financial incentives for publishers when its campaigns receive greater engagement, beyond ad or content views, sign-ups, game play, and so on. The move essentially forces publishers to assume a proactive role in embracing accountability and also inspiring creativity to effectively partner with brands to cultivate meaningful interactions with audiences.

In response to P&G's announcement, Jack Wallington, program manager at the Internet Advertising Bureau (IAB), seemed to support P&G, but added a note of caution: "It's not the way the whole market is heading, but looking at more than traffic is a good thing. But even with CPE and other statistics, people are missing a trick in terms of branding power. Even if users don't click through, they could still be engaged. I hope P&G takes that into consideration."[17]

Jerry Lloyd-Williams, digital strategy director at U.K.-based media agency Mediacom, believes that CPE requires accountability, making the media buy a more collaborative experience. Mediacom, for example, worked with Volkswagen and *Times Online* to create a CPE campaign, "A Life More Streamlined," for the Volkswagen Passat. The *Times Online* was compensated each time a person watched a video, listened to a podcast, or downloaded material.[18]

The data, of course, changes from network to network, but it is this information that must be uncovered through industry research or through direct consumer analysis to create an internal benchmark for your activity.

Charlene Li, founder of the Altimeter Group and former social analyst at Forrester Research, conducted a social engagement review in conjunction with Wetpaint of the 100 most valuable brands, as identified by *BusinessWeek*/Interact.[19] The ENGAGEMENTdb 2009 Report observed the engagement programs as well as their performances.[20]

The team critiqued the brands on the extent (breadth) of engagement across the Social Web as well as level of engagement (depth), such as whether they reply to comments made on blog posts or respond to consumers on Twitter, and so forth. Each brand was given a numerical score.

The top 10 ENGAGEMENTdb brands with their scores in 2009 were:

1. Starbucks (127)
2. Dell (123)
3. eBay (115)

4. Google (105)
5. Microsoft (103)
6. Thomson Reuters (101)
7. Nike (100)
8. Amazon (88)
9. SAP (86)
10. Tie: Yahoo! and Intel (85)

As we're enthralled in the exploration of engagement metrics such as CPE, social actions, or engagement, the ENGAGEMENTdb report did find a correlation between engagement and financial performance.

But even more interesting is that we also looked at the financial performance of the brands, grouping the companies with the greatest depth and breadth into a group called Social Media Mavens. These mavens *on average* grew 18 percent in revenues over the last 12 months, compared to the least engaged companies that, *on average,* saw a decline of 6 percent in revenue during the same period. The same holds true for two other financial metrics, gross margin and net profit.

The metrics we establish are derivative of the mission, purpose, and presence we embody throughout the organization and are truly measured by how our intentions are conveyed through the champions and advocates we empower. This sentiment and philosophy is echoed in Li's introduction of the ENGAGEMENTdb report:[21]

> *The study also looks at the engagement best practices of four companies: Starbucks, Dell, SAP, and Toyota. Some of the key findings include:*
>
> Emphasize quality, not just quantity.
>
> *Engagement is more than just setting up a blog and letting viewers post comments; it's more than just having a Facebook profile and having others write on your wall. Don't just check the box; engage with your customer audience.*
>
> To scale engagement, make social media part of everyone's job.
>
> *The best practice interviews have a common theme—social media is no longer the responsibility of a few people in the organization. Instead, it's important for everyone across the organization to engage with customers in the channels that make sense—a few minutes each day spent by every employee adds up to a wealth of customer touch points.*

Doing it all may not be for you—but you must do something.

Start you must, or risk falling far behind other brands, not only in your industry, but across your customers' general online experience.

Find your sweet spot.

Engagement can't be skin-deep, nor is it a campaign that can be turned on and off. True engagement means full engagement in the channels in which you choose to invest. Thus, choose carefully and advocate strongly to acquire the resources and support you will need to succeed.

We're learning that social media engagement is tied to all outbound forms of marketing, service, communications, branding, and relationship management. It's less about talking at people and more about collaboration and movement, which offer more value and quality to people on both sides of the equation and thus ensures measurable impact.

■ SHARE OF VOICE AND SHARE OF CONVERSATION

Establishing share of voice and share of conversation tied to sentiment is also a metric of brand health, now and over time and establish share of voice now and over time is to use the techniques shared in the chapter discussing the Conversation Prism and Conversation Index.

It recognizes the state of awareness and reputation to not only measure, but also to inspire rapid evolution.

By listening to the conversations on the Social Web, we can capture the following data using a period of time (a particular month, for example):

1. Number of conversations related to brand or product within all relevant networks (blogs, Twitter, Facebook, and so on).
   a. Categorize conversations by networks of relevance
   b. Sorted by business unit (marketing, service, product, communications, and so on)
2. Sentiment (positive, neutral, negative).
3. Repeat this process for key competitors.
4. Compare findings by first searching conversations related to the greater market. For example, if we're searching for Lexus against BMW and Mercedes, each of the car manufacturers

would represent the share of voice. If we ran a more sweeping search for luxury sedans and then searched the place of each manufacturer within the dialogue, we could establish share of conversation.

This data should be captured in the form of a matrix or report so that we can refer to it every month.

To determine share of voice and the state of sentiment, we simply capture the total number of conversations and organize it as such:

Share of voice: Total conversations in the Social Web compared to brand or competitor share:

➤ Your brand represents X percent

➤ Competitor A = X percent

➤ Competitor B = X percent

➤ Competitor C = X percent

➤ Competitor D = X percent

➤ Total = 100 percent

Sentiment score:

➤ Total positive, neutral, or negative conversations divided by total number of conversations, including positive, neutral, and negative for a particular span of time (example: 12,000 positive conversations divided by 25,000 total number of conversations = 48 percent).

➤ Compare results to competitors for each state of sentiment.

■ COMPARATIVE DATA ANALYSIS

In almost every form of measurement, the need for comparative data is prevalent. At the campaign and brand level, a snapshot of time and activity is necessary to serve as a benchmark related to the state of brand-specific activity as well as that of the competition. Whether it's the Conversation Index, the social influence score, or existing data that reveals sentiment, traffic, and activity volume, sales, action, competitive intelligence, and so forth, we must first establish a benchmark for every program by which to compare future socialization of resources and objects.

For example, how much are you paying now to acquire customers and prospects or market share using other marketing channels and using the preceding metrics?

Everything we discuss and review serves as the base to compare our work and results to internal initiatives and in direct comparison to the efforts of our competitors. Thus, we learn and adapt to create more engaging programs that are measurable and versatile. By defining what it is we need to grow or where we need to reach, we can determine what it is we need to measure, which dictates the social programs we employ and how we ultimately engage.

In the end, the best thing to measure is the estimated activity you plan on capturing. Give them something to talk about. Give them a reason to connect. Monitor, document, and measure everything that happens as a result.

■ NOTES

1. K. D. Paine, "Establishing the ROI of Social Media," *KDPaine's Measurement Standard* (May 2008), www.themeasurementstandard.com/issues/5–1–08/painelet5–1–08.asp.

2. "Return on Investment," *The Free Dictionary,* http://financial-dictionary.thefreedictionary.com/Return+on+investment.

3. Brian Solis, "The Essential Guide to Social Media: A Free eBook," PR 2.0 (June 9, 2008), www.briansolis.com/2008/06/essential-guide-to-social-media-free/.

4. "Public Relations Measurement 2010: Five Things to Forget & Five Things to Learn," *MetricsMan* (July 29, 2009), http://metricsman.wordpress.com/2009/07/29/public-relations-measurement-2010-five-things-to-forget-five-things-to-learn/.

5. K. D. Paine, "What's Important about Social Media Is What Happens Because of It," *KDPaine's Measurement Standard* (July 2009), www.themeasurementstandard.com/issues/7–1–09/painelet7–1–09.asp.

6. K. D. Paine, "The All-Purpose, One-Size-Fits-All Public Relations Measurement Program Checklist," The Measurement Standard Blog Edition (March 11, 2009), http://kdpaine.blogs.com/themeasurementstandard/2009/03/the-allpurpose-onesizefitsall-public-relations-measurement-program-checklist.html.

7. Pat LaPointe, "Twittering Away Time and Money," *Marketing Measurement Today* (July 24, 2009), http://marketingmeasurementtoday.blogspot.com/2009/07/twittering-away-time-and-money.html.

8. Chris Lake, "10 Ways to Measure Social Media Success," eConsultancy (March 5, 2009), http://econsultancy.com/blog/3407–10-ways-to-measure-social-media-success.

9. Chris Lake, "Q&A with Zappos CEO Tony Hsieh," eConsultancy (November 27, 2008), http://econsultancy.com/blog/2955-q-a-with-zappos-ceo-tony-hsieh.

10. "CPM," Marketing Terms, www.marketingterms.com/dictionary/cpm/.

11. "Cost-per-Click," Marketing Terms, www.marketingterms.com/dictionary/cost_per_click/.

12. "Click-Through Rate," Marketing Terms, www.marketingterms.com/dictionary/clickthrough_rate/.

13. Eric von Coelln, "After the Tweet: Exploring Twitter Click-Through Rate Benchmarking to Measure Engagement," Voncoelln.com (June 3, 2009), www.voncoelln.com/eric/2009/06/03/after-the-tweet-exploring-twitter-click-through-rate-benchmarking-to-measure-engagement/.

14. "Cost-per-Action," Marketing Terms, www. marketingterms.com/dictionary/cost_per_action/.

15. David Berkowitz, "CPSA: The New Pricing Model For Social Media?" *Social Media Insider* (August 4, 2009), www.mediapost.com/publications/?fa=Articles.showArticle&art_aid=111081.

16. Suzanne Bearne, "Cover Story: P&G to Pay Publishers Based on Online Engagement," *New Media Age* (September 17, 2009), www.nma.co.uk/news/pg-to-pay-publishers-based-on-online-engagement/3004452.article#.

17. "P&G to Pay Publishers Based on Online Engagement," Mad.co.uk (September 16, 2009), www.mad.co.uk/Main/News/Articlex/038fc4206a70425095eae37466f7ef37/PG-to-pay-publishers-based-on-online-engagement.html.

18. Suzanne Bearne, "Cover Story: P&G to Pay Publishers Based on Online Engagement," *New Media Age* (September 17, 2009), www.nma.co.uk/news/pg-to-pay-publishers-based-on-online-engagement/3004452.article#.

19. "The 100 Top Brands," *BusinessWeek*, http://images.businessweek.com/ss/08/09/0918_best_brands/index.htm.

20. ENGAGEMENTdb 2009 Report, www.engagementdb.com/Report.

21. Charlene Li, "New Study: Deep Brand Engagement Correlates with Financial Performance," *The Altimeter* (July 20, 2009), www.altimetergroup.com/2009/07/engagementdb.html.

Conclusion

And here we are. . . .

You and I have traveled a great distance to reach this point in time and place—collaboratively reaching a state of higher awareness and wisdom in our journey. You are to be commended and hopefully rewarded for your investment in deciphering this perpetually transforming landscape. Remember, you play an active role in its evolution and definition. As we've learned, new media is a great journey in which the destination is immaterial, but the stops along the way account for everything. The learning you've absorbed up to now and all that you will master through practice in the time to come shapes your future.

I'd like to take this opportunity to leave you with a few parting thoughts before we continue our expedition together in the other mediums that follow this book. Remember, the companion site for this book, www.engagingbook.com, will include many lessons and stories that did not make the final cut for the book, as well as current stories that continue to capture and define the progress of interactive media.

■ YOU ARE MORE INFLUENTIAL THAN YOU MAY REALIZE

The future of new media is up to you. As such, we must strive for higher standards through innovation, accountability, purpose, and the ongoing sharing of our knowledge to improve the foundation for new media literacy.

While I've shared case studies and examples in this book, remember that those stories are merely illustrations for what's possible. The true purpose of this book is tied to the ripe opportunities that await your creativity and brilliance. New media thrives on its interdependence with cutting-edge technology systems and new ideas. The channels and tools for communicating are always changing, but it's the people we are trying to reach and the need for solutions and direction that remain constant. Their actions and words tell us everything we need to know. It is your duty to build the bridges between your communities and your brand and mission, inspired by prevailing case studies, but guided by your intuition.

The problem with creativity is that it's usually constrained by spoken and unspoken rules that govern the process of ingenuity.

If I host a brainstorming session and place a box in the middle of the room and say, "Here's a box, now think outside of it," I unwittingly place parameters around your imagination. Sometimes brilliance is channeled through our fieldwork, without the limitations of the proverbial box that's placed before us.

Therefore as my good friend Chris Heuer, founder of the Social Media Club, says, in social media, "There is no box."

As we draw our experiences in this book to a close, the truth is that our partnership is only beginning. I look forward to connecting with you online and in person one day soon.

I'm grateful for this opportunity to share my experiences with you. In the process of writing this book, I, too, have learned a great deal. So, thank you.

All that's separating you from where you are and where you want to be is time and experience. Your dedication, aspiration, and motivation already serve as the foundations for success. It's why you're here.

Now, let's get to work.

Appendix

30-Day Listening Report:

A Template for Capturing and Presenting
Social Media Activity

Share of Voice

	Blogs	Facebook	Twitter	Groups/Forums	Other SocNets	Notes
Total # of Company Mentions						
Total # of Competitor Mentions						

Share of Conversation

	Blogs	Facebook	Twitter	Groups/Forums	Other SocNets	Notes
# of Industry Keyword Mentions						
Total # of Company Mentions						
Total # of Competitor Mentions						

Conversations Requiring Response

	Blogs	Facebook	Twitter	Groups/Forums	Other SocNets	Notes
Marketing						
Customer Service						
Support						
Sales						
HR						
Finance						
Executive						
PR						

Sentiment

	Blogs	Facebook	Twitter	Groups/Forums	Other SocNets	Notes
Brand						
Competitor						

Potential Impressions/Reach	Blogs Monthly visitors	Facebook Number of likes and # potentially exposed to each like	Twitter Number of people connected to each Tweet [followers]	Groups/Forums Thread views	Other SocNets	Notes
Company Mentions						
Competitor Mentions						
Keywords						
Looming Crises/Opportunities	Blogs	Facebook	Twitter	Groups/Forums	Other SocNets	Notes
Brand						
Product						
Recurring Themes	Blogs	Facebook	Twitter	Groups/Forums	Other SocNets	Notes
Brand						
Product						

Glossary

Aggregator: A tool, application, or process, that pulls together multiple feeds from content sites and brings them together in to one place.

Astroturfing: A synthetic grassroots effort; a falsely positioned, paid, or deceptive campaign to generate buzz, visibility, and word of mouth (WOM).

Authenticity: The practice of being authentic, true, and genuine in online interactions.

Authority: Someone who is an expert or recognized pundit or influencer on a particular subject.

Authority (2): The stature earned for a person, blog, content, destination, or network as measured by linkbacks (links to the particular destination) or connections (friends or followers) or comments, views, or tweetbacks (retweets or tweets of reference), or votes/thumbs up/+1s/Diggs, or a combination of some or all of these.

Being Yourself/Being Human: Part of the problem associated with social media is disingenuous behavior. Social media thrives on authenticity and sincerity. The practice of being human, being yourself, or disclosing that the persona is representative of something else that's calculated and intended. Anonymous interaction is discouraged and usually disregarded.

Blogroll: A list of related, inspiring, relevant, or friendly blogs as listed on any given blog.

Brandjacked: The act of assuming the presence of a person or brand in social networks. Squatting (taking or assuming a username before the true brand owner can grab it) in any given network is also a form of brandjacking.

Brandstream: This is a trademarked term used to describe a brand's use of an activity stream or lifestream.

Citizen Journalism: Everyday people reporting on news, events, and experiences through blogs, microblogs, micromedia, video, audio, comments, and so forth.

Cloud: The cloud is essentially a metaphor for the Internet. It ties to cloud computing and serves as the backbone and hosting infrastructure for social media applications, services, and networks. The cloud can host online applications, services, published content, storage, data, user information, and so forth.

Cloud Computing: Any application or service that is hosted in the cloud and accessed through a client, such as a computer, smartphone, gadget, appliance, and so on. Applications and services that are served through cloud computing mimic the capabilities associated with software applications, but don't necessarily require the traditional hardware and support infrastructures to create, install, and manage them.

Comment Spam: The practice of artificially and thoughtlessly promoting content or products in the comments section of any blog, social network profile, group, fan page, wiki, or content page. Strategically discussing the solution/service/person as it relates to steering content helpfully without coming across as spam, snake oil, or as a sales pitch, is not comment spam.

Connection: The link between people, themes, topics, keywords, and content.

Consumer-Generated Media (CGM)/User-Generated Content (UGC): The content created by users or consumers and added to social media properties and communities. For example, blog posts, comments, reviews, votes, videos, pictures, podcasts, online documents, tweets, and status updates are all forms of user-generated content.

Conversation: The published online dialogue that transpires between one or more people in and around ideas, content, updates, themes, and events. Conversations can be synchronous, tied to real-time updates and responses, threaded in one string of related content, updates, and responses, or asynchronous, whereby the dialogue is not tied to time and place and is distributed across social networks. (Twitter hosts asynchronous conversations; responses to blog posts or online content from other blogs, microcommunities, or other social networks through links also represent asynchronous dialogue.)

Creative Commons: Creative licensing by CreativeCommons.org offers a social media–friendly licensing architecture that allows people to use and share content based on the terms defined by the content creator or host. It frees up the usage patterns usually limited by traditional copyrights (all rights reserved) in exchange for credit, links, or some other form of gesture or recognition.

Crowdsourcing: The process of tapping the wisdom of crowds to create content, solve problems, answer questions, contribute to the evolution of a product or service, define governance associated with rules or politics, and so forth. Wikipedia is the most frequently used example for defining crowdsourcing. Digg is considered a crowdsourced news community.

Dashboard: A central hub for a variety of actions and capabilities, similar to the desktop of a computer screen. It refers to the items you place within a fixed area to streamline your activities associated with reading, publishing, responding, listening and monitoring, and updating.

Disclosure: The ethical measure of stating your intent, association, and goals associated with content or activity.

Embed: The process of integrating or adding a piece of content into another piece of content or place. YouTube provides embedding code for its videos to enable users to place an integrated video and player in blogs, Web pages, and online profiles to share and serve information without forcing the visitor to click through to YouTube to watch the video.

Engagement: The steps in participating in an online conversation through direct interaction or a response through direct or indirect words in and around the content source or publisher.

Favorite: Favoriting content or updates in social networks for review or sharing at a later date. It's also used as a form of bookmarking.

Feed: Content that can be viewed through other related or outside services. A blog updates its feed using RSS (really simple syndication) with every newly published post that can then be read by someone else who subscribes to the RSS feed using a feed reader such as Google Reader or Netvibes.

Flog: Fake blogs, comments, or reviews that promote content, products, brands, or services by pretending to be something or someone else without disclosure.

Folksonomy: The indexing of content by a greater collective of people through tags, labels, descriptions, titles, or keywords. Flickr and YouTube are powered by folksonomy so they can help others find the content they need. It's the process of matching content to content seekers and serves as the undercurrent for effective social media optimization (SMO).

Gadget: A tiny application that performs a specific function on a Web page or social network profile. iGoogle is an example of a service that provides a customized experience based on the gadgets users install on their iGoogle desktop. Gadgets are virtually unlimited in variations and capabilities. They can include mini services to check weather, interact through instant messaging clients, update Twitter, check stocks or sports scores, translate sentences or words into other languages, read RSS feeds, and so on.

Hashtag: A keyword, keyword string, or theme preceded by a pound or number sign (#) and used to index and categorize content in networks where folksonomy is not directly supported. For example, hashtags gained prominence in Twitter as a way of associating tweets to topics. This book could carry the hashtag #socialmediamanifesto or #socialmedia or #SMM.

Hat Tip: The gesture of publicly recognizing someone or something as a source of content or information.

IRL: *In real life* refers to behavior offline, or in the real world, which can sometimes be quite different from online behavior or activity.

Keywords: The word(s) used to describe content, media, destination pages and sites, and communities to boost visibility and ranking when someone searches for related information. Webmasters use keywords to describe and promote websites in search engine results, often referred to as *search engine optimization* (SEO). Keywords are also used to promote content when someone searches within a social network or a blog search engine. This is referred to as *social media optimization* (SMO).

Lifestream: A dedicated channel to aggregate the content produced on various social networks such as Flickr, YouTube, blogs, comments, and so on, into one easy-to-follow and easy-to-interact-with stream. FriendFeed, SocialThing, and Chi.mp are considered services for creating, hosting, and following lifestreams. Also referred to as an *activitystream* (related to similar activity, not necessarily sourced by the same person or brand) and *brandstream* (the channeled activity produced by a brand). The Facebook NewsFeed is also considered an activitystream or lifestream, as it collects updates from the outside networks and communities you designate.

Like: Similar to favoriting, liking is a token of gratitude and appreciation for content and updates shared in social networks such as Facebook and FriendFeed.

Linkback: A way for Web and content publishers to receive notification when other publishers link to their page or media.

Linkbait: Refers to the intentional publishing or promotion of content or destinations to provoke a response, usually in the form of a linkback. Since links contribute to the authority of a host, it helps boost their ranking and thus motivates publishers to use controversial methods to bait linked responses. If not done carefully, it can have negative repercussions.

Listening: Monitoring conversations and activity online related to keywords.

Liveblog or Livetweet: Sharing updates in real time (as they happen) in blog posts, Twitter, or other social media platforms to keep readers or followers up to date with events as they unfold.

Livecast: Streaming video or audio live to document an experience or gather viewers and publishers together at a fixed moment in time to interact around the subject.

Mashup: The fusion, mixing, and matching of two or more applications or services to create or enable something new. Google Maps is a popular service that is often mashed up with other services. For example, Twittervision shows tweets and twitterers on a map, based on any given location, to show where people are tweeting from in real time.

Meetup: A service for facilitating and discovering events related to any given topic, theme, or interest. When you host an event that is housed at meetup.com, it's generally referred to as a *meetup*.

Meme: A theme that spreads on the Internet quickly. A memetracker can channel related activity and updates in one place to follow progress and information.

Participation: Engaging in online activity and also creating and contributing content that potentially resonates with people on any given subject within related communities and networks.

Pay It Forward: The act of paying homage or respect and calling attention to someone else in recognition of their contributions.

Permalink: The permanent link or URL for a destination or specific piece of content or media.

Relationships: While they may mimic ties in the real world, social media relationships usually refer to the exercise of connecting with like-minded individuals. These relationships can be fostered as a means of instilling and cultivating loyalty, advocacy, and activity. As in any relationship, there is an expected give-and-take value associated with interaction. Much more than a two-way street, people on both sides of the relationship must view the connection as mutually beneficial and productive over time.

Return on Investment (ROI): Return on investment is the system by which we measure the effectiveness of our initiatives related to time, resources, and capital compared to what was received in return. Over the years, especially in social media, ROI has been adapted to measure specific nuances of initiatives. ROI can also stand for *return on influence, return on involvement, return on innovation,* and *relevance of interaction,* among others.

Retweet: Retweeting, or simply RT, is the process of sharing someone else's tweet so as to extend the visibility of the original tweet and also recognize the originator in the process. For example: RT @briansolis Engage! is now available in bookstores online and near you. See www.areyouengaged.com.

Social Capital: The amount of personal wealth you garner through participation, engagement, contributions, and paying it forward as measured by reputation and authority. This is referred to as *personal brand worth,* or, as Tara Hunt calls it, the *Whuffie Factor.*

Social Economy: The people and technology that contribute to and define the vibrancy, prosperity, direction, and health of the Social Web.

Social Graph: Originally used in reference to the network of friends, associates, peers, and contacts that one maintains in Facebook, the social graph is essentially a personal network for facilitating communications and sharing information and content. Social graphs can span across multiple networks or reside in one primary community.

Social Operating System (OS): *Social operating system* is a term that I initially used to refer to the applications, widgets, gadgets, and services (online social networks and microcommunities) that we use to effectively communicate and navigate within our social graph.

Statusphere: Another term I use to describe the new ecosystem for sharing, discovering, and publishing updates and microsized content on social networks and microcommunities that reverberate throughout social networks and syndicated profiles, resulting in a formidable network effect of movement and response.

Stream: A flow of information that is aggregated from a series of distributed content and presences across the Social Web.

Syndication: The opposite of aggregation, social syndication is the process of sharing one piece of content produced in one network across multiple networks without having to manually update each and every maintained account or profile manually. Ping.fm, TubeFilter, and Utterli are a few of many examples that facilitate syndication.

Tag: A keyword used to describe content in social networks and blogs.

Tag Cloud: A visual collection of the most often used tags generated by user, URL, page or profile, or themes, as dictated by either description tags or by the most often used words in any given post, site, or collection of media.

Tastemaker: Also referred to as *taste neighbors,* these individuals are considered influencers and trendsetters within their immediate sphere of activity or social graph.

Thread: A visual flow of tracking and presenting related conversations and responses within blogs and blog comments, microcommunities such as FriendFeed, social networks such as Facebook, or using special tools such as JS-Kit echo of Disqus, or a combination of all of these.

Trackback/Tweetback: Similar to a linkback, a trackback or tweetback lets a blogger know when another blogger has linked to her blog or tweeted about her post.

Transparency: Its original definition referred to honest and authentic participation in social media. Over time, I've argued that the term *transparency* can be misleading in the sense that being yourself may not be enough to warrant a desired response, or that it wouldn't necessarily support or best present the brand, company, or service represented if the individual personality did not match the corresponding persona and prestige.

Trending Topics: Popularized by Twitter, trending topics are the most current themes that people are discussing related to keywords or hashtags at any given moment.

Tribe: Popularized by Seth Godin, *tribes* refers to dedicated communities around a particular theme, cause, or movement. I believe that in life we are either hosts or we are guests. In this example, we either belong to a tribe or we lead it. In social media, we have the ability to effectively thrive in both so as to build a cross-network tribe rich with advocates and enthusiasts.

Trust: The reward for genuine participation and helpful collaboration in social networks and blogs.

Tweet: Trademarked by Twitter, tweet refers to an update shared on Twitter.

Tweetup: Similar to meetup, Tweetups refer to events organized on Twitter that result in an IRL (in real life) event.

Twit/Twitterer/Tweeps/Tweeple: Someone who tweets on Twitter.

Value: The substance and essence contributed to an online exchange or act of sharing information.

Views: The number of times a piece of content, media, or online destination was viewed by people. Many services attempt to track the number of unique views based on the IP address (an ID or Internet protocol address that's specific to a computer or device accessing the Web through any online access provider) to qualify and quantify the amount of views. Instead of counting how many times one particular system watches a video, it will only count it as one view to provide a more accurate reflection of popularity and activity.

Viral: The act of media or content getting shared within and across social networks. This is often confused with the impression that through viral marketing, content itself can elicit the desire to share. However, it's people that ultimately make something viral and they consequently require attention when introducing interesting content that offers the potential of legitimately going viral.

Virtual Goods and Gifts: Products that are made available for free or for purchase to use or share with others within social networks. In Facebook, you could offer a virtual birthday cake as a gift to recognize someone's special day and call attention to the act within your (and their) social graph. Other virtual goods include drinks, badges, games, and so on.

Virtual World: A social network that offers an immersive 3D world that is constructed outside of reality to create its own experience. Second Life and World of Warcraft are leading examples.

Vote: The act of promoting content, people, or media within specific social networks. Votes (Diggs on Digg, Stumbles on StumbleUpon) can go up or down.

Widget: A self-contained website, ad, game, network, service, or application that is embeddable on websites, profiles, blogs, and other online properties.

Word of Mouth (WOM): Not necessarily derived from social media, but most certainly practiced and studied as a part of it, *word of mouth* refers to the phenomenon that occurs when people actively and fervently share content, media, or information across the Web. As content picks up momentum, it goes viral. Word of mouth marketing is the discipline dedicated to promoting products or content through the engagement and promotion of the people; it's intended to benefit, educate, enlighten, or entertain.

Index